T0149183

authorHOUSE®

AuthorHouse™
1663 Liberty Drive
Bloomington, IN 47403
www.authorhouse.com
Phone: 1 (800) 839-8640

This is a work of fiction. All of the characters, names, incidents, organizations, and dialogue in this novel are either the products of the author's imagination or are used fictitiously.

Published by AuthorHouse 10/13/2016

ISBN: 978-1-5246-4280-8 (sc)
ISBN: 978-1-5246-4278-5 (hc)
ISBN: 978-1-5246-4279-2 (e)

Library of Congress Control Number: 2016916170

Print information available on the last page.

This book is printed on acid-free paper.

Foreword

This writing is a consolidation of dreams, experiences, stories true and fictitious, perceptions, realities, fantasies and most of all, reflective experiences. The community, Weirton, West Virginia, exists in the Northern Panhandle of the State, forty miles west of Pittsburgh, Pennsylvania, twenty-five miles north of Wheeling, West Virginia, on the Ohio River directly across from Steubenville, Ohio.

The places depicted, for the most part, do or did exist and are described with an attempt at accuracy; however, some liberties were taken to fit the story line. (Sorry and apologies to purists) The events: athletic, social, religious, educational, business and political did take place in one manner or another. Again, they are reasonably historically correct, with minor embellishments to fit the mood and personalities of the characters. A few of the events the authors experienced personally, or through firsthand accounts. (Note that authors is plural, because as you will find, this was a cooperative effort of many.)

The characters are purely fictitious, did not exist, but were created by the authors as composites of individuals they have known, met, observed, liked and disliked. While from time to time a reader, who also lived during the time of the story, in this and/or in the vicinity of the story backdrop, may feel they recognize a character from real life. It is only the illusion created by the story and the reader's backward drift to a time of adolescence. Journeys to yesteryears can fill a memory with hope, excitement, anticipation, young love, hormonal peaks and above all, dreams of what once was.

If you are Weirtonian or a Red Rider, you are not intentionally a character in the story – unless you create yourself in the pages. If you are able to do so, great. You are allowed to become your own Red Rider.

The author, Laura Chadwick, does not exist. Ms. Chadwick is a pen name, hopefully in the long tradition of the many great writers who have used this approach to enhance or camouflage their true identity for many, many personal reasons. One of the contributing authors is a 1940s Weirtonian who grewup during the 1940s and 50s in Weirton and graduated from Weir High School; therefore, the places, life style and culture of the story are from first hand experience.

The Story

The story is set in Weirton, West Virginia, a 1950s small industrial town in the Northern Panhandle of the state, an arm that follows the Ohio River beyond the Mason and Dixon line until it turns into Pennsylvania and its Pittsburgh birthplace. Weirton is more akin to Ohio and Pennsylvania than the rural heart of West Virgina. Weirton's economy and its existence is dominated by the Weirton Steel Company and related coal mining spread throughout the region. For this Ohio Valley steel mill community the 1940s, 1950s and 1960s were high water marks in development, growth and prosperity. The city was described as a melting pot, a city of churches, and the essence of ethic diversity.

It is 1958-59; the two main characters are Seniors in Weir High School. They and their friends experience the fun and frustrations of their final year in the controlled environment of public education. They move through the nine month school year dealing with academics, sports, romance, religion, friendships, social mores and their futures. They are growing from adolescence to early adulthood, with all the ups and downs that come with that transition.

Marc was born a Weirtonian, a town whose tradition places great emphasis on winning, working and achievement. Jamie has just arrived from Birmingham England following her father's career in the mushrooming global steel industry. She is adjusting to life in the United States, its fast pace and the abundance of everything. Together they travel through the trials of going from seventeen to eighteen and the prospect of the inevitable – maturity.

The unique small town atmosphere adds to the unexpected twist and turns that is their final year of youth. They respond in many ways together, but just as many in opposite directions. As they reach the final days and events of high school, everything is falling into place and is in sync, then…..

Table of Contents

Dedication

This story is dedicated to all the Red Riders; Eagles; Hawks; Tigers; Bees; Blue Birds; Vikings; Demons; Bishops; Bob Cats; Bears; Mountaineers; Cavaliers; Cowboys; Pirates; Golden Flashes; Spartans; and the hundred of other monikers of our high school years.

Enjoy

Chapter 1

Wakening

That familiar rise in the road loomed ahead—the one that seemed to bridge the two massive parts of the tandem mill. He could see the lights of the stadium off to the right where they had been for fifty, no, maybe seventy years. The lights had been there for as long as Marc could remember, but it had been years since he had seen them all lit.

He could not see all the stadium lights from the road. The towering roofs of the tin mill still blocked the view of the ones on the west side. The foggy glow from the stadium created an eerie effect as the darkness of the mill and the rising hillside behind the stadium dominated the scene and dampened the bright lights even though they reached eighty feet into the air. The lights were only visible for a few seconds as his car reached the flat peak of the overpass and started down the incline on the other side towards the town's main thoroughfare.

An unmarked mill gate on the right side curved towards a large corrugated building and back again under the bridging road. The landscape was dark and haunting. The blue-gray coating of a steel mill talcum powder bath had fallen on the buildings and roadway at the gate for many years giving the scene a touch of homeliness and despair. How could anything be that dusty? It was a bleak, three-dimensional lithograph of the industrial revolution.

It hasn't changed, Marc thought. *It's still the same as it was in the late 50s.* The short stretch of four-lane road—about two miles—still merged into two lanes as he reached the number five-mill gate and the start of downtown Weirton. Downtown? Yes, this was downtown Weirton. A row of one-, two-, at most three- story buildings on the west side, and the mill, – rising like a big, dark mountain of steel, mortar, brick, and fencing on the east side.

Could Marc find his way to the football game? He turned off Main Street at Virginia Avenue, and then drove up the hill for a few blocks to the high school. Well, it's no longer the high school. Marc wondered if there was anything still there. At one of the class reunions a few years ago, he had bought a brick, supposedly from the old school. At the time, it was being torn down, and Chris Barrie had brought some souvenirs from the demolition site. Marc had paid $10 for what he trusted was his piece of Weir High School history.

Virginia Avenue was still there; however, there were more empty lots, boarded-up buildings and parking lots for mill employees than Marc remembered. The area looked old, real old. There was the telephone office. He remembered the telephone "operators" who would go in and out of the building as he came and went from the high school. The young women in their nylons and high heels enchanted him. At the time Marc regarded them as women because they were older and out of high school—women who worked at the "romantic" job of telephone operator. All around the dilapidated telephone building, which now had a sign indicating the ISU (Independent Steelworkers Union) occupied the premises, was the discarded and unusable waste of a struggling industry and its people. Obviously, the telephone company had long since moved.

Marc reached the end of the next block. The pitch of the road was steep, at least that is the way it seemed tonight. When Marc drove these hilly streets at sixteen, they did not seem to be any more than slight rises in the road. *It's all what you get accustomed to*, he thought. Now his Jeep Grand Cherokee seemed too big for the road let alone being able to make the turn into the parking lot outside the stadium. Marc suddenly stopped the light brown Jeep. He was confused and unsure of himself and felt he was driving into a tunnel as the road ahead grew narrower and darker.

The parking lot was gone!

No, it was just so dark that at first glance he didn't see the barrier at the entrance: a rickety, one legged wooden horse holding up a partially broken two-by-four.

The lot, or what appeared to be the remains of the parking lot, was packed with cars, trucks, and buses parked haphazardly. The few gray cloudy figures standing behind the temporary gate were simultaneously motioning for him to turn away and go down the street to his left or continue up another block to the very top of Virginia Avenue. Marc was confused by the traffic controllers. He knew that climb ahead was steeper yet and he didn't want to take that vertical trip.

He turned the steering wheel sharply left, but he was already committed to pulling into the lot. He hit the brakes to avoid going any farther and in fear of the unknown darkness. As the Jeep came to a sudden stop, Marc shifted into reverse. Before he could start to backup, a horn honked and honked again. With a jolt, he slammed the brake pedal down with a forceful drive of his right foot. The red glow of the Jeep's brake lights mixed with the headlights of a car behind created a murky violet-gray collage that made forms and objects indistinguishable.

"Hold it—you can't back up. Give him a chance to get out of the way," a sharp, husky voice called out coldly and somewhat angrily from the rear.

Marc sat still for a moment as he realized that a car behind him was going to be allowed into the parking lot. The barrier was being moved aside and the car turned right into the lot and proceeded down the narrow drive between uneven rows of parked cars, pickups, and school buses. With the gray darkness hanging over the passageway through the motionless vehicles, it reminded Marc of a quick view of a cemetery corridor of large crypts.

"Okay. Come on back. Cut it hard. You have plenty of room," the rough voice said again.

Marc did exactly that. He continued at a slow, cautious pace until the voice yelled, "Okay, okay."

Marc stopped. *Why is it so dark?* He wondered. "*I can't see a damn thing. Are my headlights on? I see fine in front. Must be these new glasses—damn bifocals. It gets worse with every new prescription.*"

He turned the Jeep into the side street running ninety degrees off of Virginia Avenue. The road was narrow with cars parked on both sides of the street; there was only room for one car in the center of the road. *This is like driving through the hedgerows of England all over again*, Marc thought. The one lane created a tunnel effect that the night darkness only intensified. If he met someone coming from the opposite direction, it would be a game of chicken to see who would back-up first to an unoccupied area and pull out of the way.

"God, this street hasn't changed either," Marc mumbled to himself.

The small houses seemed tinier than he remembered. But their appearance of clinging to the side of the hill was still the same. Their fragile foothold left the impression that they could let go any minute and tumble down the hillside in unison.

On the right side of the street the houses were well above the road level and towered over everything on the downward side. They seemed to hang on edge and lean unstably forward. The slightest disruption of their perch would cause them to rumble over everything in their path like an avalanche.

The left side of the street was just the opposite. As Marc drove at a snail's pace through the urban burrow of parked cars, trucks, and an occasional RV, he looked directly into the second-floor windows or at the porch rooftops of the houses on the downside of the hill. The houses had steep stairs leading off a sidewalk that went down to a porch or directly into the front doorway. In the darkness, pendent houses appeared to be sliding away.

What an odd sensation, Marc thought: *One side falling on top of you and the other falling away.* These homes had been here since he was a little kid and had parked on this street with his dad. Was it always this dark, this tight, and this unstable? Probably so, but it certainly seemed to be at the extreme tonight.

Regardless of his feelings of familiarity and uneasiness, Marc still had to find a parking place if he was going to get to the football game. He had already come a block and a half from Virginia Avenue without finding a place to park. *Must be a big game tonight and a good crowd,* he mused. Fans were walking on the sidewalks on both sides of the street headed toward the stadium, so there had to be parking further down. *But how far? This is going to be a long walk back to the stadium*, he groaned.

Marc had left his mother's home late and this unexpected search for a parking place was going to make him late for the kickoff. *Oh well*, he thought. *So what—I'm not really here to see the game. He didn't even know who Weirton was playing. He had come to—to just what? Why had he come?*

Marc was having trouble thinking of the right words to describe the reason he—at fifty-two years old—had decided to return to his alma mater to go to a high school football game. But he was alone, on a misty night, dark as a coal dungeon.

"Oh well, I'm here now," he rationalized to himself in a subconscious whisper.

"Now, I need to get parked and to the stadium."

He drove another block. The headlights revealed the end of the parking bottleneck and an abundance of parking spaces. He seemed to have reached the end of the fan parking. He pulled straight into a curbside parking spot, got out of the Jeep, locked the doors and stepped up on to the sidewalk. He could see the dim lights of the stadium far off in the distance. It was that same dull grayish glow he had seen as he approached downtown between the tandem mill buildings, structures and piping. The destination now had a shimmering quality about it, as if he were looking through water goggles.

As he sauntered towards the stadium, the entire atmosphere took him back to another time. He had walked these streets often as a kid going to the game with Dad, Uncle Len, Paul, Vince and whoever was available on game night. The swells, the sights, the voices, the memories all mixed together.

The view from this elevated sidewalk was even more revealing. The houses on the steep incline setting were both unique and monotonous. Their ghostly appearance on the lower side left him numb and his skin slightly goose-bumpy. The houses seemed to be foreboding shells with an occasional light-filled window protected by heavy drapery that caused the rays to appear as shadowy blotches of dull whiteness. Voices from these lower tiered dwellings floated upwards clearly. The sounds seemed to race uphill, and he could have eavesdropped on selected conversations if he wanted to.

The higher side homes seemed to be like rock-ledge overhangs. They were hanging precariously overhead with their porches and entrances beckoning only the sturdiest climber. The stairs were built at such an angle that you were required to hold onto the handrail to avoid tumbling backwards and to aid in moving perpendicularly. Even with this overwhelming appearance of a jutting overhang, the homes presented a hint of comfort and warmth. Those homes with outside lights or lights in windows provided the only illumination.

As Marc moved past these contrasting houses and their settings, they took on a life of their own. With no one to talk with, he was lost in his thoughts, imagination, and memories. The soft, almost undetectable voices of the other football fans walking ahead and behind him on both sides of the street only added to his loneliness. He thought for a moment that he must seem odd to the other shadowy figures journeying to the misty bright lights and faintly audible high stepping music of the school bands. But odd or not, he had a "right" to be here. He was part of this Friday night scene. The preoccupation with his "belonging" question lasted only momentarily.

His attention was directed back to the scene of the houses both towering above and lying below. As he glanced upward, the brick, stone and cement walls that kept the trees and the postage stamp lawns at bay, created a sense of importance, achievement and protection. The steps were climbing to terraces, and the doors opened into artistic homes and warm firesides. But the lower dwellings seemed to be merely temporary and precarious domiciles with porches, few domestic comforts and a vague uncertain future for those that would enter. *Funny how light, shadows and perception influence your mood,* Marc thought.

One of these had belonged to Aunt Ida and Uncle…? God, what was his name? He was a strange, unkempt and mysterious man. He always had a dark, rumpled suit coat on and that pipe in the side of his mouth that dangled on the edge of his purplish-black lip. You waited for it to fall, but it never did. He could talk and eat, and the pipe never left its perch. Their house was near the alley that cut through these houses. But that was a long time ago. They were gone before I finished high school, mused Marc.

"Hey Bobby!"

"Wait up. Hey Bobby, BOBBY! DAMN IT WAIT UP," someone yelled from the shadows across the street, and began running with the lead feet of an elephant and the gate of a large, overweight Great Dane. As each stride hit the black top, it resonated with the steely sound of studded army boots.

"HEY, I'VE BEEN TRYING TO CATCH UP TO YOU FOR A BLOCK," the runner shouted, as he got closer.

"I THOUGHT … OH …sorry. I thought you were… Sorry. I guess it's not you. I mean, WOW, I ran all that way," he gasped for air between every other word. With a shallow, almost breathless whisper, he grunted, "Sorry" again and moved ahead of Marc in a slower but still hurried pace.

Marc watched the interloper scurry off in the direction of the stadium. His figure became faint in the limited light of the evening. Even though Marc could only see his fading silhouette move quickly away, he was fascinated by the odd, almost laughable stride. He looked like a two-legged pogo stick. The entire body was in the air like a floating plump potato, with one foot hitting flat-footed and propelling the "potato" into the air again to repeat the sequence.

Very strange and funny…I have seen that stride before, thought Marc, when something else caught his attention, Permian's Grocery. Not much of a grocery store, but more like deli. It sat on the street corner of Virginia Avenue and across from the entrance to the high school campus. You could buy just about anything that a teenager would want, from sandwiches to cigarettes. You could also "play the numbers."

Marc stopped to look at Permian's. The building was empty, the sign was worn so badly that only the first three letters were visible and the GROCERY was gone completely. The large twelve-foot high store front windows were filthy, cracked and partially boarded. The spacious front concrete slab that had once served as a rendezvous for students, was uneven, heaved and crumbling. A congregate of leaves, papers and trash was tucked up against the fence that bordered the left side of the building.

Permian's Grocery had long ago given up the ghost. Only its legacy remained.

Marc turned away from the depressing scene and took the few steps to the street corner. He glanced at the rickety partition between Virginia Avenue and the stadium parking lot. It was his first unobstructed view of the assembly of traffic wardens as they meandered around the entrance. The group was task-less now as the stadium-bound traffic was coming to an end. Their voices pierced the muffled sounds of the early evening as they lamented with each other about the growing coolness. The light from the distant stadium and the few pale streetlights cast them in a devious role. *I bet that group is like a fraternity. You can't just join; you must be voted in*, Marc thought. *A band of merry gatekeepers.*

He crossed the road and semi-sprinted up the sidewalk until he reached the divided walkway of the high school campus. This was the promenade between the school buildings and the amphitheater for much of the socializing that came with the teenage scene. Even on this dark and chilly evening, the parade ground had a charm. Most of the large, half-century-old maple trees were still standing in between the two corridors of pavestones on either side.

Entering the boulevard-like passageway, he could see the almost leafless canopy stretched ahead creating a funnel-shaped walkway. With the light brighter at the far end, the sounds of the stadium were rushing toward him with a megaphone-like effect.

His step was quicker. Adrenaline from expectation sharpened his awareness. Fellow journeyers in small groups also picked up the pace, like some prod was suddenly being used to heighten their interest. The goal was in sight and the sounds were creating an almost adolescent-type excitement. But even as Marc's enthusiasm quickened, he sensed a feeling of emptiness. Gone were the buildings—the high school of his youth was gone!

The freshman building, the band Quonset hut, the shop complex and senior high buildings were all gone. They had lined the walkway with intersecting paths that crisscrossed the green. Buildings that had been symbols of stability, security, comfort, joy, excitement, frustration, boredom and education were gone. The ground where they once stood was empty and functionless. Even in the dull evening, the overgrown stubble of weeds, saplings and deadwood intertwined with the littered debris. Disuse and misuse was evident, and the void it depicted was the quality of an abandoned strip mine. The message was depressing to anyone who recalled that former landscape in its prime, and disappointing for those who would be hopeful of renewal.

Many of the cement entrances remained embedded in the turf, as if waiting for someone to restore their doorways to purpose. Even the wide stairways that carried students, faculty, and visitors between the campus ground levels to the bus depot and the parking lot were still intact. In the twilight, they betrayed their uselessness. The destinations of the walkways had been obliterated.

Marc could see himself bounding up those steps; in a hurry to get to friends, to practice, to a dry or warm hallway, to a love, and periodically to class. As he passed the stairs at an ever-lengthening step, he realized that they were many and steep. His breathing was already slightly elevated. *If he had to, could he climb them tonight? Yes, but slowly,* he thought, *very slowly.*

Clearly in view, a short distance ahead, was the end of the promenade. The landscape that had once been the home to teenage castles of learning was narrowing and its appearance gave no hint of what had once stood so stoically. The shortened distance to the back of the property brought the red brick alley that ran behind the removed buildings, into view. Surprised that it was still there, Marc slowed his pace to get a confirming view. A series of fans brushed past him in a rush. Marc came nearly to a stop as he focused on the once hidden model-T-accommodating lane. The block wall that kept the hillside at bay remained. That back causeway had always been the gathering spot for all the cigarette junkies, wayward class truants, lovers, delinquents and pandering town folks. When it was dull inside the ivied halls, you could usually find some colorful event happening in the alley.

Back and side exits from all the school buildings led to the alley. Dressing rooms from the gym emptied into the back lane and provided the quickest access to the athletic field, which for the most part was the stadium. The stadium in those days served as both practice and playing field. A single purpose gridiron was a luxury in the 1950s.

Would-be heroes sauntered, jogged but rarely ran out to football, track and maybe some baseball practice along the uneven, rut-ridden brick roadway. Cheerleaders in bikini bottomed outfits with short skirts restricting a direct view of their rumps, would bounce, hop and giggle their way to the stadium grass—more interested in being seen than perfecting their inducements for success and victory. Band members parachuting out of the World War II hanger that served as their practice, dressing and storage room would zigzag down the passage as if they were a gaggle of geese on their way to nowhere. Some were bellowing on their instruments, others playing tuning chords over and over in a mishmash of discord—especially the percussion section. Drum rolls tended to drown out all other sounds. If done in unison, rat-a-tat-tat could rattle your teeth like a hailstorm on a garage's tin roof.

All those contrary minstrels, even though they made no music, could stir your blood and make you feel alive, destined and invincible, even if only for a moment, until the reality of the drudgery of practice commenced. Then everyone was fighting for space on the only green pasture bigger than first down yardage for city blocks. The band captured the midfield; cheerleaders, the nearest goal post, and the football team the distant corner. Each went through their paces, eventually returning to the bosom of their locker rooms, practice hut and dressing rooms by way of the back alley.

On the evening of game day, that trip was a journey to Bourbon Street at Mardi Gras, to Fifth Avenue in New York City on Thanksgiving Day, and doing the stroll on American Band Stand all at the same time and in unison.

WOW, I still can see it, feel it and hear it, Marc reminisced.

"Damn it," Marc said aloud. He had stumbled and nearly fallen as he stepped off the paved sidewalk into the cindered parking lot crammed with cars.

"You all right?" a baseball capped gal asked.

"Yeah…Yeah, I'm fine," he mumbled in some foolish soprano pitch.

"That's the news for tonight. From all of us here at ABC have a good evening and an enjoyable weekend. I'll see you back here on Monday. Good Night."

"This has been ABC Evening News with Peter Jennings."

"See yourself in the Ford of the future. Take that test drive at your Ohio Valley Ford Dealers today and be driving your new Ford tomorrow. Don't wait you'll…"

She pressed the remote volume button and reduced the TV sound to a bare whisper.

"Do you have a favorite show you like to watch? It doesn't matter to me, besides I have to finish the kitchen."

"Oh, let it be Jamie, we have all evening. It doesn't matter to me. I keep the TV on for company since Dad died—just to have some sound in the house. I'll watch anything. Whatever."

Whatever, Jamie thought. *Wonder what that means. I know that she has her favorites. I'll just keep it on ABC; there will be some mindless game show soon.*

Jamie waited until the advertisements were over and then pushed the control to raise the sound. "And now it's time for everyone's favorite show of fun and prizes: WHEEL OF FORTUNE with Pat Sajak and Vanna White."

"You watch this don't you mother?" Jamie asked, forcing her voice to be as sincere and accommodating as possible. She always stumbled, well maybe choked on the word "mother." But mother-in-law was too—too something—and to keep peace with her husband and her 80 year old evening companion, who was the grand matriarch of the family, she had acquiesced many years ago. Keeping a low profile and conversation to a minimum was critical to her sanity and getting through the evening. It was just the two of them in the house now that "hubby" had left for an evening of football. Her mother-in-law always referred to her own son as Jamie's "hubby." Why such a reference was another of those American slang terms that even after 30 years of American residence, Jamie never understood.

She pulled herself out of the marshmallow cushion of the faded blue sofa. The spring support in the living room furniture piece had lost all tension years ago, so that once you were down, getting up and "out" was a major chore. You had to push with both arms and leverage the weight of your lower body with the calves of your legs against the sofa's front frame and raise yourself with body pressure and a jerk.

Having escaped from the octopus-like couch, Jamie turned from the living room and moved toward the kitchen where duty called. As she glanced at the hallway, the 1950s décor filled her vision and her mind. Nothing in the house had changed since her first introduction to the family homestead thirty years or more ago. The carpet throughout the main first floor was still a bright absurd flowered pattern of reds, blues and greens with turquoise and violet hues as accents. Besides the ostentatiousness of the gaudy colors, the years of use and misuse were evident in the pathways from the front door and the stairway to the upstairs. It had not been cleaned in years, and to even try to do so now would probably destroy the brittle fabric.

However, despite the decades old décor and the dilapidated furniture, the home had a charm of its own. The building styles of the mid-1930s accentuated strength, roominess, functionality, and most of all, a subtle richness. The woodwork that framed the doorways and created the floorboards, the stairway banister, and the large heavy solid doors were creamy marbled cherry, very rich and warm cherry.

The workmen, who created this home with its whimsical woodcraft, had artistic talent beyond being carpenters. Their workmanship remained the one redeeming quality that made this house a home of pride and compassion.

Jamie had always admired the exquisite appointment of her in-laws home and had a sincere fondness for its roominess and eloquence of function. The warmth that filled its rooms over the years could be sensed the moment you entered. Her in-laws and the tight knit family that used this home as a gathering place had played out scenes of comedy, tragedies, pageants, vaudeville, but most of all life. What stories these walls could tell—what they had witnessed. In this home a family had started, grown, multiplied and was now starting to disintegrate.

Entering the kitchen, Jamie immediately caught sight of the stack of dirty dishes, cooking pots and pans covering both the kitchen table and the sink counter. *How could dinner for three create such a mess?* She turned and glanced through the doorway to the dining room and realized that there were even more dishes on that table in the form of coffee cups and dessert plates. *It's going to a sizable task to get this all cleared, washed and returned to the right cupboard,* she thought. Every visit the clean-up duty always fell to her. When her father-in-law was alive, he would always help, and they had some of their best discussions between the soapy water and the dishtowel. But he had been gone for a number of years and this task had become hers alone.

This old house, despite all of its charm and character, had many flaws and the lack of a dishwasher was one of them.

Jamie allowed herself a silent, resigned "sigh" and started to organize the mess. In the living room the WHEEL OF FORTUNE was in full swing and the volume set at such amplitude she could hear every groan, moan, laugh and applause of the studio audience. She would have to put all the noise in the back of her mind and concentrate on something else. Jamie loathed game shows. She walked back to the kitchen entrance into the hallway and pulled the pocket door closed. At least part of the TV noise would be muffled. Turning into the dining room, she picked up the dishes and stacked them on the kitchen counter. It took a couple of trips before the table was cleared and she could shut the door to the dining room, closing off the kitchen completely.

As the hot water filled the sink, the detergent transformed it into a milky soup of bubbles. In went the first batch of dishes and back went Jamie's thoughts to her earliest memories of leaving England, journeying to the states and to the place called Weirton, West Virginia.

It was a journey that was supposed to last only a year—maybe two at the most—her father and mother had said. It was Dad's "job and a good opportunity." Weirton Steel was a world leader in the manufacturing of tin, and the chance to experience the innovative techniques it had produced would be a boost to his career at Birmingham Iron and Steel. The move was called a "rotation of assignment" arranged between the two companies. Mother and Dad considered it a great chance to see America and "have an exciting adventure." That may have been fine for them, but not for a sixteen year-old girl just trying to fit in at a new school.

Thoughts of the farewell party hosted at the St. James Club flashed into her mind. In a room filled with friends and business acquaintances of her father, she found few women in attendance and no other young people. Nevertheless, it left a lasting impression. Jamie recalled the old-world charm of the prestigious hall, the dark wainscoting rising to a towering ceiling beamed with heavy arches. Various dignitaries of past generations graced the walls; their visages smiling benignly from ornate gilt frames. Dinner had been served on an enormous trestle table that extended the length of the room and involved several courses. What a send-off for her father! He was so pleased that the top executives were there to wish him well. *I can almost smell the cigar smoke after forty years,* mused Jamie. *I wonder if the St. James Club still exists?*

Shortly thereafter, the family had embarked on Jamie's first real trip through England. Jamie remembered her reluctance and fear to leave the safety of home and her resolve not to enjoy any of the trip—first to London and then on to Plymouth where they were to board the steamer for the United States. Dad had thought they should spend a couple of days in London first, and despite her resolve, Jamie found herself fascinated.

As the taxi drove them from the station to their hotel across town, she found herself glued to the window. People queuing for vegetables from stalls right in the center of the street, clothing stalls, fresh fish and game hanging on hooks, and persons of all nationalities dressed in native outfits, Indian, African and Chinese intermingled. Streets so narrow that she gasped at times thinking they were only inches away from oncoming traffic barreling toward them at a terrifying speed. All of this complicated by bicyclists with huge baskets across their handlebars filled with fresh veggies and loaves of bread. Birmingham was nothing like this—a steel based town, it stamped more of workers and home life and lacked the cosmopolitan atmosphere and excitement found in London.

For Jamie, it seemed the two days allotted to see this fascinating city went by far too quickly and all too soon, they found themselves off to Plymouth. Leaving the city behind, the train slowly wound itself through the countryside passing through quaint little towns each clustered around the churches, their tall spires rising above the cottages and farms. As they approached the sea, the countryside began to appear more rolling with hedgerows surrounding the fields creating the appearance of a patchwork quilt, each hill providing a better view than the one before—so charming. Why had they never explored Devon before?

She could smell the sea even before the train began its descent into the station. Nothing had prepared her for seeing the ship from the dock. Just looking at it and realizing that she was going to spend a week at sea and was actually going to America—*why I still get excited recalling walking up the gang plank,* thought Jamie. She could still hear the deep whistle and feel the tugs bumping alongside churning the water, guiding the huge ship out of the harbor. She had stood with her mother, father and little brother, all of them silent, along the rail as their homeland got smaller and smaller and finally disappeared into the horizon. They were at sea and had left everyone, friends, family and home behind.

Jamie came back to reality as her hand slipped into the sudsy water. She had recalled the Atlantic crossing many times over the years, and as usual, the memory was clear and precise. The company had actually provided their family with a fairly large suite that enabled her parents a room of their own. Jamie slept on a pullout couch in the sitting room, with her little brother curled up alongside in a sleeping bag.

A balcony opened off the far end. The first night she could not sleep as thoughts raced through her mind; sadness at leaving home mixed with excitement of the trip and fear of the unknown town waiting for her in the states. She ventured onto the balcony and was enthralled with the scene awaiting her. The moon was full, creating a trail across the sea, silver fish were jumping through the waves, but the best was the sky. Millions of stars seemed to just hang over her head. She had never seen such a sky. That night she had grabbed her blanket and watched the sky and sea until she finally fell asleep.

During the remainder of the journey she had let herself flow into the shipboard activities, dinner at the captain's table, shuffleboard and even slide shows in the evenings presented by a retired Navy commander relating his exploits and travels through India, across the Himalayans to China, Japan, ending in Australia. *I thought it sounded so boring, but I actually allowed myself to enjoy everything from visiting with little old ladies to even babysitting one evening—weird,* thought Jamie.

The ship had actually seemed dwarfed by the towering skyscrapers as they approached New York harbor. Jamie remembered how she had craned her neck to see the modern exciting city. As they passed the Statue of Liberty, the passengers stood as a body in awe of the Lady Liberty who seemed to be raising her torch just for them, welcoming all to this new land.

Once through customs, her father, now anxious to reach his new destination, would not succumb to either his wife's or Jamie's pleas to stay in New York awhile. He immediately hailed a taxi for Grand Central Station. What little they were able to see of the city differed so from London that Jamie could not even count the ways—but the traffic was not much different with the many taxis weaving through at breakneck speeds.

Everything seemed new and shiny. Tall skyscrapers, wide boulevards and shops with glittering window arrangements caught her eye, and the people seemed to be dressed in the latest fashions. Lights danced on the marquees. One could hardly look in every direction at the same time. It was nightfall when they finally boarded the train for Pittsburgh and settled themselves in their assigned sleeper berths. Jamie was so tired; she fell right to sleep without seeing any more of the city as they sped westward.

As dawn arose, they found themselves crossing the Appalachian Mountains. Summer was in full swing and the trees even at this altitude were a kaleidoscope of deep green, sea green turquoise and teal. Even so, it seemed empty. As they traveled across Pennsylvania, there seemed to be no towns. Jamie thought wistfully of the patchwork quilt charm of southern England dotted with quaint towns and farms and wondered how she could ever get accustomed to this wilderness.

She had watched the rugged landscape silently as the train wound through the mountains, waves of homesickness sweeping over her. After a long hard day, the train approached Pittsburgh. High hills dotted with house after house loomed over them as they wound around the riverbed toward the center of the city. Somehow it seemed more familiar. Smoke from steel mills wafted across the skyline and there was grayness and a grittiness in the air—Birmingham! It was very similar to home. The train crossed a huge bridge where three rivers seemed to converge into one and then suddenly it plunged into the darkness of the station.

As they gathered their bags and headed along the track, they noticed a large bald-headed man carrying a sign over his head with Dad's name in bold lettering. As they approached, his face broke into a huge grin and he hugged everyone. "Welcome, welcome to you all. I am Gus, chief supervisor of plating," he beamed. She had warmed to him from the start and he had become and remained an important part of their lives. *How long ago it seemed.*

"I have a house for you. Marietta and I picked it and it is very fine; up in Marland Heights, the best area." A Porter was swiftly dispatched to get their travelling bags and take them to a waiting car. Gus made sure all the personal items were packed safely in the boot, or trunk, as years of Americanizing had taught her.

He arranged for the larger travel trunks to be loaded into a waiting Weirton Steel cloth-covered truck. He gave the driver the directions to their new home provided by the Company and forcefully told the man to go directly to the house and make certain the trunks were immediately taken into the house. Dad and mother were impressed and flattered with all the attention lavished on them. Jamie had the same feeling.

Uncle Gus, as Jamie would later call their first American greeter, made everyone feel comfortable with a box of cookies, baked by his wife

Marietta, and a "pop." Once everyone had caught their breath and sat for fifteen minutes or so with the goodies, Gus started the car and off through the streets of Pittsburgh they motored, across the three rivers by bridge and into the countryside they went. Closer and closer to the adventure destination. Jamie knew her mother was nervous and indeed frightened as they traveled the narrow, winding roads to Weirton.

The houses looked so tiny and unkempt with cars, tools, and animals just laying around the yards, large front porches with washing machines in plain view. *How could they live here? Yes, there were parts of Birmingham that were poor, but this was slovenly*, Jamie worried. "Almost here, now," said Gus as they turned down the main street. The steel mill dwarfed the town with huge pipes crisscrossing the mainstreet and soot covering sidewalks and streets. Yellow smoke created a haze so thick you could hardly see the storefronts. Even in remembrance, Jamie could taste the sulfur grit of this thriving American steel mill town.

Then Gus turned the car and immediately began to climb a steep hill. Up and up they went. You could not help but notice the neatly groomed homes and gardens, blooming trees and flower boxes. The entire surroundings changed; for the better.

Jamie remembered holding her breath. Then, there they were, turning into the driveway of the place where they were to live for the next year. She and her mother had caught each other's eye and simultaneously had let out a sigh. It was fine. A sturdy, dark Tudor style home with leaded glass windows covered with ivy, surrounded by a hedge and even a garden in the front. Jamie had not expected anything like this; to be honest she had not thought about the house at all—just the entire uprooting of her life.

"Jamie, Jamie," the voice from the living room sounded distressed.

Jamie reluctantly pulled her thoughts from the warmth of her memories and almost ran into the adjoining room. She found her mother-in-law on her hands and knees in the middle of the floor. "It's Okay, I'm fine. I just had a light spell and found myself here and I can't get up," she rasped. Jamie gently helped the frail lady to her feet and led her into the bathroom where she had been headed. After making sure she truly was fine, Jamie pulled the door behind her and let out a low sigh.

Her own heart was still pounding as she dropped down on the couch. She marveled at how delicate and truly bony she found Elsie and worried anew about her living alone in this house. Something like this was precisely what they had feared would happen and had been a topic of discussion for the past two years among the family. Jamie's sister-in-law wanted her mother to live with her in Virginia, but that would mean Elsie leaving her home of sixty years, and most of all, her extended family. Jamie did not even want to think about Elsie coming to live with "Hubby" and her—privately, one of her oldest nightmares.

To Jamie, the solution seemed obvious. There was a beautiful new complex just up the next hill that would fill all their needs for Elsie. The care level was graduated, starting with apartment living, then assisted living, followed by skilled nursing if needed. They had even visited the director and toured the facilities. If she moved into one of the lovely apartments, the view from the window would be the same view into the woods and down the hill that she had now. Her own furniture would surround her and she could have her dinner with other residents, join activities, and best of all, have companionship and someone to look in on her and give her the care she needed. Jamie and "Hubby" would be spared the constant upkeep of the old house and they could still take Elsie home for dinner and visit as often as they did now. All of this seemed to be out of the question as Elsie refused to even listen or discuss the idea and would only respond with firm "No's."

Despite this rational solution, in her heart Jamie knew that to her mother-in-law, her home was the most important thing in her life and she would never want to leave. She, herself, knew only too well that feeling and again, allowed herself to drift back in time.

The trip through the parking lot was like maneuvering a maze of cars, trucks, and buses sardined into every nook and cranny. As Marc reached the entrance to the stadium, he started up the incline and found what appeared was the shortest of the three lines to buy tickets. Everyone moved quickly now, including the ticket seller in the small wooden booth, as the kick-off time approached.

"A general admission ticket please," Marc asked as he handed a five-dollar bill through the moon-shaped cutout in the window.

"That's $4.00. You got a buck coming back."

Marc took his change and the ticket and moved off to his left and entered the gateway into the stadium. After handing over his ticket, he took a few steps onto the gray cinder walkway and stopped to take in the stadium that he had not seen for decades. It was the same, but different. The atmosphere and the sensation of just being there were invigorating, exciting, and sad at the same time.

He took a few steps over to the three-foot high inner-fence that cordoned off the playing field from the outside track. The steel linked fence was the same as it had been in the 1950s. It was bent, scarred, and had not been painted for who knows how long. He noticed the three-station concrete water fountain sitting at the gate. It had long ago stopped serving its main purpose and now was strictly a sentinel of bygone days. It had been freshly painted red, white, and black—the hometown's colors and stood out against all the spartan surroundings.

Inside the gate stood the large flagpole, still surrounded by a group of Boy Scouts serving as a color guard. They held a folded flag in readiness of unfurling with the playing of the Star Spangled Banner. At that moment, a squeaky voice came over the inadequate public speaker. It was hard to decipher exactly what was being said, but the band coming to attention and spectators stopping to look towards the flagpole, was message enough that the two high school bands were about to play the national anthem.

As the music started, Marc could hear voices behind him picking up the familiar phrase "*Oh Say can you see by the dawn's early light...*"

The flag was raised faster than the music and reached the top of the pole halfway through the national tribute. When the combined bands finished, the sound of the passing crowd immediately picked up and Marc turned to see the inside of the stadium for the first time in at least twenty-five years.

"Damn," he said, "It hasn't changed."

The main concrete block stands were right where they had always been. The press box, or better called the enclosed coaches box, was at the top and middle of the grandstands. The stands covered the area between the ten yard lines with the grassy, roughly corrugated hillside stabilizing the ends. The stadium builders had carved the grounds and the grandstand structure out of the steeply sloping hillside and used the natural topography to enhance the spectator capacity. There had been many Friday nights when grassy seats were the only ones available to general admission latecomers. *But not tonight,* thought Marc.

He glanced to his left, and sure enough, the concession stand was still there. There were lines trying to get stadium hot dogs, a box of popcorn or something to drink. The concession stand looked as if it would fall over at any moment and probably had not been worked on for the past forty years. He made his way through the crowd of high school or younger students who were grouped in bunches or running about helter-skelter. Their voices were loud and young, and the decibels of sound were high even though they were outside. There was a school booster's booth with a sign advertising sweatshirts, hats, jerseys, and all kinds of football paraphernalia. He walked over and glanced at the merchandise.

"Can I get you something?" asked a rather short, chubby woman dressed in one of the large red sweatshirts.

"I don't know," said Marc, "just looking."

"Well, let me know," said the attendant.

Marc looked around and decided to get a sweatshirt for himself with the high school colors and logo.

"Can I get a sweatshirt?" But he was ignored as the chubby red-clad saleswoman talked to her co-worker.

Marc raised his voice, "Miss"—after shouting the fifth time, she turned—"Yeah?"

"I'll have one of those red sweatshirts with the Indian horse."

"What size?"

"I need a XXL," said Marc.

"We are all out of those," she chuckled.

"How about an XXL in the Black?"

"Nope, no XXL in anything."

"OK, thanks," said Marc somewhat deflated by the idea that he wasn't able to make a purchase. Forty years ago he had had a waist size of thirty-two inches and now his bulk meant that he could not even buy a sweatshirt.

He stalked away in frustration and moved over to the chain fence. The kick-off was about to take place, and he wanted to get a good view. He leaned against the fence realizing it was the same that had existed when he was a player—wobbly, unpainted and for the most part, dilapidated.

He squeezed in between a couple of other fence-leaners and glanced down the field as the purple-clad visitors kicked off to the home team dressed in their red and black uniforms, trimmed in white.

The aroma of the freshly cut grass mixed with the moist evening dew and the acidic steel mill set the reality of the place and time. The voices and cheers, even the distant sounds of pads and helmets, almost made time stand still. The memories rushed through him with lightning speed and caused a moment of breathlessness. The kick-off was over and teams began the struggle of the evening—to overpower, dominate and eventually defeat the opponent.

After a few plays had been run, Marc left the fence and wandered to the grandstand and started up the staircase. He wanted to be at the top to get the same perspective of the game that he and his father, uncle and cousins had shared many years ago when they attended ritually each Friday night.

The concrete stairway was cracking and crumbling with years of use and weather. As each step brought him closer to the top, he realized how sparse the crowd really was and how their dress and mannerisms differed from his. He had not been in the midst of his old hometown citizenry for many years. As he neared the top, the stadium seats were almost empty, the wooden benches sagging with the invisible weight of past occupants. They had a gray, dull color, sprinkled with splinter-like shades of raw yellow wood.

He reached the walkway at the top of the stadium and turned to the vista of the distant low bleachers on the far side of the field, and the rising gray-black iron ore-covered corrugated buildings of the steel mill. Beyond the steam-belching exhaust funnels, the hills that encased the valley could barely be seen. The hills seemed to blend into the dark western sky creating an ethereal feeling. As his eyes focused, he could barely see the ridge of the road that he had traveled over the tandem mill just thirty minutes before. Marc again felt the loneliness of being in a lost world that either he had passed by or that had passed by him.

The crowd's noise picked up and brought Marc's attention back to the field. The two teams were in the middle of the gridiron with a purple-shirted sprinter streaking down the sidelines. It was obvious that the ball carrier had the speed, as well as an open field in front of him, to go all the way, and a few seconds later, he had scored for the visitors. The two teams gathered at the end zone with the purple knights attempting the extra point—missing! Five minutes into the game and the home team was losing 6-0.

As the teams trotted back to the mid-field area, Marc gazed down at the green field, noticing that it was anything but a continuous carpet. The middle of the field was worn to dirt with larger patches of dirt scattered along the sidelines. The dirt had a smattering of brown hues, but was predominately black with the soot of the mill.

The crowd in the stadium seated below was shocked and seemed very dejected. The home fans had been startled by the quick scoring of the visitors. The lack of any audible reaction, except for a few moans and guttural utterances, implied a familiar discontentment as well as acceptance. They had experienced this sour start before. It was frustrating, but expected.

Marc leaned against the guardrail separating the stadium top walkway from the thirty or so rows of bench-seating, stretching from his pedestal to the gray gravel running track below. From this mantel he could survey the field, the stands, the rooters and the football revelry.

"Ouch, damn it," Marc blurted out unconsciously. He had slid his hand along the railing separating the lower stadium seating and the top shelf walkway and the rickety old temporary stands. His quick movement had sent a sliver of rusty iron into his hand and thumb.

He jerked back as a reflex to the sudden prick and pain. He put his thumb in his mouth in an attempt to ease the discomfort and sooth the distress. The wound was more of a scratch than a laceration.

"The fence get you, too?" a voice remarked. The fellow was standing in the background. He was rather robust. Marc knew he, himself, had a slight fifty-year-old paunch, but this stranger resembled a snowman, with a pudgy, round face and a very large potbelly with legs somewhere underneath. Immediately, Marc noticed the filthy, torn grayish jacket the snowman wore, and he was sure he could smell it along with liquored breath.

"That rail has gotten me a couple of times, the damn thing hasn't been painted for years."

Marc took his thumb out of his mouth and looked closely at the reddish pencil line near the center of the thumbprint. "That hurt. It caught me good in two places," Marc said as he noticed scraped skin and blood on the palm of his right hand.

"It'll do that," snowman said with a smirk.

Both looked back to the field with Marc re-examining his hand and thumb to make sure there was no splinter lodged in the wound. There did not seem to be, but the hand and thumb pulsated with discomfort. Marc shook his hand in a waving motion to shoo away the tingle.

"I usually sit over there with that bunch," the snowman blurted out. "Want to join me—at least you won't risk another cut and you can take a load off."

"Well—ah—that sounds okay—if you don't mind," Marc stammered.

"Hell, come on."

They moved towards the center of the field and took the stairs down a few rows from the top. There were a group of five or six guys scattered in a loosely defined semi-circle. Marc and snowman sat behind the top man in the group. Nods all around went to the snowman and a few high fives followed. The snowman mumbled a few names with a glance toward Marc in the gesture of an introduction. Marc half-heartedly raised his right hand and waved it back and forth a few times. One big fellow sitting in front looked familiar. Marc realized that this was Mr. Big who had yelled at him as he walked towards the stadium.

A split second later they were all looking towards the field and the continuing game. The visitors had scored for the second time with ease. The home crowd groaned in unison, but took the opponents' score in stride, once again.

The home team had the ball, but their offense made a number of mistakes and was so ineffective that they lost ground. The fourth down punt sheared off the kicker's foot and barely carried twenty yards beyond the line of scrimmage.

"What the hell was that!" was the outburst almost simultaneously by three or four of the men. "You've got to be kidding me," yelled the big fellow sitting in front of the snowman. "Damn, they get worse each week. I can't believe it. We haven't had a winning team in years. Damn it!"

"They're just no fucking good!" blurted out a baseball-capped malcontent off to the right.

"Easy, Easy," said his companion. "Watch your language."

About two dozen spectators turned around and looked irately at the entire group. A few of the men stood and let the culprits know their foul mouths would not be tolerated.

"Hey, you with the big mouth… We have families here. We don't need your kind of cheering," said one of the incensed.

"Yeah, Yeah, sorry," said the big man in a mild manner. He leaned forward and in a calm, but sharp, voice warned: "Chris, if you don't watch your mouth, I'll throw you out myself. Every time I get home for a game and meet up with you, something goes wrong. So, shut up!"

Chris adjusted his cap and remarked, "Okay, okay, but they ain't good." The scrawny little man was determined to get in the last word.

Mr. Big turned around to snowman, "Your cousin is going to get me really mad. One of these days and I'm going to lose my temper like we did when we were kids."

"I know," said snowman, "cool down."

Big man and Marc were staring at each other—both searching their memory.

"I know you!" said Mr. Big.

"I think so," replied Marc. "You yelled at me on the street tonight."

"Right, I thought you were Bobby" – pointing at snowman. "No, I know you from someplace else. You from Weirton?" he asked.

"Was many years ago, grew up here, went to Weir High class of nineteen sixty—no, no nineteen fifty-nine," Marc answered.

"Me, too," Mr. Big blurted out, his eyes popping and his face showing some crimson shade of excitement. "Scotty Stockdale," his hand outstretched, "and this is Bobby—Bob Moffit," he announced pointing to snowman.

Marc reached out and grabbed the bear-sized hand firmly. "You son of a gun— Marc Floreau." Marc, too, was grinning to see two old classmates and lost childhood friends. They all chuckled a little and Marc asked Mr. Big, "Do they still call you 'Sage'?"

It was warm in the bedroom and stuffy. She opened the two corner windows in the hope of getting the cool evening air to counter the furnace that was set at an absurd, steamy high seventy-five° temperature. Jamie's mother-in-law was always cold, summer, winter, fall, no matter the season or the outside temperature.

The house was always "closed up." The storm windows were on year round, the windows covered by heavy drapes, with seldom a window open. That was a problem even now. Jamie had opened the windows but the storms were fastened shut and stuck. She went back to each window and checked the latch on the storm windows. Sure enough: closed and locked. She struggled to loosen the catch and with some pushing and pulling weakened the resistance holding the outer glass casing in place. Her hands firmly gripped the small shanks on both sides and forcefully pulled upward. The protective frame and glass creaked and shrieked raucously as it lifted, allowing the cool breeze to rush in.

Fresh air at last, Jamie thought. Now the other window needed her attention.

"Jamie – Jamie, are you alright? What was that shriek?" It was Jamie's mother-in-law from downstairs.

"Everything is fine, Mother," Jamie tried to hold her tongue as she walked out of the bedroom and stood at the top of the stairs. With less bitterness, Jamie explained that she was opening the windows, and as they had been stuck fast, she had to yank them open. She told her mother-in-law she had one more to open and turned to do just that.

"You be careful. Those windows are old and could break and cut you. Be careful," was the reply.

"I will," Jamie shouted.

As she returned to her window duties, Jamie thought of her granny's home in Berkswell. The ancestral home was anything but modern by any standards, with its 19th century idiosyncrasies, much older than this house imbued with the history of generations. She could almost smell the musty aroma of the hundred years plus, stone and timber framed home.

As a child, frequent trips to her father's parents' home meant a drive through pretty villages oozing with the charm and the atmosphere of a by-gone era. Even in her youth, Jamie was delighted with the leafy lanes from Birmingham to Berkswell. The hour and a half trip took her family through some of the most beautiful countryside in the Midlands of England.

It was always a treat to leave the dusty, grimy metropolis that was Birmingham. It wasn't called the city of a thousand trades for no reason. The center of England's industrial might, with its smells, sounds and sights, was known for its grinding prosperity in the nineteen fifty's. Vocational character encompassed every aspect of city life.

Fortunately for Jamie and her family the "grannies" (as the family called them) homestead provided a respite. Birmingham was a commerce center with all the benefits of corporate prosperity for her father and the drawbacks of manufacturing dinginess for her, her brother and her mom. At least it was positioned with easy access to the scenic, refreshing country seclusion and hearth of family.

It had been a long time since Jamie had taken a quiet moment to remember Berkswell and Granny Tolliver's home. Good memories, longings, and some regrets.

When she arrived in the United States in nineteen fifty-eight, she could only think of home, England, friends along Warwick Road, Wake Green School, her dad's birthplace – Berkswell, and her granny and grandpa. She had missed them all so. Why Dad had to come here to work, she never really understood.

Dad and Mom said for "only a year or two." Now, nearly thirty-plus years later they were all still here in the United States: Mom and Dad in Georgia, and she married with grown children and still living in West Virginia. Tonight, Jamie was back in her first American hometown—Weirton, Weirton, West Virginia. She was waiting for her husband to come in from a night out and about in his old haunt.

Well, Jamie was not going to stay up. She would leave that task to her mother-in-law. With her asleep, "hubby" and his mother will have a chance to talk when he gets home, probably about her.

Now, if only the torrid heat in the bedroom would subside and the cool evening breeze would overtake the room's environment, she could sleep. This sultriness is worse than sitting around granny Tolliver's AGA, the enormous fire burning stove, in the Berkswell kitchen.

The old friends had talked about past times, their respective careers, the decay of the Ohio Valley, their restlessness, friends lost and forgotten but mostly about their high water mark, Weir High School. The stadium crowd had been dwindling since the half-time band performances. The few who were still seated were parents of the players and some visiting fans enjoying the obvious outcome.

"Sage" and Marc finally decided to part. Their conversation exhausted, they would go their separate ways. Sage was going to stay with Bobby and the others. Mark shook a few hands and said his "see yah's." A couple husky replies followed his jerky gait down the stadium stairs to the running track.

Marc maneuvered towards the exit with the remains of the throng. It had been an evening of veritable remembrances; a stab of the past, which rendered both rewards and regrets. As he strode at the pace of the disinterested quiet clump, he realized the game was in its final moments. He paused and looked up at the scoreboard.

Visitors 33 / Red Riders 0

Chapter 2

Encounter

Wake up little Susie wake up... We both fell sound asleep... movies over, It's four O... Wake up little Susie ..., a song by The Everly Brothers, "Wake up Little Susie," blasted away on WEIR – AM. The reception faded a bit as Williams Drive sloped into a meadow like park. The drive continued past a two story reddish brown brick and granite stoned circular structure on its way to Williams Country Club. The Grecian architectural building and grounds housed a municipal pool surrounded by a park of grassland and woodland.

Marc strained to hear the words and rhythm of the music on the radio. He slowed, turned right before he reached the pool and let the car drift onto the gravel driveway of the parking lot.

The lot was packed. Cars and an occasional pick-up crowded into the sloping and ridge-filled terrain. It always was crammed on hot steamy summer days. The gravel under the tires crunched and crackled like Rice Krispies cereal. The stones in the lot topping were loose in hot tar after nearly a week of summer heat and humidity. The rattling thunder of "rap," "smack," "whack," "whop," and "tap" made the sultriness even more repressing and the temperamental radio barely audible.

The front and second rows were all filled, but spotting some openings in the back row, Marc drove to the rear and maneuvered the car sharply to get the angle to back into the open space. He quickly snatched the towel that was on the front seat and exited. Wow, it was hot. The heat radiated from the stony surface, the cars, the dirt, even the small patches of grass. A stifling haze captured the feverish temperature. His egg white, short-sleeved pullover shirt and the seat of his sandy brown khakis were sticking to him.

Driving with all the windows down had not provided adequate ventilation to overcome the scorcher. He tugged selfconsciously at his clothing to release the cloth bound to his body. One advantage to parking in the hinterland was the shade provided by the red maple trees on the boundary. While the car was not completely shade covered now, it would be later in the day as the sun drifted lower.

Marc sauntered through the coupes, sedans, occasional pick-ups and a few convertibles toward the pool. His six foot plus frame was muscular, slim and athletic; his face compact with a subtle nose and light blue eyes. His cinnamon-blond hair was cut very close on the side with a flat top crown, held upright at his temple with gel. His face, arms and neck, were reddish-bronze in color from all the summer sun. As he crossed Riverview Drive, which separated the parking lot and the Marland Heights Municipal Pool, his pace quickened. He could hear the swimming crowd all a buzz with fun filled screams, laughter, and music over the park-wide sound system; mothers' voices calling and directing children and an overall babble of scores of bathers trying to cool themselves with a dip.

The sounds would get louder as he neared the building and would become even louder when he worked his late afternoon to evening lifeguard shift. The noise from all the malarkey that went on during a busy, tropical summer day at the pool was always irritating. Worse yet, he might end up nursing a bunch of twelve year olds left there by their mothers.

Regardless of the frustrations with the job, at least he was paid and his friends were always around. If he hadn't taken this job, he would be home probably toiling in the garden that consumed the back yard, working more hours at the gas station, or even worse, his dad would have arranged a job for him in the mill. All of those alternatives were real downers and boring. At least here, something was usually happening.

Up the walkway he continued. The blacktop walk was even hotter than the gravel, but at least the large maple and ash trees in the garden strips that separated the wheel-spoked sidewalks, provided shade and dropped the temperature a few degrees. Actually the landscaping was very nice—much better than around home. His mother might not agree, but these grounds were landscaped and tended by a score of gardeners from Weirton Steel.

The "Company," as it was universally called by everyone in town, provided most people with, not only their jobs, but also with most of the really nice things in the town—the pool, its gardens, the country club, the community center, the holiday parades, the hospital, and even one of the mill executives served as mayor. Marc reflected for a moment on the question that was often asked around the dining table: *What happens if the Company leaves or goes under? Heaven forbid!*

He could smell the fragrance of the flowers planted along the path. There were beds of petunias, impatiens, and geraniums in full bloom. Large colorful creamy white and rose red rhododendrons centered one of the garden spots. Bright fire red marigolds and feather lime grasses bordered low shrubs gathered in decorative small terraces and oval shaped landscaped centers. The grass had been cut in the morning and the freshly mowed musky scent remained. Together the ambrosia of the garden was sweet and a momentary refuge from the vapor locked stagnation of the day.

As he drew closer to the main promenade which encircled the pool entrance, the swarming crowd of swimmers resembled a disorganized rabble. A family approached him, headed to their car. All three were lobster red. Mother's forehead and shoulders looked scalded and the two pre-teen youngsters were even more roasted. They may have cooled off in the water, but their afterglow was going to make the evening even more uncomfortable.

"Mom, I don't want to go yet," moaned the stick-figured boy as they passed. "It's too hot to go home now," he mumbled into the ground.

"I told you we would leave after lunch. It's time to go."

"Aw, MOM."

"Your sister is tired and I have to get supper on the table for your dad," was the snappy reply from Mom as she rushed by Marc holding the hand of a very lethargic sun burnt little girl.

Not a happy bunch, Marc thought, *after a day of supposed fun at the pool.* Marc turned his head slightly to let them pass and then focused back on the pool entrance. He noticed a group of girls gathered in a cluster on the stone patio outside the arched stone doorway. They were partially blocking the walkway causing the traffic to squeeze into single lanes to get around them.

The feminine cluster had found a small patch of leafy shade and was holding its ground. Their chatters were distinct from the other noises. The voices were familiar, and as he got closer, so were their faces. Marc started to feel a little selfconscious. One of his classmates recognized him and waved for him to join them.

"Hi Marc, you on today?" she blurted out.

"Yeah, I have to close today."

"Me too, we'll be together and at least we can cool down at the end," Niki quickly responded with her tantalizing voice. Her raven hair was held in back with two small pony tails, a look that accented her enormous, deep brown eyes. Dressed in a white peasant blouse and bright red "short" shorts, she looked extremely fetching, *as always*, Marc mused. Not only was she a looker, her outgoing personality and friendliness to everyone enabled her to be one of the leaders of their class. In truth, she had probably been one of his best friends for years. Their mothers were fast friends, and their families had even vacationed together. The two of them had dated a bit, but found they remained just friends.

Just having her attention made Marc uneasy. He stopped short of the group and drifted in small shifting steps towards the gathering of girls. He was the lone guy, and while he knew them all, he had misgivings about intruding.

"Marc have you seen Will? He's looking for you," someone uttered over the constant din of noise.

"No," Marc responded, not knowing yet who he was answering.

"He was just here and said he had to talk to you," Sarah said as she scooted around the fringe of the crowd and wheedled her way towards him. "He went into the office and was talking with the Coach," she continued until she finally was standing right next to Marc. "He was talking about going to the golf course and meeting Ronnie. He needed a football from Coach Warren. I'm not sure he ever found one, but he was still looking the last time …," Sarah rambled on and Marc tuned her out. Sarah was always babbling and following him around. She was a tiny, mousey girl with a pug nose covered with freckles; cute enough, but Marc found her constant chatter annoying. Sarah was always wound up like a spinning top and never seemed to run down.

"Yeah, I was going to meet him before I started work. I'll find him in a few minutes," Marc imparted, as he tried to move away from the five foot tall chatterbox. Sarah was clad in pea green Bermuda shorts, white knee socks, white kid sneakers and a multi-colored open blouse, with nothing to see inside. The shorts were lengthy and somewhat baggy—a new style for the summer of nineteen fifty-eight? He immediately thought Niki's cute shorts were much more eye catching, especially on Niki. Sarah was good company by herself but less genuine when with others.

Sarah stopped suddenly as she realized Marc's waning attention, and slid back into the pack. She immediately bubbled on to another topic with a new girl Marc had never seen before. He stood in utter amazement watching this strange new person. She was dressed from head to toe in what had to be very hot and sultry clothes, and she appeared to be from another decade. The unfamiliar face was ablaze with pepper-red piping, and beads of perspiration were dripping from every pore. Her bright reddish hair was plastered to her head and brow both from the sweltering heat and from its own volume. Her mane appeared as a tangled mop rather than the feathery swirl favored by most of the girls in their class.

Marc only had a momentary glance at this unknown homespun miss but her overheated misery was unmistakable. *Boy, she needs a long cold shower,* he thought. *Those horsehair clothes don't help. Who is she? What is she doing with that faddish bunch?*

As quickly as he could, Marc darted through the crowd of bathers, family escorts, and water logged nomads, bronzed colored mermaids, and red skinned frogman, each headed on their personal journey with no regard to traffic patterns. Marc needed to get through the roman-arched doorway of the entrance and make his way to the employee's locker room, which doubled as a storage area for all the pool cleaning equipment.

Once inside the gothic styled colonnade, the temperature dropped ten degrees. The shade of the arcade was welcome to all. Marc felt welcome relief in the new found coolness and a healthy dampness.

The sting of the chlorine and sodium from the purified water startled Marc's senses, as it always did. In the cavernous below-pool setting, the aqua acidic smell was pronounced in an intoxicating way to bathers. The undirected chatter and water soaked bodies meant heat relief was available just above their heads in a giant blue lagoon like pool.

Marc quickly made his way to his locker that was really more like a big wire basket locked to steel framed, floor to ceiling shelving. Marc still had more than two hours before his evening life guard shift started, so he stored his towel and swim suit in the basket, put the padlock in place and went off to find Will and the others.

"Well Mum Ah can't wear these. Niki n the others wíll think Ah'm daft.

Ah'm so domestic n they are all so brilliant n in." Jamie bellowed. "Niki wants me to go to the swimming bath with her today. All my frocks n jumpers are too hessian n not on." Jamie's voice shrieking as she continued in a deep Birmingham, England dialect.

"These aren't wozzers Mum. They are right tidy."

"Why did we leave England?" Jamie whispered rhetorically. "It's a bloomer. Ah miss granny n Birmmie. This is all fishie n Ah bloody want to go ..."

Jamie was tall slender teenager, with an angelic oval face, short forehead and strong cheek bones. Her hair was very long, reaching the center of her back, tightly packed with ringlets, and somewhat disorderly. She had a creamy, snow flake complexion, accentuated by contrasting crimson hair, and a maturing feminine body. Her posture and manners telegraphed the transformation taking place.

"Ah'm tired of your mucking about," her mother said sharply, stopping Jamie in mid-sentence tirade.

It had not been easy for the Toliver family from the day Francis was offered an opportunity to come to the states to take part in the development of a new steel making process. Francis was so excited when he phoned from across the Atlantic in some part of the United States called West Virginia. Birmingham Iron and Steel had sent Francis on a two month trip to the United States to learn how these steel producers were able to roll steel slabs to nearly paper-thin thicknesses and still maintain the alloy's strength and form characteristics. The process had many names and many different manufacturing approaches. In the West Virginia setting it was called "double reduced tin" and was starting to compete very effectively in the beverage and food container market.

From the moment Francis sent his first letter back to his wife, Ellen, from the small steel mill town on the Ohio River, his excitement in this career adventure was evident. Francis was so engrossed in the metallurgical breakthrough that he was learning about, that he courted the idea of remaining in the states and being in on the "ground floor" of the innovation.

As Francis's stay was extended, and discussions between the British and American companies explored some joint cooperation, the possibilities of Francis's visit being more long-term became apparent. He returned to his West Midlands homeland and family at Christmas time to announce that he was being promoted to oversee the coordinated efforts of the Weirton Steel Company in Weirton, West Virginia in the United States with the Birmingham Iron and Steel Company of Great Britain.

With pride and some trepidation, he told his wife a day before he made the announcement to their two children, Jamie, sixteen years old, Harry aged twelve, their grandparents, and close friends. For most it was a bombshell—a shock beyond words—producing long moments of silence.

From that wet wintery day in Birmingham to this sultry summer day in Weirton, the Toliver family had been on a whirlwind adventure that only seemed to intensify daily. The latest issues confronting them were home furnishings, clothes, local foods that were not familiar to them and the August heat—the extremely oppressive, humid heat they had never encountered in England. With Francis at work most of the time, these testy conflicts were all on Ellen's shoulders. Right now, Jamie, the one least agreeable to the move from the start, was struggling with just about everything in her new surroundings.

"You know Ah can't do anything about your fabrics today. We only've one motor car n me without a driving license. You'll just've to wear your trousers n brogues until we can've a shop. We've other doodads to get first," Ellen rattled off sharply. She was a forty something year old woman, only five foot two, who suddenly found herself shorter than her daughter. Her face was full and very light toned, framed by tightly permed curls in her brunette hair. Her bright blue eyes darted sharply through her wire framed glasses as she responded to Jamie's outburst.

Jamie's shoulders slumped even more and her head drooped. In a soft and weeping voice she moaned, "Ah can't go dressed like a hen. Ah just can't go."

Ellen heard the faint squawk and took a deep breath to calm herself. She realized the struggles Jamie was dealing with. She was struggling, too. The move from England to the states had been sudden and traumatic. For Francis it was exciting. He had his new job, but for Ellen and Jamie it was turbulent. Everything was alien to Ellen and Jamie.

However, for Harry it was different. The twelve year old adjusted quickly, once the good-bys were said, everything new was exhilarating. He had already made friends and the issues of clothes, language and surroundings seemed to have no importance at all. In the few days they had been in their new home, Harry had found a number of new mates. He was already exploring the woods and the hills in the neighborhood and was spending most of his time out and about with his new sidekicks.

To twelve year old boys, how you turned out, or what zany words and phrases you used, didn't matter. Running, climbing, sporting was all that mattered. Harry was making the transition in a good natured way while Jamie kindled a fire at every turn. She had met a friendly group of girls her age, but they were American to the core in speech, dress and manners and Jamie was the munchkin trying to assimilate.

"Ah need to understand the cooker this afternoon so we can've minced meat stew with stick beans. Ah can't fancy any links at the shops, so we will've to make do. The temperature positions are all over the top. Ah ruined the beskets n salt beef yesterday n Ah was hard done by you all. So straight away for me on the beef roll or it will be another dog's breakfast tonight. Wear what you've until we can've a proper shop. You'll've your jam tomorrow," Ellen rattled off as she left Jamie standing forlorn.

"Blimey," was all Jamie could quip as her mum left her abruptly.

Her mum had always been there for her, but now she, also, was tired and depressed. Mum had done nothing but layabout since the family arrived in their American home. Ellen missed her family terribly and had become very melancholy during the first weeks in Weirton.

The house the company had provided was very modern by Birmingham standards, filled with furniture and appliances beyond their grandest dreams. The house in its plantation-like setting was high on a hill overlooking the Ohio River as it made a sharp turn south. The river looked small from this distance; however, it was anything but. From the back yard patio, the Tolivers could see well into the state of Ohio. At night the faraway lights of homes, industry and roads, reminded them of the Birmingham sky from the top of their terraced home and the circus of Colmore. While the scene was breathtaking, it was not yet their home.

Jamie remembered her mum more light hearted and amenable in their English home and longed for that willowy personality to return. But right now Jamie had to decide what to do about meeting Niki and some other "yanks" at the "bath house."

How hot can it be? I'm blistering. It's boiling hot and this woolly frock is stifling. I can't breathe! I should have borrowed the shorts and lace top Niki offered, Jamie pondered silently. She felt embarrassed needing to borrow someone else's clothes, especially from the daughter of her dad's new boss.

Niki Stewart was her first American friend, these initial days in Weirton. Niki was very kind to her and had introduced her to a number of other girls who would be her classmates in high school. Even though each of the half a dozen new schoolmates was very good-natured and accepted Jamie into their fellowship, she needed to find a comfort zone with Niki and the others.

Jamie could see that this new lot was very status minded. Their dress, chit-chat, homes, interests were looped in with each other. Jamie felt that she could fit in over time, but presently she was nervous around them and felt as dull as dishwater.

Jamie, Niki, Sarah, Amanda and Allison had walked over to the Marland Heights Pool. They weren't going to swim but just have a walk about to see what was going on and, more importantly, to be seen. Niki was a life guard at the pool and would have to work that evening so their time was limited.

As they had walked towards the pool, Jamie tagged along at the back of the parade and concentrated on the king sized homes that lined the neatly landscaped roadway. Jamie was still taken by what she was seeing and experiencing in the states. She compared everything to what had been her English life style just a few weeks ago. Here everyone lived in a house that was on its own plot of land, with its own garden. Every house had its own garage for at least one auto, and every auto was an estate car.

Her mind drifted to home and Birmmie. She could see the Birmingham dwellings. They were all locked together in a single structure that captured an entire city block. This sweeping ulitarian architecture was on both sides of the street, on every city street, in every city, especially in Birmingham, England.

Birmingham streets were dusty, aged and most notably enclosed, canal like, carriageways. The two, three and four story unbroken structures limited the light, even on the sunniest day, and created a sequestered atmosphere. The buildings were built right up to the road bed, with no front greenery, just bricks, mortar, stone and gray dirt moving with the slightest breeze. From the pavement and the footpath, the stone and block steps led into a common entrance into each living-space, called "flats."

Jamie was surprised at how she now visualized her home and the place she longed for. It seemed so different in her memory. She wanted to get back as quickly as possible, but as she thought about it, "*What" exactly was she missing?*

She missed the people, her granny and grandpa, her school mates and even a few of the blokes she admired in a puppy-love way. *What was she doing here?*

She could smell the fine English gardens in the back of the flats. Horticulture was a major part of Birmingham and English life. She missed the cologne of the summer estate yards and the soft haze of rain on the veggie plants. Even where the backyard plots were small, the greenery skills of every English man and woman were evident. Every household had flowers, vegetables, herbs and a patch of lawn, at least enough to lounge on.

As picture perfect as Jamie's memories were, she realized that the stamp size grounds of her home were no match for the expansive lawns and well manicured bushes, flower beds and landscaping that were part of the American homes. Green grassed lawns surrounded each home as if it were a public park for individual families. Such expanse was only found in the English country settings and in the small rural hamlets, but even there the plots were smaller and certainly not as manicured.

As the parade of teenagers trudged along, Jamie's pace slowed as she thought of home. She considered her long dishrag hair that was sticking to the side of her face, her neck and now her forehead, and watched the lot of hens out in front acting daft. They seem to be so carefree and loose, with no concerns at all. Jamie felt nothing but concern. She didn't want to be bloody-minded! She had always been a little daft herself, but not now. "Bloody hell," she said in a soft and nearly teary voice.

Jamie became very self-conscious of the peep of a sound that came bubbling out. She raised her eyes slowly to spy on the ladybirds. They were still boldly moving forward with laughter and a skip now and then. No one heard her shaky plea. Her heart started to beat again and she took a deep breath. She needed to get her wits about her. She had to be herself again and not some withering thing. Where was that "keep your pecker up" her granny was always talking about? She couldn't get her knickers in a twist in front of these new bright sparkly friends.

She whispered to herself her mum's favorite expression when she felt low, "Tart Up, Tart Up, Tart Up." Jamie repeated the slang over and over in a soft, muted hush. She was calming. Her feelings of frustration, anger and melancholy were subsiding. She raised her crest fallen head and looked to the forest off to her left.

The guard rail provided a barrier between the road and an expansive green lawn that sloped steeply to a forest of maple, oak, spruce, fir and locust. The woodland was a noticeable distance away, but because of the extremes of elevation, the crowns of the trees were at eye level. Jamie took in a full breath—Ahhh. The tears on her cheek evaporated and she concentrated on the sounds of her new friends chatting away and the louder echoes of the bathers as their group of sprightly lasses was in sight of the red brick pond, the municipal pool.

This was Jamie's first trip to the Weirton Municipal Pool, but she had heard it described as "the place to go in the summer." Everyone met at the pool. She quickened her pace to catch-up with the others. They were turning into one of the spoke-wheeled entrances to the grounds and the main entrance. Her short sprint made the hot day seem even hotter. Her body was soaked with perspiration and her face, forehead and even her eyes, felt like they were on fire. Finally, Jamie was walking directly behind the weary pilgrims. They were complaining about the heat too, but they did not seem to be as devastated by the murky heat as she was.

The fairway was clear. Not a golfer in sight. The steamy conditions were chasing all the duffers into the clubhouse or more specifically the lounge. The browning of the grass because of the two week heat wave caused a crunching sound as he ran around the third green and down the sloping approach mound and into the treed divide between the fourth and fifth hole. He headed to the large open grassy plateau that ran alongside the fairway of the sixth hole. He was sure he would find Will and the others if they hadn't decided that it was too hot to work out and had gone swimming instead.

As he got closer to the plateau, he heard a comradely chatter in the distance. They were there. Marc quickened his pace. As he hurried into the clearing, the dozen or so bare chested, able-bodied buddies were running in all directions, footballs flying about.

"Hey Marc," a shout called out.

Marc spotted Will off to his right and jogged over.

"We looked for you before," Will panted, short of breath and red faced.

"Got busy at home. Ran into the others at the pool, they...."

"Watch," Will spit out, reaching over Marc's head to defected a spiral. They both ducked as the ball tumbled past them and hit hard on the caramel concrete like ground. It bounced high and right back at them. They both flinched and Will snatched it out of the air.

"We've been here about an hour," Will said with a huff and bent to rest his elbows on his knees, "I've had it." Will's face was beet red with sweat dripping from every pore, his nose, ears and chin. He looked peaked with his face muscles strained stone crimson. "Wow, the sun is like a laser. I'm beat, let's take a swim," Will stammered breathlessly.

"This is a damn furnace! It's worse than the open-hearth," someone in the gathering crowd aspirated as he sat with a thud in a patch of shade from a drooping little elm. Two more priming football hopefuls dropped in the same skimpy shadow. All three were tired, hot and finished exercising for the day.

The entire group of gritty athletes was suddenly sitting under the sparse shade, breathing hard, unwilling to move and unsure of their next move. They were despondent, languishing in their fatigue. Marc remained silent as one by one they bitched about the unrelenting heat during the workout.

Each resembled a glistening semi-bronzed statue with perspiration dripping profusely to the ground, but their stoic deep breathing revealed the truth of their exhaustion. They were a dozen or so teenage football players trying to get into shape for the fall football season. It was the agonizing August ritual being carried out for the glory of high schools large and small.

Marc was glad he had missed this informal practice called by the team leaders, Will and Ronnie. This was a miserable day to be running with a football for no good reason. Will and Ronnie were "gung-ho" and always ready to make the sacrifice, but Marc was more laid back and not enthusiastic about calisthenics, running sprints and all the other shaping up activities. However, playing the game itself was a different thing.

The idea of swimming was unanimously agreed to by everyone resting in the shade. So the shirts, footballs and the few bottles of water and pop were picked up and everyone started back to the pool. The links remained empty as the call of cool refreshments had captured the golfers.

Will and Ron were Marc's best friends. The two were very athletic and handsome with stone like bodies. Will was Marc's height, but Ron was two or three inches taller, with wider shoulders and chest. Will always had a radical hairdo that changed with his mood; today the sides and back were shaved and the top was a mop of curls. Ron was the gentleman of the three and his hair was always tapered on the side and two to four inches long on top. It always was combed, with a part on the left side. Each had brown eyes, a tanned face with an intellectual air, although Will's character was more carefree.

Marc walked back with Will and Ronnie. They were a closely-knit threesome who seemed to do everything together or at least in concert with each other.

"I can't believe that practice starts in a week or so," Ron said. "The summer's over; hell, baseball's almost finished. We only have one or two games left."

"No, No there is only one game left and then the tournament starts," Will corrected Ron.

Marc spit out, "Hell, I don't even want to play baseball anymore. I'm sick of it. It's too slow and boring. The games drag on and on and on."

Will cut him off, "Okay, okay, we know baseball is not your favorite. But you're the catcher; all you do is catch the ball and throw it back to the pitcher."

"The hell with you, ass. And I'm the second string catcher so I sit on the bench most of the time. That's real exciting. Only time I get in is when Carl pitches. Big deal," Marc jumped in.

"If you were better...." Ron started.

"You ass," shuddered Marc, stopping in his tracks with a glare at Ron.

"That's enough. The football season starts in what? Three weeks," Will chimed in to settle the give and take of the musketeers. "We need to get in shape and ready. Everyone was huffing and puffing out there like they were a bunch of girls. This is going to be a rough season. Everyone will be waiting to beat us after last year. Scotty and Bobby were winded from the start. They look fat and slow. Coach is going to run our butts off. I don't even want to think about the first day. He'll make the two-a-day's killers," Will tried to keep the peace.

Ron panted, "The heat is too much for anyone today. It's one hundred degrees out here. Look at you, you look drained. You were throwing ducks out there."

"My hands were all sweaty. I couldn't get a good grip," was the mumble from Will. "I was tired and it was hot, but we are still in bad shape."

Marc looked disinterested as he drifted ahead of the other two. He looked back and leisurely strolled onto the powdered dirt that served as the horseshoe pitch. "Hey, it's like this every summer. After two weeks of football camp, we will be ready. The first days of practice are always tough, but we get through. It can't be this hot forever. Let's get wet and cool down."

The three wandered through the park grounds. There weren't many people at the picnic tables and no one cooking on the barbecue pits. Everyone seemed to congregate under the shade trees simply sitting silently and still. The pool ahead promised a refreshing soak.

"Niki, are you taking the last year of French?"

"I have it on my schedule for third period, but I'm not sure I want to. I don't see a reason to. There is always a lot of homework and I want to enjoy my senior year—not work my tail off. I already have three years of French. Not much opportunity to use French unless you go to France … that will be the day!"

"I'm going to be in the class. I like French. Miss Darby is fun in class and makes speaking French fun. You can't leave the class. It's going to be a very small class and mostly conversational French. It will be fun."

"I don't know. I'll wait to see. I just don't want to be that busy."

The exchange between Sarah and Niki was interrupted by: "Je sera dans le class aussi. Je vous assistez avec le travail." The French was smooth and articulated without hesitation. "J'ai parle le français tout ma vie. Nous avons les langues pendant le premier de l'école. Et, j'ai été a la France et la Belgique et les autres places ou on parles le français beaucoup de fois."

It was Jamie, who hadn't said a word for most of the afternoon. She struggled with the heat and looked squirrelly with her hair and clothes matted to her body. She had been doused with perspiration by the heat and the intense muggy air. But the opportunity to use her fluent French language skills gave her a lift. Her voice was soft but confident for the first time.

"Boy that was great. You're even better than Miss Darby. She uses French in class but only with sentences she has practiced," Sarah responded in a surprised and surreal voice. "What did you say? Ah, say something else. I love to hear people speak another language." Sarah was staring directly at Jamie with the look of a shocked puppy.

Jamie glanced away surprised by the sudden attention and by her own spontaneous outburst. "Ah said that Ah will be in the same French class n if you would like, Ah could help you."

"You really do speak French?" Was the query in unison from Niki and Sarah, who added: "I love your accent, it is so cute!"

"Aa, well brilliant, Ah do speak French. Everyone in Britain speaks French. We 've to because France is right there. Ah also speak German n Spanish," Jamie replied.

"Wow, all those languages! I wish I could," said Sarah. "We don't have any choice. It's either French or Latin."

"E difficile parlare latino," Jamie spouted in Italian, which neither girl understood!

"You are something," Niki said, "you surprise me every time we get together."

"Hey you guys," someone shouted from outside the covered picnic area. The sun was shining so brightly that the girls couldn't make out the figures as they came in under the shade of the roof. The three girls had been sitting in a large covered picnic area with a dozen picnic tables and a large fireplace at one end.

The area was also protected by a woodsy mix of oak and maple trees that helped to keep the sun at a distance. It was still very warm, even in the heavy shade, but nowhere near the scorching temperature of the direct sun. The intruders went directly to the water fountain in the middle of the building. Each took a long drink and went back for seconds. Marc, Ron, and Will had finally made the trek from the golf course to the pool area.

"Where have you three been?" questioned Niki. "You look terrible! Why would you be out in this hot weather running around? Are you crazy?"

"Well, the season's only a few weeks away," Will spit out as he wiped his mouth and attempted to take a deep breath. "It was dumb to be out there, but I'm going to take a swim and cool down."

"Have you seen Amanda? Is she swimming or something?" Ron chimed in.

"No, I don't think she's here," Niki said. "She was, but went home for some reason."

"Oh," was Ron's reply as he started to walk away.

"Hey, where are you going?" Will asked.

"Swimming, come on, let's go, it's too hot."

"Okay, I'm coming. See you'ens later."

"Not if we see you first," was Sarah's quick reply.

The two hurried off, while Marc made his way back to the water fountain for another drink.

"What was all that about Amanda," Marc blurted out inquisitively as he looked back towards Niki.

"All what?"

"Ronnie asking about Amanda and then walking away. I think he was mad or upset or something."

"He did seem to be upset," Sarah added.

"He was hot and wanted to take a swim; that's all. Maybe he needed to talk to Amanda about something," Niki responded raising her hand and waving it in a good-by motion. "So what do you care?"

Marc glanced at Niki and made a grimaced smile and said, "I don't care about anything." He waved his hand in a similar nonchalant gesture, turned and walked away.

"Hey, Marc, are you going to swim before our shift," Niki asked quickly. "I think I will!"

"Well, if you're going to go, we should go now," Marc mumbled as he left the shady cover.

"I'll be there in a minute," she shouted.

"Jamie, I've got to go. Can you get back home?" Niki inquired as she started to get up.

"Wait, what's this Amanda thing about?" Sarah quizzed with interest.

"I don't know. I, ah, I heard they have been dating more often. That is all I know. Don't make a big thing out of it; it's nothing, nothing."

"Why didn't I know about them? No-one told me."

"Sarah, why would you get upset? There is nothing to know."

"Well you know, I'm supposed to be Amanda's best friend."

"Cool it, I have to go. Jamie, can you get back to your house?"

"Yes, yes, Ah can."

"Don't worry, I'll see that she finds her way home," said Sarah with an angry muffled voice.

Niki left towards the pool at a quick step and suddenly was out of sight.

Jamie felt lost, but didn't say another word and sat at the picnic table for more than just a few minutes. Sarah sat silent also but with a deep frown. Sarah was staring at the woods that were alongside the pavilion. For the first time today there was a breeze blowing. Jamie felt coolness spread over her; relief at last. Sarah didn't seem to notice the change, but was in some distant place. Finally Sarah sighed.

"I don't like it when people keep secrets from me. I can keep a secret. Amanda tells me everything and I tell her all my secrets. Why didn't she tell me she was dating Ronnie? I think that's nice. Everyone likes him and he is so cute," Sarah continued with a monolog that covered every puppy love romance that had sprouted and faded over the past year.

Jamie just sat and listened. She did not know most of the people Sarah mentioned but was getting a good tutoring about her future classmates. The shade of the large summerhouse with its open three sides and the high leafy cover was a welcome reprieve from the heat even if she had to listen to Sarah's fast paced woeful tale. Jamie's mind wandered. She was more interested in who the three tall well built guys she had just seen were, especially the one Niki left with. He seemed totally unlike most of the boys she had ever known. Finally, Jamie grew tired of sitting and listening and even Sarah was slowing down.

"Ah need to get back home. Mum will be getting the meal on the table."

"Yeah, you're right. I need to go home, too. Boy, Jamie you do have an accent," Sarah replied as she squirmed from the table with difficultly. Her legs were stiff from sitting so long.

Jamie stood, was going to tell Sarah that she did also, but Sarah was moving off quickly.

"Hey, stop running. HEY! I said stop running," Marc shouted as the two saggy swimming suit clad boys ran in behind him and slowed down to a trot. They smiled at Marc and lowered their faces as they started a half hearted laugh.

Marc glared at the two and then looked back toward the water where his eyes needed to be. Life guards were the police, baby sitters and nurses at this large city pool. During the summer, the pool was the daily destination for every youngster who could convince his parents that it was worth a dollar or more to get them out of their hair. The parents were only too glad to have the house quiet and the kids using up all their energy swimming. Today with the steamy weather, the parents needed a dip as well, so the pool was crowded even in the evening. Kids, moms, a few dads and even some babies with their guardians were in the foot deep soaking pool.

Marc needed to keep his eyes on the water and less on two energetic boys. There were only two of them on guard at this hour of the evening as normally most families were home having dinner. Not tonight. More concern for the heat then eating.

"I said stop running. Stop running," Marc bellowed sharply. *Damn kids*, he thought. *I don't need the frustration*. Marc was watching the shallow end and the baby pool while Niki was in the ten foot high guard's chair at the deep end in between the two low diving boards and directly under the high board. All three boards had lines of swimmers waiting to show their talents. Most were just merely jumping when it was their turn, but a few were doing jackknifes and swan dives from the twenty foot high board.

Wow, that was a good one, Marc reflected as the small splash hid the entrance of the diver. Oh, no wonder, that was Danielle. She popped up a distance from the boards and began swimming with her silk-like stroke toward the side. Marc was lost in watching the mermaid wiggle for the ladder.

Danielle was beautiful. She could swim like a fish mastering freestyle, backstroke, butterfly, and the breaststroke, the favorite of all the guys. Danni's face was slim with dark blue eyes, and dimpled cheeks. Her figure was one of a kind. Her hair was shoulder length, and a golden brown, a little bleached on top from all her time at the pool and her swimming ritual. She was also musically very talented, and a strong gymnast. Danni was only a junior this year, but she had been chosen to be a cheerleader. Marc and Danni had been sweethearts off and on over the last few years, but this had changed in recent months. Her parents were very strict to say the least. She was not allowed to ride in Marc's car; she was not permitted to go to school dances; and holding hands and kissing were taboo. Marc found it hard to have a sweetheart without the sweetness of affection. He missed having a reason to be with Danni regardless of the restrictions. She was a real beauty and fun to be with. Maybe this year would be different. At least they would see each other at school and at church. Marc convinced himself that romance with Danni was possible and only a moonlit night away.

A yelling mother brought him back to the moment. It was Anthony again. His mother was trying to find him and get him to help her pack-up and leave. Anthony was nowhere to be found. Marc quickly decided that this was an opportunity to start to clear the pool. He drifted toward the swallow end where the water was only three feet deep. There was Anthony, crouched down into the water with only his head showing and hiding behind other swimmers with his buddy beside him.

"Tony, your mother is looking for you—NOW," came out of Marc.

"Tony, I see you and you can hear me. Now get over here."

"Why?" Tony responded as he stood up straight and pounded the water, splashing everyone close by.

"Why? Because I said so, now get over here—NOW. You too, Ralph."

"I'm coming, but it's not fair. Why do we have to go home? It's still early."

Tony and his friend trudged through the water like their feet were in cement.

As they reached the ladder, Tony looked up with sad eyes. "It isn't fair."

"Your mother has been searching for you for the last hour. Talk to her about fair or not fair."

Tony was out of the water and he and Ralph stood with water dripping into two puddles. Marc reached out and grabbed Tony by the arm and the three started for the other end of the pool. As they approached the family area of the pool, Tony's mother spotted them.

"Where have you been? We need to get home. I told Ralph's mother he would be home by now. You two get our basket and towels, fast … move," she bellowed.

Marc looked at Tony and Ralph, smiled and said softly. "See you next time."

They both smiled back and ran off to help Tony's mother.

Marc smiled to himself and said silently under his breath: "They are not bad, just devilish—like me." He walked over to the guard's chair and tickled Niki's toes. She looked down and took off her sunglasses.

"You want to change places? I'll walk for a while," She said.

"No, no just wanted to say hi."

"Lot of people to watch, and they are all over these boards."

"They sure are; stuffed into the whole pool. Busy night."

"Buzz… any other news? I just hope we don't have another accident off the boards. One rescue is enough for me."

"Gee, I thought you had fun that day," Marc said with a smile.

"Okay, wise guy, enough of that. It's not funny."

Still smiling, Marc turned around and headed back to his post, laughing inside as he remembered a Sunday last month. He was working the afternoon shift with Niki, Danni and Rick when two divers, one off the high board and the other off one of the low boards, hit in mid-air. Both divers were stunned and had difficulty in getting back to the surface. Niki and Rick had to go in deep and bring the swimmers back up and help them over to the side. Rick brought his swimmer up quickly. The boy was conscious and under his own power, able to climb up the ladder and out of the pool. Niki had some difficulty getting her diver back to the side and to the ladder. When the second boy tried to climb up the ladder, he had trouble. Niki was still in the water and tried to help by pushing him up the ladder.

That's where the real problem and the fun started. The swimmer had lost his trucks in the deep water, so Niki was pushing him up out of the water with both her hands on his bare ass. This pushing, with others pulling from top of the ladder, went on for five or more minutes. Niki kept pushing on the nude bottom but the swimmer would make it part way and fall back on top of Niki, ass forward. Finally, he successfully got out of the pool and some good neighbor covered him with a towel.

Neither of the divers were hurt, just dazed. But the scene of Niki pushing up on the nude butt brought laughter to everyone. Poor Niki had ever since suffered the jokes, as the story was told almost daily. No one had seen the poor fourteen year old eighth grader since the accident. Marc laughed again and tried to focus on the pool and the people swimming as he returned to his end of the pool.

The evening passed slowly, and the crowd thinned. Marc spent most of the time at the very end of the pool leaning against the chain link fence separating the main pool from the baby's wading pool. He did more daydreaming then guarding. He noticed Niki standing on the foot rest of the high guard chair. She stretched her arms and twisted her frame. She had been sitting for about two hours and she was stiff. She raised both hands with her fingers spread wide indicating ten minutes to closing time. Marc looked at the large clock behind the board to find she was right, ten minutes to nine o'clock.

Niki looked striking standing high on the chair with the sun setting behind her. They had dated recently, going to a few spring dances and a couple of summer parties. It was a relationship of convenience. They were friends and enjoyed kidding each other. As far as any loving, Niki enjoyed kissing Marc on the cheek. They did have one brief make out evening that Marc cherished in his memory and would like to relive and expand. Maybe tonight?

Niki blew her whistle. "The pool's closing; everyone out of the water. It's nine o'clock; closing time."

The same message came over the loud speaker and everyone started to get out of the water and move toward the stairways to the dressing rooms. Marc and Niki waited until everyone was gone from the pool area and walked around the pool finding a few towels and other items left behind. They tossed what they found into the lost and found basket with other forgotten items. Both walked over to the guard chair and took off their whistles. Niki quickly dove in and started to float on her back, enjoying the coolness. Marc dove in and came up next to her. He shook the water from his face and wiped his eyes.

"That feels great. Long night, hot," he said.

"That last hour was very long and I have to teach swimming tomorrow at ten in the morning," Niki replied as she took a few back strokes, "then, I am on the evening shift again."

They swam for a few minutes cooling down and washing the day away. As they treaded water, Marc glanced at Niki and the cute grin that seemed to be sculptured in her face. Her eyes were blinking the water away, which made the deep brown hue even deeper. Behind those puritan eyes Marc was sure there was someone with adventure on her mind. She was an independent soul, and she knew it.

"What's with you, you're staring at me."

"No, just thinking about something."

"Yaa, right. I know you."

"Who was that, ah, person, the girl, you were with, in the shelter? She was really different, kinda odd."

"Oh, that is Jamie. She's English, from Britain."

"British?"

"Yeah, she moved here from Britain. Her dad works for a British steel company and is studying some process being done here at the mill. She's only been here a few weeks."

"She looked like she was going to melt away, and that hair wow."

"She has never lived where is it's so hot. She says that she doesn't have summer clothes like ours."

"Buzz… no kidding? That outfit was ugly and hot," Marc abruptly pounced.

"She's going to be in school with us, so you better make nice."

"Nice, I'm always nice," Marc responded "okay"' with a smile.

They treaded water for a few minutes as the loud speakers blasted a dumb song about a lion sleeping in a mountain *Oh wema-way-wema-away home.*

"We better check the dressing rooms," Marc mumbled with water in his mouth. "You want a ride home?"

"Sure; I'll see you downstairs."

Both swam to the nearest ladder and headed for the dressing room stair cases; Niki for the girls and Marc the boys.

Mum was finishing the dinner and da and Harry were hanging around the kitchen table. Jamie could tell they were both very hungry and frustrated that the food was not ready. "Hiya everyone," she nearly whispered as she entered the kitchen.

"Well, where have you been? Your mum needed your help with the stew n using the new cooker," her da reacted sharply, somewhat angrily staring at his daughter.

With tears starting to fill her eyes and her face showing the pain of his censuring voice, she sucked in a deep breath and turned to leave saying, "Ah legged it all the way home!"

Her mother turned quickly from her stove and glared at her dad. "Francis, that's enough of your bullying. Leave her alone. Ah told her she could go to the bath house with her new mates. She doesn't need your sass," the words were sharp and her voice shrilling.

Everyone stopped for a split second. Da's face turned sheepish red and he and Harry turned and marched into the living room and were out of sight before the rebuff had settled.

Jamie caught her breath and walked over to the stove to where mum was stirring a pot of boiling water with peas and carrots. She waited for her mum to look up from the steaming mix. When she did glance at Jamie, her eyes were soft and the lips parted in a knowing smile. "Make sure the table is spot on n the flat cake is cut," mum said sweetly in her easy voice.

Jamie went about the business of getting the table in the yellow and blue kitchen set and ready for dinner. All of a sudden she was famished and the aroma of her mother's cooking settled in her nostrils. It smelled like home. Her mind cleared; the anxiety that tugged at her heart all day seemed to float away. Her mum's support, the coziness of their new home, the smells of English cooking, and even the sulking of her da and brother, gave her new life. Maybe this could be fun—an adventure. "Mum, the tables ready. Let's eat. J'ai faim."

"C'est prêt," mum replied playfully.

Dinner was very good and Harry made it fun as he described all that he had done during the day with his new mates. He mixed terms from American baseball and English cricket that brought laughs to everyone, including himself. He was enjoying these odd, and at times silly, American games. Football and Soccer were not the same game, but had similar names for different things. Harry kept repeating that the "Americans were daft," but he certainly was getting a kick out of all the fresh experiences.

Even da revived some of his lost sense of humor. Half way through his meal he snickered at Harry's stories and he shared his own American/British anecdotes. He told of all the misunderstandings that happened at the mill because of language, terms and customs. He laughed so hard in telling stories about different words in describing the use of a telephone: busy signal or engaged signal, pound key or square key, call transfer or call diversion, that he nearly choked on the pudding. Even if Jamie didn't understand every yarn da shared, she laughed along with the family. All four enjoyed the great homey meal and the shaggy-dog sagas.

With the meal and the cleaning-up finished, Jamie went off to her room. She was enjoying the large home, which provided more privacy than she was accustomed to, especially the modern air conditioning feature, almost unknown or even needed in England, on this sultry day. It had taken her some time to cool down after walking all the way to and from the pool. She needed some American summer clothes and a proper bath costume. Now that she had eaten, laughed with her family and cooled off, she was comfortable for the first time today, both physically and mentally. She took a shower, another comfort of her new home, got into her nightshirt and went downstairs.

She found her mum and da sitting in the sun room at the back of the house. It had started to rain and a cool breeze was blowing through the screens of the open windows. The rain was already dropping the temperature and the beautiful view out the back yard was fog covered. Her parents had just finished mapping out how they would move forward to adapt to Weirton and the living style in the states. Her da left the room and Jamie and her mum sat quietly for an extended time, listening to the soft rain.

Finally, Jamie broke the ice and said, "Ah met someone Ah liked today."

"Tell me, tell me more."

It had started to cool and there were dark, low thunder clouds off to the west chasing the red tinted sky. Rain was starting and the parking lot was almost empty and Marc's black nineteen fifty Chrysler Windsor was almost camouflaged in the shadows at the back of the lot. It had taken more time than usual to clear everyone from the pool dressing rooms and to get them to leave the main lobby. The entrance desk was closed, the snack bar shuttered and locked, and the evening watchman had arrived. It was a few minutes after ten p.m. as they opened the car doors, let some of the warm air escape and jumped in, Marc on the driver's side and Niki on the passenger side.

Niki moved away from the window towards the middle of the front bench seat, but not close enough to Marc to be considered any more than a friend. They rolled the windows down and could feel a slight breeze and some rain drops. Marc started the car and drove past the few cars in the lot and out onto the street.

The trip would be a short one since Niki lived on Marland Heights, only a few streets from the pool. The radio was on and the instrumental record *"Sleepwalk:" a song by Santo and Johnny* filled the air. Both Niki and Marc were keeping time with the soothing sounds. Marc opened the conversation and asked Niki why she was friends with the new girl from England.

"Well, my dad made the arrangements to have her father work here. He made sure they had a nice home to rent on the hill and even got some furniture for it. They have been to dinner with us and my dad thought I should help her to get to know some people before school starts."

"Where do they live?"

"Over around the Riverview area, almost to the end. It's a nice house that no one has lived in for a few months. I think the company owns it now."

"So, you're babysitting?"

"No, we are friends. She is as old as I am, maybe even older. She's already finished their high school and will be in our senior class. She did not want to go directly to college since she knows nothing about the states," the reply started tartly, but calmed at the end.

They were in front of Niki's house. Marc stopped the car and shut off the engine. He started to lean towards Niki, hoping for a few minutes of passion, but that was not to be. Niki smiled, and quickly leaning over towards him, pecked him on the cheek. Before Marc could even react, Niki had opened the door, slid out and was running up the steps through a little rain to the back door.

"See you tomorrow," Marc shouted.

"Maybe. Thanks," was all that came back.

Marc sat for a moment reliving Niki's fast getaway. He started the car and the radio came to life with *Eddie Cochan singing "Summertime Blues:" I'm gonna raise a fuss, I'm gonna raise a holler…there ain't no cure for the summertime blues…Sometimes I wonder what I'm a gonna do…Sometimes I wonder what I'm a gonna do…*, and he drove away to his home on the other side of town, Weirton Heights.

Not my day, a phrase that continued to repeat itself in his head as he drove through town. It started to rain harder and before he was home, it was pouring.

Chapter 3

Preparation

"You have to get lower than the defensive man. You can't let him move you straight back into your quarterback. You people look like this is your first time with a helmet on," the words were uncompromising. Coach Mendel did not appear to be angry, but anxious. It was the third day of summer football camp. Mendel held his breath for a short pause, fought to calm himself. The start of camp was not going well, a fact that was obvious to everyone: coaches, players, trainers and even the two dozen or so fans who had come to watch this year's team get ready for the season.

The squad was silent and solemn. Afternoon practice was nearing the end; energy was bottoming out and the attention span had been lost in the August heat and showers of grass, dirt and sweat. The fifty or so varsity hopefuls were scattered near the south end goal post of the pasture-like grass field that was as much dirt as grass, in complete disarray. Most of those not directly involved in the mock scrimmage were on one knee, helmet off, hair matted and dripping with sweat. Movement was slow and without urgency.

Coach Mendel closed his eyes for a moment. He took a deep breath and replayed mentally the past two hours of practice. The rewind was not pleasant. Three days of morning and afternoon practices had almost been regressive, not as the coaching staff had anticipated. He was not angry but more anxious. Football camp was meant to create the foundation for the season. Team comradeship was critical to that foundation being firm. So far, unity, gusto, spirit and just plain get-up and go were missing. The entire group was just going through the motions. Everyone seemed to be mesmerized in some venue far away from the practice field and the up-coming season, which now was only two and a half weeks away. With the end of the first week of camp only a day and a half away, time would start to be limited to get ready for what was a very tough schedule.

Mendel took a quick look around at the band of dust covered, lifeless, aspiring high school athletes. They seemed either awestruck or dazed. Their posture was evidence of their gloomy outlook. Even his coaching colleagues were showing signs of detachment. It had been a long three days since they had arrived on the West Liberty State College campus to begin getting ready for the nineteen fifty-eight Weir High School football season. The weather had been hot, the dorm room sleeping arrangements unfamiliar, and the cafeteria food a new experience for players and coaches.

He reflected on the need for this "camp setting" to be a positive experience starting soon. But right now the need was to finish the afternoon practice on the up-beat.

"Let's get the second team in here; quickly, come on let's go. You, too, Glickman, I want you at right tackle," Mendel hollered out as he grabbed one of the dawdling shoulder padded uniformed players standing near him. "Get your helmet Glickman. You're going to need it." Glickman moved quickly to reach for his helmet and stumbled to the gathering huddle. Coach grumbled something under his breath, shook his head and lowered his eyes in apparent discontent.

"You too, Richards, get your helmet on. You need the practice. MOVE PEOPLE, GET UP OFF YOUR BUTTS!" Moans and grumblings could be heard from many as they started to budge.

"Hey, I'm not here to cajole you. You want to play football? Well, with this attitude you'll get your asses kicked in Charleston and on every Friday night. Now move or go home."

"TODAY FOLKS—TODAY," Came a sharp pitched voice from the back of the forming huddle.

Coach Warren, a graying five foot-ten inch tall, fifty-three year old head coach with a slight pot belly, thinning hair, and a full round sun-reddened face had been silently watching the semi-contact scrimmage that was concentrated on run blocking overseen by his assistants. Practice was divided into fifteen minute segments with drills directed at specific objectives. The three assistant coaches had specific responsibilities so that Coach Warren could monitor the overall performance from a distance.

His firm and demanding voice had been quiet for most of the practice. He seemed to be a spectator, walking in an out of drills, watching from a distance and kicking at the turf and adjusting his baseball cap over and over again. He was always soft spoken, seldom yelled at anyone, and normally had his assistants run the practices. He played the role of the conductor. The backs and ends were his special interest, and he spent his direct coaching on them. But suddenly, he was on the prowl and that usually meant trouble.

Marc had watched the Coach over the last ten minutes as the chief focused on the overall performance of the practice and started to pace behind the main group with increased frustration. Coach's attitude was changing and he was about to lose his cool.

The sound of his frosty words and voice caught everyone's attention. The message was very clear –he was mad. Once he had their attention, he turned away and glanced skyward, gripping his anger, clamping it down; he would not lose his cool. Marc and a few other teammates who had experienced a few years of playing for him recognized the inner strength of their coach and the need for something to change. He was very even keeled and a raised voice was out of character. When it occurred, it usually changed the atmosphere dramatically. Marc felt the energy level leap to a higher level.

With his intervening, the white clad, dirt smeared uniformed group quickly formed an oblong circle serving as a huddle. Coach Mendel stepped into the center of the gathering and began giving instructions and encouragement. Finally, he stepped out of the huddle and gruffly shouted, "run it."

The defensive side of the scrimmage was getting lined-up and ready for the next play. Coach Romeo, who was in charge of the defense, was joking with some of the lineman. For this exercise, he was in charge of a ragtag defense, made up of the third team freshmen and sophomores that were untapped for any offensive spot on the depth charts. Coach Romeo enjoyed taking untried, eager new additions on the defense, and teaching them the fun of rough and tumble football, especially against their own offense. He was the only black coach on the staff. He was tall, muscular, with graying hair, a small pencil thin mustache, with long legs that caused his walk to appear as a trot. His voice was clear, deep and compassionate. When he spoke, you listened.

Coach Romeo saw the offensive huddle break, jumped back from the ball he had been standing next to and looked around at the makeshift defense. He clapped his hands and pragmatically bellowed: "Here they come, get low linemen and make them work. Let's see what damage you can do. Go get'em."

The formation was a slot right with the offside end wide to the left. Quarterback Ray Williams looked to both sides, squatted behind the center, Bobbie Richards, and shouted out the defensive set – "fifty-two – fifty-two" – meaning that the defense was in a five man front line and that there were two center linebackers. The call allowed the offense to mentally configure their blocking assignment.

"READY—SET." Torsos bent, finger tips rested on the soft grass, helmets snapped up, and bodies steadied as statues ready to unwind. From his one-knee position off-center behind the offense, Marc saw an offense poised to uncoil in unison. "Settle in, settle…." Before he could finish his thought, the left side of the line moved, the halfback stumbled forward and Ray Williams was knocked on his ass by his own center, who had lost the ball somehow.

"What was that? Who can't count to two? TWO – TWO." Mendel was bellowing like a steam engine. The words were flowing without stop. He walked back and forth, head down, talking more to himself than any of the players who were moving slowly away trying not to catch his eye. In their all-white garb, they reminded Marc of sheep trying to escape nips from the herding dog.

"Does anyone want to tell me what the problem is? Are you too tired? Or maybe you ate too much lunch? What pray tell me is wrong?" Mendel barked as he stared at the gathered would be athletes. No one was looking in his direction. The players were penitently scuffing the ground with their spikes or staring skyward; each trying not to make eye contact with anyone, especially Coach Mendel.

Looking straight up into the hazy powder blue sky, Mendel seemed to wilt a little. He flipped the clipboard in his hand so that it spun around to land softly back in his hand. He looked at the clipboard, to the ground and finally towards Coach Warren. Coach Mendel was in his third year of coaching. He had attended Weir High School in the early nineteen fifty's, had played college ball, and then returned to his alma mater to teach and coach. He was young, energetic, and fit. He appeared to still be in playing shape. His full head of hair was covered by a baseball cap and his eyes with sunglasses.

Mendel turned his back to the mass and walked slowly towards Coach Warren, who stood stoically ten yards behind. The two chatted for a few minutes, looking out on the vast green grassy field that almost reached to the horizon. The woods at a great distance sprung-up out of nowhere and feathered into the green and brown low rising hills that reached quickly to the lazy cream colored sky. Not a deep blue cloud anywhere. The few clouds that were in the sky stretched like floating pale blue-green ribbons and string.

It was a picture perfect, semi-steamy August afternoon in the Appalachian foot hills of the West Virginia panhandle. A soft wind kept the atmosphere in a constant state of movement and the temperature comfortable, even in football garb.

Warren made a simple hand wave to the other coaches and staff, calling them away from the squad. As they started to gather, he called out, "everyone take five and a knee; bring some water in." The coaches joined up to talk in muffled tones with few gestures. They appeared to be at ease and even laughed somewhat silently. What started out to be a moment of anger for Mendel and Warren had changed unhesitatingly when all four coaches gathered. The four strolled a few more yards away from the squad that had almost in unison taken a knee, unsnapped their helmets, and were starting to yak about nothing in particular.

Marc was still on one knee, helmet on the ground, the palm of his left hand on the new white and red stripped head gear for support. He was separated from the main body of the troupes and only halfheartedly paying attention. His thoughts were on everything but football. The nice day took him back to the carefree days at the pool, the pickup games of baseball and basketball; his decision not to play legion baseball this year, the girls that only wanted to be his "sister-like friend," and the reality that the summer was almost over, football practice had started and his senior year was about to begin—only a week and a half away. *Wow, that is a load,* he thought, *and I'm only seventeen.*

He watched as most of his team mates headed toward the trainers and the water. It was obvious to Marc and most of the veterans from past seasons, that there was no enthusiasm in anyone on the practice field.

This was already the end of the third day of summer practice. Marc was tired and malingering about what the summer should have been like. He had enjoyed the relaxing summer days, but something had been missing. He wasn't certain what he had neglected to do these past three months, but there was a deep shallow pit inside him that felt unfilled. It was difficult to concentrate on anything. This unfulfilled perplexing desire was consuming his thoughts.

Mid-August always brought football practice, with two per day sessions and chalk talks every evening. But this year it was different, more intense, especially in this isolated camp, devoted to nothing but football. Rather than the two week summer practices at the high school field, the boosters had arranged for a two week true football camp at West Liberty College. So, now it was football day and night. The team was housed on campus. It was football for breakfast, lunch, dinner, and all the time in between. Marc liked playing football, but twenty-four hours a day was unsettling for him and the others, even for the coaches.

They had only been on campus for three days and the uniqueness had completely worn off. Practices had not being going well. For a team that last year had won the Division I-AAA West Virginia State Championship, they performed appallingly. The practices were sluggish. Even the calisthenics were feeble. Today had been the worst. They had their first full intra-squad scrimmage. Execution of an offense was disappointing. Marc had played so poorly that he had been replaced by some sophomore he did not even know.

Marc had played football and just about every school sport since he was in the sixth grade along with just about everyone on the team. Sports were his life. It always had been football in the fall, basketball in the winter; baseball in the spring and summer, as well soccer in the community church league. Last spring he even ran on the high school track team in between baseball games. But, without a doubt, last year's championship football season had been the high point for him, his friends, and the entire city.

There were fifteen returning letterman from last year's undefeated state champs, and they were touted to be just as good this year. So, the start of camp had been a letdown as the coaches said, "unworthy of their past." Marc agreed. However, he knew he was still preoccupied with everything but football practice, and that seemed to be the norm for the entire squad. Being isolated, thirty miles from home and away from all distractions, was intended to provide the opposite results; so much for good intentions.

In the three days at camp, the little spirit they had at the start, was now lost. Marc felt disagreeable towards everything associated with football. He was exhausted, irritated and most of all peeved. Nothing was like it should be; nothing like it had been last year. That was fun; a lot of work, but fun, a team working together, excited, with some piss and vinegar. This year everyone seemed to be weak, and almost feeble; no pep or bounce. Now even the coaches were confused and ticked off. The water line was getting shorter. He heaved himself up—drink time.

Starting to stand, Marc was vaulted to his feet as whistles splintered the silence with screeches and the coaches shouted – "gassers" – "everyone to the hill." "Gassers, now, let's go people" – "go, go, move." Marc started off in slow recoil, but as the shouts and the whistles became louder, he broke into a startled sprint towards the "hill."

"Oh, I hate these damn things. Why do we always end practice with these killers? They choke the life out of you. I'll never make it," someone behind him was complaining already.

Marc's subconscious was racing faster than his stride. He reached the bottom of the "hill," actually more a mound than a hill. He doubted that the incline was more than about five degrees, maybe twenty-five yards from top to bottom, but running up it was torture; especially at the end of a two hour practice. Typically the players would run up the hill three or four times, one after the other - drained.

"Backs and ends in the front line." Coach Warren's piercing voice howled. "Run all the way to the top; come back down on the outside. The harder you run, the fewer we do. Watch out for the gopher holes in that high prairie grass. You can twist an ankle or break a leg."

"Oh, thanks for the good news," someone in the back row mouthed off in a sassy voice.

"Ready – Set," the whistle blasted a loud – Wzzzzzz shrilled across the field and the front line of crouched contenders lurched into a sprint. Up the incline they rose; the faster runners separating from the body; but, everyone struggling with the heavy grassy terrain and the effort needed to scale the "hill."

A few stumbled, but all eventually reached the top panting for more oxygen. They turned to the side and staggered down to the bottom. The second column was already being launched with the Wzzzzzz of the whistle. This row included all linemen with a little more weight to carry, and as a result, a slower pace. They sped up the "hill" with the same determination and laborious breathing. The misery continued until the fourth dash was completed and everyone was bent over holding their sides and needing to fill their lungs with fresh air.

"Alright, hit the showers; good job on the gassers. Remember dinner is at six and position meetings at eight-thirty," Mendel called out. "If anyone needs the trainer, see me first."

Everyone staggered towards the locker room, water, a shower and a spot to sit in the shade. About a third of the group crouched low, blessedly dropped to one knee, before they reached the field house. A few dropped like rocks at the first shady grass, their aching legs and lungs giving way.

"Ah like the orange color. It … it shows your face so brightly. You glow."

"Oh Mum, it isn't orange, it has more of an amber or a tea color."

"Regardless of what's the color is, Ah like it on you. It's brighter than anything you've now. You should get the lot of them. They fit you handsomely. They are really bonnie."

"Ah can't get all three shades of the same blouse. It's too much of the same thing n Ah don't want to look the same every day. They will think Ah'm daft."

"Well I think they are all cute and all the colors look wonderful with your ivory cream complexion," their new American friend, Marietta, blurted out from her chair in the corner of the women's dressing room.

"See, Ah'm on target n Marietta should know," Jamie's mother said quickly, piggybacking off the supportive comment of their Weirton and American semi-tour guide.

"Ah don't fancy the yellow n blue ones. They are a fancy frock for just grammar school. Ah will look like a Mark's n Sparks high tea dicky bird," Jamie snapped back with frog in her voice.

"Well then you should be wearing Harris Tweed. You don't need a new wardrobe bin of clothes. We've enough of them now. So let's be done with it," her mother responded brusquely. "Ah'm wasting my day n quid on new frocks n jumpers. You'll look tidy enough with all your English clothes. Marietta, let's go home now, let's be done with it," Ellen snapped loudly and firmly. "See what Ah've to sort out Marietta. Ah just can't sort it out; the house, food, schools n the clothes. Ah'm ready to pack it in."

"Oh Mum, those are ugly cloaks. None of the birds wear that bloody cotton wool over here," Jamie stammered, turned in a circle trying to hide her tears and compose herself. Her voice now clearly in a sobbing mode, "these are just.... just not on. They're a pack of saftness. They're bloody ill."

She looked at her mother with tears running down her cheeks. Ellen's expression was stern, but she, too, had signs of starting to weep. She turned away and lost eye contact with Jamie. They each stood their ground for a few moments trying to moderate the tension. The move to the states had been improving as the summer days went by, but school and clothes for Jamie were difficult issues for mother and daughter. The education system in the states was so different than that in England, and for Jamie, it was a step back. Rather than going to college, she would be a senior in high school, taking studies she had already completed in Birmingham. She wanted to return to England and go to college, but her mother and father wanted her to stay with them and acclimate to the American way of life. It was a sharp point of disagreement, only second to the question of her wardrobe.

Jamie turned away and quickly moved along the clothing racks that spread out in a confusing matrix. She reached the large plate glass windows at the front of the store that looked out onto Main Street. Through the mannequins and displays, she could see the sun's rays bouncing off the parked cars and a large church cathedral on the far side. It was a bright sunny summer day, like most she had experienced the past three months.

Summer weather in America was wonderful, with many more full summer days than in England—certainly more than in Birmingham.

After a few moments of sunshine gawking, Jamie turned away from the store front windows, moved slowly along dozens of clothes racks that created narrow pathways leading to tables of blouses, slacks, women's tops of all makes and colors, and finally into the shoe displays. The number and styles were bewildering. The women's and young girl's department covered the entire first floor.

Shopping in America was beyond her understanding of reality as compared to clothes shopping in England. There were more choices, the fabrics softer, styles more modern, and a rainbow of colors. England was starting to show more variety, but only in the most expensive shops and no way to this extreme. Shopping and dressing could be so exciting here, but Jamie felt her mother was still holding onto her English roots. She refused to change her style, had not purchased a single piece of American clothing for herself, and not much for Jamie. Her father, who had been working in the states for nearly a year, had adapted completely and his wardrobe was American from his hatless head, to his well-shined wing tip shoes.

She stared back across the women's department and could see her mother and Marietta standing where she had left them. They seemed lost and forlorn. They were looking towards Jamie with impatience. Her mother had a look of dread on her face. Tears began to fill Jamie's eyes, and she was breathing in gasps. She wiped her cheeks and slowly returned to their side.

Looking directly at her mother she abruptly burst into a storm of words: "Ah didn't want to come here. You n Da know that. Ah'm done with it. Ah'll go back straight away myself n live with Granny in Berkswell. Ah can get on as a charlady n go to university." Her voice was cracking and rising in volume. The conversation was now carrying to other shoppers and clerks. Heads were turning in their direction throughout the entire store of Stone and Thomas.

"You're going off, Jamie, please be quiet. Pack it in," her mother said sheepishly.

"It's brilliant for you n Da n even Harry, but not me," Jamie blubbered out explosively. "Ah have lost all my friends. They've stopped writing, n these clothes are ratty. They etch in this weather n look as dull as muck," she shrugged pulling on her slate wool-tweed sleeve. "Ah 've passed all my "O" level exams n should be in university not going to some American High School. Ah'm going home," Jamie's voice quivered and began traveling off.

She walked away again; this time toward the exit. Before she went too far, she stopped, her shoulders dropping, and returned soothingly and said: "Mummy you carry on about our need to adjust to Da's new goffer, n Ah want to, but you don't let me fancy anything jolly new."

Marietta had walked over from her corner perch. She stood barely five feet tall and moved as though she were on air. Her floral dress with a swing skirt fell softly from shoulder to ankle and the matching purse was tucked inconspicuously against her small frame. Marietta Brandon was the wife of a mid-management engineer for Weirton Steel, and along with her husband Gus had been asked by the company president to "host" the English metallurgical engineer, Francis Toliver, and his wife and two children.

Marietta, a thirty-six year old mother of two teen age boys and a longtime resident of Weirton, was always dressed smartly. Today, she looked classy, well groomed in heels, not high but sturdy and comfortable for all the walking that shopping required. She had a small busy profile hat that messaged her commitment to Ellen and Jamie to help them get ready for the school year and settle into an American life style.

The small statured woman was serving as a pseudo American /Weirton Steel host. Gus Branden worked directly with Francis, Ellen's husband, and was mentoring him in the ways of the American Steel Industry. Both men were metallurgical engineers with unique skills and background in the new and expanding double-reduced tin process. This nearly paper thin steel product was revolutionizing the container industry of pop-top liquid cans and was starting to be used for interior car components.

Gus and Francis were leading an American/England project to capture the markets in the United States and Europe for this new pioneering process. It was a critical venture for both the Weirton Steel Company and for Birmingham Iron and Steel. The steel industry was changing in the post-World War II decades and both companies needed some new products to stay competitive. Success for Gus and Francis could be career making and Marietta and Ellen needed to keep the home side as smooth as possible. Marietta seemed to recognize that more than Ellen. This discontentment needed to be settled.

"We all need to get some lunch and talk this over. What if we went to the Club for lunch and plan our attack on a shopping spree for both of you."

"You mean the Golf Club?" Ellen asked, both surprised and thankful for relief from the tension.

"Yes, Williams Golf Club. You have been there with us for dinner. It is exciting at lunch with all the golfers, and many of the wives will be enjoying a day out. Is everyone game for some relaxation?"

"Oh, me, that would be grand, indeed. Yes, would that be alright with you Jamie?"

"Yes, are we dressed right?" Jamie's face was still crimson and puffy from all the tears.

"Yes, you are fine. They have a lovely women's luncheon room and some wonderful desserts. We can talk about solving this clothing issue, maybe plan a trip to The Hub or even the Pittsburgh department stores. That will give you an even larger selection and some of the newest styles. It'll be fun and I need a few things myself."

"Yes, right."

Ok, it's settled and I am hungry," Marietta laughed and led the way to the exit, the car, and a ladies lunch at Williams Country Club.

"Everyone gather around, on one knee. Make a circle. Make room over here so everyone can hear."

"Good practice this morning. We are starting to see some good hustle.

This is the end of the first week of camp. We have had some good days and some bad ones, but overall the results have been encouraging. Now, I have some good news and some bad news. Let' start with the bad news. We all know that a number of your teammates have been absent from football camp, because they have been playing baseball in the American Legion regional tournament. Well, they lost in the finals last night and their season is over. We are sad for them. No one likes to lose in any sport after they have worked so hard over the season and in tournament play; but lose they did, and that is good news for our football team."

Cheers went up from some of the squad, a few groans, and a couple of damns. Coach Warren stepped back for a moment and then went on: "That means that those football players who were playing baseball for the legion post will be at practice next week with a lot of catching up to do. Also, next week's camp will be our last chance for two a day practices and evening blackboard sessions. So, rest up over the weekend and come back here prepared for a busy week. We have to get ready for not only Charleston but for the entire season, and we only have five full practice days left of summer."

He stopped for a few minutes, and then looked around the circle of sweating faces and dirty uniforms and said in a kind and fatherly voice, "I know that teammates not being here for the first week of camp has been difficult and welcoming them back will be odd. Their absence has kept us from having a full complement and did not allow us to progress as a total team. But next week there will be a dozen more bodies and ten of them are lettermen from last year. Everyone who filled in for those missing this week did a lot of extra work, and we appreciate that. That extra work will help you play more and also to play better this coming season. Thanks for a good week."

"No gassers today!!"

Again cheers from the circle; very loud cheers.

"Now get your showers. We will have lunch and the buses will leave at one p.m. from the field house. Be on time." Coach Warren took off his baseball cap, turned away, and walked towards the other coaches.

The circle broke-up and some of the guys started running to the locker room for water, a shower and their lunch. There was some yelling and loud talking as a long week of football practice was over. Marc walked slowly with his helmet swinging, his right arm at his side. No gassers was great news, he sure wasn't going to miss them. He had been involved in almost every play today on offense or defense. His jersey was stuck to his back with sweat and his entire body was covered with dirt and grass stains. It had been a long, tiring week and going home sounded good.

He wondered how the baseball team felt about losing and returning to football. His decision not to play legion ball this summer haunted him at times, especially as they went further in the tournament; however, he had enjoyed his summer freedom from practices, games and travel.

Now that they, and there were some very important "theys," were going to be back next week, the practices would get better, more intense, and more serious. Marc knew that the team needed everyone back if they were going to contend for another state title.

He said in a very soft voice, almost inaudible, "Wow, home for supper. Two days to do whatever, the pool tonight, maybe a date?" And then reality set in and he thought, *with who? Or is it "whom"?*

The view from the Tolliver's back yard stone patio was breathtaking. They had enjoyed the scene from the moment they moved in. The back yard was wide and long. From the moment you stepped off the patio, green grass flowed like a velvet path to the entrance of the sloping forest that fell away to the river. One could not see the river while sitting in one of the lounge chairs, but could view the wide vista of the distant hills of Ohio. The glass kitchen door, which opened onto the patio, was a portal into a world of leisure.

The Tolivers had nothing like this home and its grounds in Birmingham. There the yards were no bigger than the patio, if a yard existed at all, and the scene was the back of the terraced flats on the next block.

Both Ellen and Jamie were content to lounge in the warm sun and watch Harry and a few of his new friends run from one yard to another tossing an American football. Harry had learned a number of new games, all American versions of some English sport. His new favorite was baseball, primarily because it was somewhat like cricket. He was getting good at it; though with the seasons changing, this funny oval-shaped football started to get kicked about by him and his buddies. The silence was broken by Harry asking about lunch and wanting permission to go to the pool.

"Everyone is going for a splash. Ah, can go, right?"

"After lunch. Ah guess Jamie n Ah can muddle through without you," his mum replied somewhat sarcastically, but with a smile on her face.

"When are we going to eat lunch? The guys will be leaving soon on their cycles."

"What's this, the 'guys?' You're becoming Americanized right quickly," she kidded. He smiled and turned his head to hide his blushing and said, "the chaps."

All three laughed in unison for the first time in months. Harry ran off and Jamie looked with empathy at her mother. "He asks after you when you're sad n there's rain about you n Da."

"Right, Ah know…but maybe the shopping with you n Marietta have give'n me a turn."

"Brilliant. These past few days 've been a good tonic." Jamie chimed in. "We had great fun n bought a load of new clothes, n we still have to go to Pittsburgh next week to the big city stores: Ah'm so happy."

"Right, indeed, we've had a jolly good time. Even Ah 've some new American things," she paused and started to get up; but sat back down, "are you a little more bright now?"

"Oh, yes. Ah'm getting excited about school, even though Ah know Ah'll be retaking some studies…Ah'll meet new people n see new American things n that should be spot on."

"Good indeed… that makes me happy too… now it should be better for Harry. He watches you closely…we better get Harry lunch."

"Oh, Ah'm going to pop around to the pool this evening n meet Niki after she works," Jamie said.

"Yes, do carry on," was the reply.

Sprinting up the stairs, bouncing two steps at a time, he reached the visitor's promenade. The pool was only sparsely populated, mostly by middle school age boys who would swim all day if allowed to by their parents. The twin low diving boards had a half-dozen faithful working on jack knife dives. As he watched them, it was obvious they were already better than he was and more daring.

Marc could see Niki on the opposite side of the large egg shaped pool. She was working the late shift of the life guard schedule. She waved and yelled something that was lost in the song blasting from the park-wide sound system. Someone had turned up the usually lower volume level, probably because the pool Manager, Coach Baker, had gone home. The neighbors would not appreciate that.

The visitor's concrete deck perimeter walkway was nearly empty except for two family groups sitting on the wood benches that lined the outside wall near the children's wading pool. Marc started to move along the substantial steel pipe fence that separated the visitors from the swimmers. As he glanced off to his left into the park below, he spotted a group enjoying a picnic in the gardens of the west side ravine. *A very peaceful sight,* he mused.

The sun was low and sunset was not far behind. Marc had watched that scene from the elevated pool many times; but after the week he had just spent at football camp, living in a stuffy college dorm, the view took on a special air.

"Hi, how was practice?"

Marc was startled and he twisted around to be looking at Niki, only about two feet away.

"Ah – well," trying to catch his breath. "Good, that is okay."

"Did I scare you? You look surprised."

"No – yeah, I guess so. I was just looking at the sun."

"The sun? Oh, I see, it looks nice. It could be a little warmer. These kids swim in ice water after the sun goes down."

"It's not that cold, Maybe chilly, but not if you're swimming."

"Hi Niki," Another voice joined the conversation.

"Hi, I've been looking for you," Niki's voice went up a few decibels and was very chipper. "I was hoping you would get here early so we could … What did…well, cool… what… you look so... wow...different. And a new outfit too. You look grand."

The visitor's face started to redden and her smile expanded with just about every word from Niki. Marc just stood there listening to the two girls talk in a blaze of words, laughs and compliments about hairdos, jumpers, dresses and shoes.

Marc thought about leaving, but he was enjoying listening and admiring this unknown person standing next to him on the visitor's side of the railing. He thought he knew her. She looked familiar, but also unfamiliar.

Regardless of knowing or not knowing her, she was something, he thought. He would add his "WOW" to Niki's, if he were in the conversation. Musing about her, Marc concluded that she was cute and pretty at the same time. She was dressed in a variety of blue shades. The pants were knee length that had a bow tied at the knee somehow topped with a matching summer jacket. The entire package highlighted her blue eyes. But it was really her face, hair, complexion and her funny language, voice and phrases that captured his attention.

He studied her face. It was heart shaped with her hair curving around it like a furry hood on a coat. *Her hair was red, no, reddish brown or maybe a golden auburn, and it changed with different angles of light,* Marc silently debated with himself.

According to the conversation she was having with Niki, she had just been to a hair stylist and her new cut was called a "bob." It was chin length, short on top, with curls and front bangs. Marc was infatuated with everything about her; she was intriguing in so many ways. The oval face with a natural ivory complexion and the ogling baby blue eyes and the scarlet hair mesmerized him. Her voice slurred every other word and was difficult to understand, but sophisticated and fresh. The effect made Marc unsettled.

"Hey, I need to walk around and do my thing. I'll see you about eight fifteen. Stay with Marc and ask him about football. He's one of the stars," Niki lectured to them both and pointed to Marc. She moved away quickly, needing to make-up for her long pause.

"Yeah, star—that will be the day," Marc sniggered halfheartedly.

"Your a foot-baller?"

"A foot…baller! Not sure what you mean?? I do play football," Marc responded with a quizzical voice and face.

"Do you like playing n being on the pitch?"

"Pitch? Did you say pitch…what is a pitch? You're talking about baseball. You pitch in baseball…not football!"

"Blimey…Ah' am daft…there's a boob," Jamie's face was in full blush as she tried to find the right words. "You're a footballer on the pitch…on the grass…the grass field."

"What are…I mean where are …you're not from here…who are you?" Marc was now very confused and perplexed.

"Ah'm Jamie. We've met before n you are Niki's bloke," her sensitivity very obvious. "We've seen each other at church."

"Cove Church?"

"Yes, indeed. At the bible school."

"Oh yeah, you're Niki's and Amanda's English friend. Now, I know who you are. Okay."

"How is camp going? Has it been rough?"

"WHAT? Oh hey, Ron you're back! It's okay, but rough without you and the others."

All of a sudden the spectator area was filled with ten or fifteen classmates with more coming up the stairs. The entire bunch that had been lingering outside the front entrance had decided to invade the visitor's perch. It was noisy, crowded, with multiple conversations, and the top of the stairs became completely blocked.

Jamie had moved away or been crowded out and was already talking to Amanda and Sarah. About a dozen girls created a clog at the top of the stair, where they had stopped to chitchat. Finally Marc and half a dozen football players moved further down the terrace to make room and continued a discussion of team, practice, sore arms and legs and everything but girls. The group joked together until the floodlights in the pool came on indicating that it was almost closing time.

As the evening sun was getting ready to burst into a yellowish, green and blue star, the crowd drifted down the stairs. More music was vibrating out of the park-wide speaker system, now with *Sam Cooke*, charming everyone with: *Cupid draw back your bow and let your arrow fly…*

Marc joined the others leaving the observation patio. Cooke's soul searching words captured more than his attention, they were a serenade of his emotions. Jamie was in the front of the parade, out of sight.

The group disbursed as they passed the admissions counter and concession stand. They exited the red stone and white painted concrete post building heading into the park grounds. They scattered like tumble weeds, but most of them drifted towards the usual evening rendezvous, the stone and wood shuffleboard shelter. It was the perfect place to meet, mix, tell stories, flirt and just be. It provided an entirely open space with four courts away from others, benches along all four sides, and a roof cover in case of rain.

Half way there, a voice on the loud speakers gave notice that the pool was closing and the entrance doors would close in fifteen minutes. Niki and the others would soon join the group. Marc spent the next hour or so wandering from one cluster to another. Niki had settled in with a girly bunch in a corner. Their laughter was loud and almost contagious. They seemed to be in the best mood of the entire pack.

As the sun disappeared, the girls left in two's and three's. Marc moved toward the corner batch and Niki. Slowly, he took his place with the gathering and waited. Finally, Niki said: "I'm tired. Time to go home." Marc took it as a queue and quietly asked the question everyone expected, "Need a ride? I need to get going, too."

"Sure, can you take Sarah and Jamie home, too?"

"Sure, no problem," was his quick response. Sarah was always a tag-along, but Jamie was a surprise addition, and he didn't even know where she lived.

"Come on, we have a ride with Marc. Let's go."

They said good night to the others and moved down the center tree lined walkway to the gravel parking lot. As usual, Marc was parked in the last row, his habitual spot under the trees.

"Shotgun!" Niki called out as they approached the car.

"What is that? Shotgum?" Jamie asked

"Shotgun," Niki corrected her. "It means I get to sit in the front passenger's seat. You and Sarah sit in the back."

"Yeah, I always have to sit in the back and be the one to crawl into the back seat over everyone! Damn it," Sarah snapped, but with a smile.

"At least you get to ride," was Marc's response as he slid under the steering wheel.

The three of them laughed and Jamie was again confused by these American customs. She and Sarah wriggled past the folded half front passenger seat into the back of the black Chrysler coupe.

Marc started the car and the radio instantly piped in some rock and roll. The blast was: *a song by Chuck Berry, "Sweet Little Sixteen:" They're really rockin' Boston in Pittsburgh P.A. Deep in the heart of Texas and 'round the Frisco Bay... All the cats want to dance with Sweet Little Sixteen… Cause they'll be rockin on Bandstand… Way down in New Orleans… Sweet Little Sixteen.* After the few blocks to Sarah's, Marc stopped in front of the driveway. Niki jumped out and moved the front seat out of the way so Sarah could get out. Instead of letting the front seat settle back and leaving Jamie sitting by herself, she called, "Come on up front. We can all fit."

Jamie quickly hopped from the back to the center of the front bench seat and gingerly sat between Marc and Niki. The ride to Niki's house was only a few minutes. As soon as Marc stopped the car, Niki dashed out of the door, calling good-night as she sprinted to the back door.

"Where do you live?"

"Down at the other end of this street. Ah'll show you."

"Ok, just point me in the right direction."

Jamie stayed in the middle of the front seat. The radio had been playing one song after the other since they got into the car. The disk jockey at WEIR was chatting up each record and the music shifted from rock tunes to love songs.

"You've such big cars here. Our cars are tiny n very bumpy to ride in," Jamie finally broke the silence.

"You have a car, over there?"

"Oh, not mine. Ah don't drive. Only my Da drives…n it's a very small car."

"By the way I am not Niki's 'bloke' or whatever you called me. I'm not even a 'bloke' to anyone. Niki and I have been friends for a long time. We have dated, but we have only kissed twice… maybe three times."

"This is my house…right there."

Marc pulled into the driveway and stopped. The radio filled the sound waves with: *I wonder, wonder who, bi du du, who who wrote the book of love, a song by The Monotones, "Book of Love."*

Jamie started to move towards the passenger side door, stopped and leaned back towards Marc and kissed him softly on the lips. Before Marc could react, she had jumped out the car door and was running towards and into the house. He sat there stunned, wanting to pull her back, wanting to say something to someone, anyone, Jamie. Finally, he backed out of the driveway, stopped and thought: *What a night! What a week! What do I do now?*

Tell me, Tell me, Tell me, Oh who wrote the book of love, I've got to know the answer, Was it someone from above, I wonder, wonder…Who wrote the book of love…

Chapter 4

Flirtation

The road was filled with curves and more curves, hills large and small, and valleys, each intersected by a stream. As they drove through cross roads, they passed were small towns of probably a dozen homes on picturesque creeks with unique names, but all called a "run." There was Radcliff Run, Wolf Run, Wilding Run and this one was Little Sandy Run. The streams were all the same, very snake like, usually set in a steep ravine, bordered by small wood or brick framed houses of every color and just as many trailer houses anchored on stones, cement blocks or dirt piles.

They had been traveling for only two hours and Jamie was already tired. Yesterday, they had driven about four hours along the Ohio River through a number of cities of some size, but today the towns, or what appeared to be towns, were merely a few homes clustered together around a country store or gas station. When the trip bordered on the river, they could see fishing boats, tugs, barges and even an occasional houseboat. Today, all that was gone as they cut across West Virginia towards the capital.

Jamie felt alone and a little sad. Everyone had been talking earlier; but now all were quiet except for some hushed conversation between Niki's mother and Miss Walker, the cheerleading coach. Niki was almost asleep with her head leaning against the opposite window. Molly was taking her turn in the back middle seat trying to read, an almost impossible task as the car shifted from side to side mimicking the road and jerked over the constant bumps. Her hands and the book were in a constant hop-skip motion, her eyes moved like a bunny trying to stay focused. Jamie felt devilish and wanted to laugh out loud at the jiggling sideshow. Instead, she snickered inside and said silently, *that could make you go blind.*

She turned to face the window again gazing at the countryside spotted with houses, barns, cows, horses and farm fields. In some ways the landscape was very picture-perfect; however, it was also boring. Already the three day trip had been an adventure, but this stretch was dull. Last night's stay in Parkersburg had been fun as she, Niki and Molly Bouchard shared a hotel room, just like a slumber party. Jamie and her new American friends laughed, told stories and had talked well past mid-night so waking-up was difficult. But the night had ended on a sour note, as her new friends did not understand or accept the big differences between England and America. They had so much here in the states. Neither of them appreciated it, and could not realize that many people didn't have as much. She had tried to tell them how lucky they were, but they teased her for being so serious. Jamie had fallen asleep crying in her pillow and thinking of home, her real home, *England.*

Tonight in Charleston would be another late night and another sleep-over atmosphere following the game. They'd be even more tired on Saturday morning with another long road trip back to Weirton. She was tired just thinking about the Saturday trip. The enthusiasm of yesterday had turned to gloom for Jamie. She was more than just homesick, she was melancholy for her past life, her Birmmie friends and the especially her extended family. Hopefully, all would go well when they arrived at this thing called a football game. Maybe she could shake the blues at the game, just maybe. Her mother would advise her "not to get her knickers in a twist."

Jamie's thoughts turned to all she was being exposed to: new friends, new school, new clothes, even a new country and now a trip to Charleston, the capital of West Virginia, and her first American football game. She would have a lot to write about to everyone back in England. They would never understand all she had seen and experienced. Even this big car, the Stewarts' family Desoto Firedome station wagon that they were riding in was beyond description to a Brit. There were three girls in the back seat of the shiny red bodied and white topped mammoth auto, each seated without rubbing up against the other or sitting on top of someone. American car seats were as big as the English train seats, or larger.

Last night their bedroom had its own bathroom with a shower, and the menu at dinner at someplace called Howard Johnsons was so big she could barely hold it up straight. Those were things you only found in the real fancy places in England, certainly not in the bed and breakfasts and pubs in Birmingham or in the roadside taverns anywhere in the British Isles. She had not even experienced that lavishness on her trip through London and on the Atlantic ship crossing. America seemed to have everything, certainly more than England.

What would tonight be like? How would people at the game treat her? She would be with Niki, Molly and the other cheerleaders at the game. What do cheerleaders do at football games? Certainly practice, which she had watched, for them was strenuous and they did a lot of yelling, jumping and running about. What is a game of football like and what will she do while they are playing? Then her thoughts drifted to Marc Floreau.

He was very cute, handsome really. He was tall, maybe six feet or more. The flat top haircut, with the front standing up straight, made him seem taller. The hair was light chestnut, although the summer sun and swimming had bleached some spots blond. His smile was what she noticed from the first time she saw him at the pool on that very hot summer day. Her kiss to him about a week ago was unplanned, just a reaction to his charm or her need for affection.

She had looked for him at school those first two days, and at church last Sunday, but had only seen him from a distance. She heard Niki and others mention that all the boys were camping some place for football, but that only confused her. Ever since that night in his car when he drove her home, he had not been around. Maybe he was upset or he didn't like the kiss. She wasn't "getting off" with him, it was just a kiss because she was happy and he was "fit."

"I can't read anymore, it hurts my eyes, neck and even my back hurts."

"You girls alright back there? We will be stopping soon to stretch and get gas. Everyone okay?"

"Uh, yes Mrs. Stewart. We are fine, just tired of riding," was Molly's reply.

"What dear? What did you say?" Voices did not carry well between the front and the back.

"Tired of riding all these miles," two voices boomed and whined in unison.

"Yes, yes I know. We'll stop soon," was the front seat response.

"Boy, am I tired. We went to sleep too late last night. I'm, 'yawwwn,' going to fall asleep right in the middle of the game," grumbled Niki in betweens yawns, as she tried to shake off a slumbering nap.

"Yeah, that was fun, but we could use more sleep and this ride is making it worse."

"Well, why are you trying to read? Your eyes will be blood shot tonight," Niki barked at Molly, who placed her book on the floor of the back seat. Molly was a cheerleader. She was cute, upbeat about everything and very sports minded. She danced, took gymnastics, and even played basketball with the boys when they would let her. She kept her hair cut shorter than most of the girls, which gave her a "Tomboy" look.

"Those stories you told about England and your friends were a riot. I laughed so hard I almost got sick. You were hilarious," Molly uttered as she turned her attention to Jamie. "I still don't believe half of what you told us."

"Well, they're all true, n not funny to me."

"Funny is not the right word. What you said was sad… I guess. England seems to be behind the times… It's not modern, and that's a real surprise," Molly struggled to smooth over the discomfort she could see on Jamie's face. "Not funny, but different…you know...odd maybe," Molly continued to step all over her new friend's tender ego.

"Daily life was hard there. Here, it is so much easier. What if you're Mum had to shop every day for bits n bobs. Our ice box only held what we could use in one day. Your Mums buy enough for a week."

"Well, now you're here, and that is great. You can enjoy the American way. Molly was only enjoying hearing about England, and so was I. We don't want to get you upset like last night. We're sorry, Jamie. We like you and enjoy learning all about your life in England and how different life is here for you. Please don't get mad at us."

Jamie's face softened and a smile spread across her face. "Some of the stories are funny, even to me when Ah think about them now. Not funny, ha ha, but funny, odd. But Ah didn't tell you them to be funny. Ah wanted you to know how difficult it is for me to feel like Ah belong here. Everything is so different here. Life is easier here for me n my family. You Americans 've so much. Houses are newer n bigger…you can buy so many things in so many different shops. You carry on about everything. Ah feel fagged just listening to you.

"That's because it has been this way all our lives," Niki butted in. "But please don't get mad with us just because we like the way we live. Your way just seems so old and some of the things you talk about just don't seem real. We know there are people who are poor and still live the way they… the way you lived in England. But, that's not us, thank goodness. Molly and I are sorry that we thought what you were saying was amusing. You were serious. We were wrong and we're so sorry. We were really stupid and unkind. Please let's make up? Ok?"

"Okay, we Brits don't get mad when we've had a row with our birds. We don't stay mad very long," Jamie replied. "Cheers, to you for being my friend. Remember the bag-roll."

"What is that again? I should remember." Molly struggled to remember what the English term meant. They had laughed about it last night.

"It means toilet paper," Niki exclaimed to the delight and laughter of the other two. All seemed to be well between them after a few moments of friction that was a carry-over from the rocky end to last night's marathon gab session.

"I didn't know that I was a bird," joked Molly, "hope I'm a Robin."

Giggles were heard from all three.

"What's so funny?" was the question from the front seat.

"A girl thing!" was the back seat reply.

The teenagers continued to compare cultures, but without the flare-ups of last night. Jamie described how she had to use a pay phone on the corner, because her family didn't have a phone in the house. They still had a ringer washer and no clothes dryer. Her mum and everyone in the neighborhood only had clothes lines in their narrow back yards that were actually called gardens. Most of the neighborhood women did laundry by hand. "Ouch" was the reply from Niki and Molly as they listened to Jamie contrast her American life with life in Birmingham.

When she told them about rationing, which had only ended recently in England, the two American girls were flabbergasted. Rationing was something they read about in history books and in stories about World War II, not in their lifetime, "wow that must have been a bummer."

The laughter from the three started to get contagious when they traded unique names and words: Bonnet (of a car) – Hood; Boot (of a car) – Trunk; Bottom drawer – Hope chest; Loo (toilet) – John; Chips – French fries; Jelly babies – Jelly beans; Lorry – Truck; Trainers – Sneakers; Football – Soccer; Maize – Corn; Bloshy – Horny: Bloke – Guy/Boyfriend; Eraser – Rubber (no, Niki blurted out: "condom"). These last few caused an intoxicating roar, hoot and hard outburst of the laughter. They were laughing so hard that Niki's mother and Miss Walker each strained to look around.

"Is everything Ok? You sound like you're having fun. What's so funny?"

"Oh, nothing mom," Niki sputtered in between chuckles.

"Well, the restaurant is close and the other two cars will stop with us. We need to eat and get gas. We'll try to be here only about forty-five minutes, so we can get to the hotel by 2:00 o'clock or so, eat an early dinner and get over to the stadium at least an hour before the game. So don't dilly-dally with lunch!"

"Don't worry mom. We will be ready when you are. We want to get there more than you do."

Everyone was quiet for a few minutes, making sure they were ready to stop. Jamie was a little fidgety. As the stop was in sight, she said in a low voice: "Will we 've any chance to see the footballers before the game?"

"Well, maybe. It depends on what the stadium is like and where their dressing room is… maybe, Why?"

"Right…brilliant. Ah'm just interested in what the night n the game is going to be like. Ah'm really amazed at all this excitement."

"Don't worry about it. You're with us, we will take care of you," Niki assured her.

"Cheers to you. Blimey you're wicked. Do you 've a bloke?" Jamie asked as almost a second thought.

"Have a what?" was Niki's surprised reply.

"A bloke or a special mate? Maybe Marc?"

"Wait. Wait. What are you ask…"

"Ok, we're here. Forty-five minutes, not a minute more. Everyone out."

"This is your gym? For your…eh…high school? It's…it must, eh be new?" Marc turned his neck from side to side and tried to focus in the low light while he spun 360 degrees looking up into the steel rafters.

"Aye, this is only the second year we have had it. Nice, huh?"

"It looks so...looks really big. Can't see the other end in this light. This is something. You could have a football game inside this place. Kicking off and punting and everything. All you need is grass," Will added his two cents as he, like Marc, was stretching his neck to take it all in.

"Aye, there are three full basketball courts. A running track above the practice courts and a swimming pool."

"A swimming pool? All right here?" Marc questioned his host.

"Aw, come on, a running track inside a gym? This I have to see," Will queried in an exasperating voice.

"Well, it's a field house, not just a gym. It's like the ones at a college. This building is far more than just a gymnasium. It's bigger and newer than the one at WVU. It even has handball courts, classrooms for gym class and special meeting rooms for the athletic teams," came the bragging reply from Marc's and Will's host Jon, a member of the Charleston High football team.

Marc, with his head tilted back, eyes focused on the high steel girdered ceiling and the permanent stadium seating that stretched on both sides of the massive wood floor to just under large glass windows, jabbed Will in the ribs with his elbow, "damn, this is something."

"It sure is, hell, it is beyond anything I have ever been in," Will whispered as he and Marc turned around again slowly, gawking at the scene and acting like tourists in a museum.

"It's a great basketball court. The Charleston College plays here also during the basketball season. They also use our football stadium."

"Yeah, I thought your stadium was a little too nice to be a high school field. It didn't have a dirt spot on it. Ours is all cut up with half dirt or coal dust. We practice on it, and during the summer they play Little League Baseball there," Will jabbered.

"Our stadium is ours and the College only uses it for their games. We are on it only on Thursday before games and on Friday night," Jon popped in quickly and very defensively and then cooled quickly. Jon was a very dapper high school jock, stocky, taller then Will and Marc, with styled blond hair. He was very friendly and seemed to enjoy their company.

"Maybe during basketball season you'll get a chance to play us here. We should be really good this season. We were runner-up in the state last year, and we have almost everyone back," Jon informed them with pride. Marc and Will did not respond but were whirling around for the third or fourth time still gawking at the size and layout of the facility.

"We would give you a better game in basketball than we did tonight in football," He continued.

"Do you wear gold basketball shoes like your football cleats?" Marc asked with a half snicker.

Their host caught the drift quickly and said with a smile, "yeah, didn't you like them? They are our game shoes."

"Yeah, yeah, I did like them and wish we could wear them. But not in Weirton. After one time they would be gray from all the mill soot and coal dust," Marc answered and all three laughed. Will added with a chuckle, "we only have one set of cleats, to be used for both practice and for games."

"You know I would…it would be great to play here. That would be great. I hope we get a chance to play you in this gym. Will, wouldn't you?"

"Remember it's a fieldhouse," Will responded a little sarcastically, with the emphasis on fieldhouse.

"How could I forget, a fieldhouse."

"Haw, Haw, Haw," was the mocking response from their Charleston social coordinator. "You guys want something to eat or drink? The boosters always have food in the far corner. The teams and the cheerleaders can get it free at the snack bar over there," Jon pointed towards the far end of the basketball court.

"Food! Now you're talking…I'm starved," Will hooted and was off at a quick step towards the free goodies.

"Willie doesn't have manners when it comes to food. We didn't get much dinner. It's a long story about our dinner or lack of dinner, but I'm hungry too. Can we really get something to eat over there?" Marc stammered trying to be polite.

"Yeah, we sure can, let's go. I'm hungry too!"

Marc and his Charleston escort moved quickly, but well behind Will, across the gym floor. They had to weave through all the other fans, players, the Charleston band and the student body, all of whom were either dancing to the loud music on the PA system or just standing in clusters, bellowing. Everyone seemed to be talking with no one listening. This was the post-game dance and social with everyone celebrating their own being.

Every high school seemed to hold these after game parties regardless of the outcome of the contest. This was the first time Marc and his teammates had attended an opponent's festivity. Surprisingly, no one seemed to be a spoilsport even though the home team had lost and the party was hosting the victors.

Weirton had won the first game of the nineteen fifty-eight season by a score of 20 to 6. The game did not seem even that close. Weirton scored early on a fumble by the Charleston quarterback that had gone straight up in the air and Sage, a big defensive end, plucked the football out of the sky and ran it in for a thirty-five yard touchdown. The other scores came on long runs by Weirton's two halfbacks, Carl Miner and Tom Kec.

Marc felt that he had played okay, but nothing outstanding. No passes were thrown his way. His blocking was effective and Carl's touchdown had come on a run behind a decent come-back block by Marc. He had a few tackles and the entire defense had been strong.

As he made his way around the crowd, Marc spotted the coaches sitting at a table off to the side watching the revelry, giving special attention to the behavior of the Weirton troupe. The team had been cautioned to be on its best behavior and the coaches were on hand to make sure everyone understood the admonishment.

His teammates seemed to be clustered around the free food. Everyone was famished, not only from the exertion of the game, but because of the sparse meals provided during a very distressed bus trip.

Willie was already at the front of the line. Marc spotted the cheerleaders, Niki, Molly, Mandy and a few others being mobbed mostly by Charleston football players. The gaggle of beauties was attracting a new batch of admirers and the Weir High cheerleaders were enjoying all this attention.

Marc finally saw the deep red hair fluff that he had been searching for since he had entered the building. Jamie was in the center of the Charleston groupies and chatting loudly in her sweet British tongue. He stood still, just watching her and saying a detached "Hi" to a few friends as they walked by. Suddenly, Jamie looked his way and a big smile covered her face and she waved.

Marc stayed where he was to just watch her bubbling in conversation with everyone she could. He looked away attempting to get his bearing on the starting point for the food line. He pondered his next move for a few minutes, abandoned the food and started towards her.

"Hi, oh this is brilliant! Ah'm having a jolly good time. All the cheering, singing, n now dancing. Saw you in the game, it was brilliant."

"You made it…great. Your first football game."

"Aye, great. Football is very rough. Everyone gets down n up n then again. Does it hurt?"

"Well, sometimes, but it's exciting. You have to enjoy knocking someone down or even getting hit. I really like to tackle and block someone. It's fun, especially if you win."

"You really beat them hollow…and so thrilling…so cuffed."

"Cuffed? What are you saying? Did you really enjoy it?"

"It was really smashing, so brilliant n intense. Ah've never done anything like these last two days. Ah want to see all the matches."

"It's, it's not a match: it is a game. Where do you get this match idea? It's a football game."

"It's a match between you n them. It's what we call them…in England."

"Well, we call them games, and we play every Friday night."

"Ah know, Ah know, Niki and Molly told me all about it. It's just so right, a honey of a time."

"I'm not sure it's a 'honey' of anything, but it is a lot of tackling and hitting the other guy."

"Right, n with that big steel-like hat. Does your head hurt after you run into someone? Ah was so scared when Ah saw you hitting your head, especially when you were knocked down."

"It can hurt sometimes, but not really bad. That's why you wear a helmet. Our hat is a helmet. The helmet is so you won't get your head hurt."

"Those things cover everyone's face. You 've a cage in front of your face n Ah couldn't see your face or even find you on the pitch sometimes."

"Well, I was there," Marc replied a little sarcastically. "You need to look for the numbers. Mine is forty-four."

"Right. Ah know you are forty-four in the red polo shirt."

"Well, red yes, but that was tonight. Tonight we were in the red colored jerseys, but other games we will wear white jerseys with red letters. And they are jerseys, not polo shirts, wow I have to explain everything to you. I..."

"It's all new to me. Ah don't know anything about your football," Jamie suddenly had less of an accent, but that went unnoticed by them both.

"Just remember that my number forty-four."

"Right, n the same forty-four in the white shirts, right?"

"Yes, yes. The same number, but don't worry about that tonight." Marc wanted to change the conversation. He wanted to talk about something other than football. He was smitten somewhat by this English diva. Just hearing her voice with the British brogue made him feel weak and uncertain. Her words had a twang about them, and they excited him. He wanted to talk about her, not football.

It took him a while, but eventually he was successful in turning their conversation to more personal topics that went on for nearly an hour. Several "Hi's" were constant interruptions from teammates, cheerleaders, and even a few of the Charleston players, who wanted more of a conversation with Jamie than just a passing "hello." It was obvious that most of the guys were more interested in attracting Jamie away from Marc than in meeting an opposing player. She looked darling wearing a short red jumper that almost matched the cheerleader outfits, a red and black sweater top, and black pumps highlighted with tiny shining red bows. Her blushing auburn hair danced with slightest movement of her head and was partially tied back with a wide bright red and white twist ribbon. She was Weir High from top to bottom, and sitting next to Marc in his crimson shirt, appearing under his opened red and black state champion leather jacket, the two of them appeared as the ultimate Red Rider fans, together as a couple.

Marc had been able to maneuver them through the food line and into a somewhat dark corner table. Their location avoided much of the traffic of interlopers and the loud conversations. The need to mix with the crowd was not on Jamie's mind either. She had made this two day trip to have a chance to "really meet Marc." It was the first opportunity she had to talk with him and get to know him. She noted that he was about six inches taller than she was, with a lean, well built body. He smiled so easily, with a peach tone in his cheeks. She realized that his athletic appearance was not just in his football uniform, but was his true stature. He was a "bobby-dazzler" in the language of her fellow Birmingham birds.

The music was filling the massive gym with the *Sonny James' classic*: "*Young Love.*" The light dimmed as on cue, their hands joined and they danced in place as the words floated over and through them: *They say for every boy and girl there is just one love … Young Love we share with deep emotion … Just one kiss from your sweet lips…* As the dance came to an end, they stood for a moment, staring into each other's eyes. They continued to hold hands, walked over to an isolated spot, sat on the bleachers and just talked, talked and talked.

Jamie shared every detail about the trip from Weirton to Charleston. She described the drive, the restaurants, the room in Parkersburg, the Charleston Hotel that they would stay in tonight, and even the tit for tat problem she had with Niki and Molly, although she called it an English "howay - haway!" After talking non-stop for fifteen minutes, she finished her story. Now she wanted to hear about Marc's journey and what the team had done to get to the game. "Where did you stay last night?"

Relating a long story was not Marc's style. He was far more introverted than many others thought; however, her cutesy way of asking and pressing him to tell more, brought out the highlights of his two day trip. The festive atmosphere was magical in loosening his narrative proficiency, and he told her his tale of adventure.

First, he told her that the team had traveled by a chartered Greyhound bus, along with a few accompanying cars carrying some coaches, school administration folks, parents and some veteran team fans. It was a small, informal caravan.

The team had stayed in Parkersburg on Thursday night at a couple of churches where they were served dinner and then slept on cots that were scattered between the two churches that sat across the street from each other. Everything was okay, the food good and plenty and they slept well; the only drawback was that the showering and bathroom facilities were very limited on Friday morning. Breakfast was again at the church with the players being assigned kitchen duty. From the churches, they walked to a grade school and had a walk-though practice of sorts. Following drinks and fruit while sitting on the playground field, they boarded the bus for Charleston. The caravan had grown with a few more cars joining the parade sporting pep signs. Someone had also created large "WEIR HIGH RED RIDERS" signs placed on both sides of their bus.

Finally, he hesitated a few minutes before he began to relate a story of an incident that occurred in Parkersburg that really bothered him. Marc said that after dinner on Thursday he and half a dozen teammates asked Coach Romeo if they could take a walk in the downtown area of Parkersburg near the churches, just to stretch their legs before bed. The answer was yes, although Coach Romeo cautioned them to stay out of trouble, not to go very far, and gave them a curfew.

They walked for a few blocks, enjoying the downtown scene and the exercise. Then they decided to get a coke or maybe an ice cream, so they entered a small mid-town diner. They were immediately stopped by someone who said he was the owner, and that he would not serve "coloreds" in his place. There were two black teammates in the Weirton group. The entire group looked at each other, turned and all left together grumbling about the unkind and biased treatment. None of them had ever experienced such an incident at home, and following their return to the church, there was an open discussion about race and the different treatments of whites and black. It was a very open discussion that continued with a conversation with Coach Romeo about what had happened and the resentment they felt. The exchange about race relations continued until the lights-out call came. Coach Romeo, the only black coach, helped them to process this nasty experience.

Marc described to Jamie his ire with people who have such prejudice. Jamie detected that inside he was struggling with the ugliness of society cruelty. This was the first time she had seen him serious. For a few moments, he was different in some way. He had seen the reality of the back street alley, and it didn't jell with his life on mainstreet. She would tuck this snapshot of his humanity deep in her memory.

The funniest part of Marc's travel log, at least to Jamie, maybe not to Marc and the team, was the breakdown of the Greyhound Bus between Parkersburg and Charleston around noon. Marc described the bus starting to have trouble climbing the hills. It would slow down and barely get to the top of any climb and then cough and sputter during the entire descent.

Going downhill was easy but going up was agony, for the bus, the driver and the passengers. Everyone was wondering when the bus's engine would die and the roll backward would start.

Finally, the air conditioning in the bus stopped and they found that most of the windows did not open. Quickly it became stuffy, sticky and hot; everyone in the bus got mad and frustrated. Finally, the bus died in a gravel parking lot of a small country store and gas station. That was the start of a nearly three hour wait for a replacement bus, a lunch of very small cold sandwiches, pop and potato chips.

What was even worse was that the lost time meant that there was not enough time to have an evening meal and get to the stadium in time for the kickoff. Instead, cooked cold steaks wrapped in wax paper were passed out with more pop, milk, apples and chips to be eaten on the second bus en-route between a hotel dining kitchen and the stadium. They arrived with just enough time to change into their uniforms, do a few calisthenics and take the field for the kickoff. But, even with all those problems and the lack of a real meal, Weirton was ready to play. And play they did—very well.

Marc's anecdotes about the three hour wait in the heat, eating cold steaks in a moving bus, dressing in a stuffy steel hut with no lockers, just wall hooks, two small shower heads for the entire team, kept Jamie in a constant state of laughter. As they finished their hour of story-telling and eating chili-dogs, pretzels, potato chips washed down with coke, they were at ease with each other. Marc was starting to understand Jamie's Birmingham accent and some British words and phrases. He was enjoying the uniqueness of her twang and the fun way she had in expressing simple ideas. But it was her eyes that captivated him, eyes that were like diamonds, casting a spell over him. He couldn't stop staring directly into them; their deep blue radiance seemed to beckon a promise.

Their conversation dwindled, and they danced continually as the evening coasted to an end. When the music stopped, they separated, each looked around to see if anyone was watching them and to take a moment to catch their breath. Nearby, Will and Niki were in a deep embrace, still dancing very slowly even though the song was over. The embrace was more like cuddling and dancing was more swaying. They were an unexpected duo. Was this a new couple arrangement or just a comfort stop?

Marc was surprised, "Will and Niki. Wow, but good for them," he said. Jamie was not surprised, smiled at Marc nodding towards the union. "That's grand. Over the moon," she leaned forward and whispered in his ear. Small groups were moving towards the doors, as the lights came up. Most of the Weirton cheerleaders were all in a bunch motioning for every one in their troupe to come together. The Charleston football team hosts were pacing at the doorway waiting impatiently for their overnight visitors. Charleston's party time seemed to have ended earlier for them then it did for their guests. Losing will do that.

"Ah 've to go…sorry."

"Yeah, yeah, me too. Go, go, catch up with the girls. I'll see you in school… or maybe church on Sunday."

"Brilliant. Yes, brilliant."

Jamie sprang forward and standing on her toes rapped her arms around Marc's neck and kissed him on the lips for thirty seconds at least or maybe it was a life-time. He barely got his arms around her when the kiss ended, she recoiled and started skipping away, body bouncing, hair swaying, her face twisted looking back at him.

"See you on Monday, at school or maybe at church this Sunday. Cheers," were her last words as she ran to join the Weirton contingent and out the door she went.

Marc was again stunned, watching her dash away. He was confused, in a happy way. *What a day, what a day*, he thought as he began walking toward Will and Ron. More had happened in the past twenty-four hours than during the entire summer. He was dazed.

"Gee, I have been looking for you all week at school. I thought we were going…"

"Sorry, so sorry, this week has been right daft. Ah tried to find you in the hall, but we were both carrying on so. Ah wanted to talk with you n Ah even went with Niki to choir practice on Wednesday night but you weren't there."

"Boy, I thought we were going to be, well you know…going to be friends," Marc bellowed loud enough for heads to turn.

"We are friends, we are mates, oh please don't be mad! Don't think Ah don't like you," Jamie's voice became weak, cracking with a sob. "Ah'm sorry. My timetable changed at school n Ah am now in all these A-level classes, with special seminar groups. Ah had most of your school's courses already in Birmmie. They put me in these small chat-group classes. Some of them in the back of the auditorium behind a screen," conveying her frustration through a whimpering voice.

"Are you that smart? You have to be in special classes with all the really brainy kids? Gee..." his voice still feisty.

"Ah'm not...Ah'm not at all. We had advanced classes in England n Ah already graduated from public school n 've completed my sixth form exams. Ah passed the GCSE n the A-levels. If Ah was back in Birmmie Ah would be in university now. Ah was a swottie for the past three years. Ah..." She said slowly, apologetically.

"What...wait, I don't understand any of that. What is a "swot" or "smootie" or whatever you said you were? And the "A-levels" of what," he interrupted with passion and irritation.

"Ah 've a British accent n use British words when Ah get excited! And Ah am smart...a 'wiz kid' to you. Ah was in all the top classes there n should be in higher level schools n move on to university. Maybe Ah am a wizard or whatever you called me," Jamie responded as her voice trailed off.

"You sure must be to be in special high level classes. I'm barely getting through our school system. I'm on the dummy side," Marc's voice now almost a whisper and implying embarrassment.

They both took a few minutes to look around to see who was watching them. No one was really looking at them, although a few standing nearby had obviously turned away to keep from staring. They were standing in the middle of the Community Center's basketball court waiting for the post game dance to start. The crowd was growing and the lights were being dimmed.

Finally, "You played smashing tonight," Jamie muttered trying to change the conversation.

"Yep I guess so. Yeah, but it wasn't much of a game. A win is a win, even if it was only Toronto. We were too much for them. Now next week we play Steubenville, that will be tough," his zest returning to his voice.

He reached out and let his fingers touch hers, moved a few inches closer to her, looked at her tenderly. "I missed…"

Jamie took his hand, but broke his comments off in mid-sentence. "Ah brought my Da n Harry to the game n they really fancied it. They thought it was wicked. It was great fun for them with all the cheering n the band playing, marching, jumping and all nuttery. My Da said it was like a football match in Birmingham, you know, English Football. He should know. He was always going with his old chaps."

"Well great," he responded, more mesmerized with her eyes, the feel of her hand, the sweet scent of her hair, than her words. "Can I take you home tonight after the dance?"

The music was starting and the dimly lit basketball court was turning into a dance hall. It seemed like the entire school was jammed in, some dancing to the jukebox music, most standing around in small clusters, talking, laughing, enjoying the victory atmosphere—the girls in their huddle and the boys in theirs. The couples were spread out into the darker corners. Surprising was the duo of Will and Niki dancing to a rather fast paced jitter bug, doing the "slop." Charleston had sparked something.

Finally there was something slow to dance to. Marc and Jamie came together, their arms around each other attentively. Their hips moved slowly in a semicircle with Marc placing faintly more pressure on Jamie's lower back and Jamie moving her cheek only a inch or less from Marc's. The music was; *"In the Still of the Night, I'll remember", by The Five Satins: I remember that night in May … I remember … in the still of the night I held you tight … so before the light … In the still of the night.* Her auburn hair was soft on his forehead and her aroma very soothing, also hypnotic. Marc and Jamie moved cheek to cheek, and as the music and dance ended, Marc whispered in her ear, "That's our song."

"Right, yes." was the response.

They stood still for a few moments looking directly in to each others eyes. "Can I take you home?"

Her shoulders drooped. "No, sorry my Da n Harry are still waiting outside for me."

"Can't you just tell them?"

"No, no, Ah can't. They've been waiting for a long time. Ah need to go with them or Da will really get bonkers. Next time...right, next time."

"Gee, Jamie, come on, your parents need to lighten up. I was hoping..."

"Brilliant, so was Ah. Ah know, but Ah've to go now, right now. See you next week or maybe at church."

"Well, yeah, well, I..."

"Cheers!" Off Jamie went. This time without the kiss. She just left and vanished in the crowd towards the door.

The Weirton Daily Times captured the reality of the football struggle between the Ohio Valley perpetual powerhouses: Weirton Red Riders and Steubenville Big Red. The paper predicted a titanic like struggle and they were right. The 13 – 7 Weir High victory over the dogged Big Red before more than ten thousand standing room only fans at Weirton's Municipal Stadium resulted in the permanent retirement of the twenty-five year old trophy between the long time rivals, recognizing the Red Rider's three straight victory years of the cross-river game.

Marc had scored one of the touchdowns on a sixth-seven yard touchdown fourth quarter pass from Will, and kicked the extra point. But, he had missed the first extra point following a Carl Miner touchdown on a long punt return early in the game. Following the Red Rider first quarter score, the game turned into a defensive slug fest until each team scored on long passes late in the game. Marc's early missed extra point could have been critical, but happily for Marc, it was not.

The team, the school, the fans and the community were as excited as they had been a year ago when the Red Riders won the state Division I-AAA Football Championship on Thanksgiving Day nineteen fifty-seven. Since the Friday night victory dance and into the early Saturday morning extended parties, Marc and his teammates had been in an excited state. The euphoria of such an achievement was hard to switch off, especially in a football crazy steel mill and coal mining community. Winning was expected and celebrated by all.

On Sunday, as Marc drove with Ronnie in the shotgun seat, Niki, Amanda, and Jamie in the back seat of his black Chrysler coup, the celebratory mood was still with them all. The mood was festive and all seemed right with the world. WEIR was playing the National Top fourty Rock and Roll songs, and the car was filled with their voices as they sang along with: *I told the witch doctor I was in love with you ....Oo ee oo ah ah ting tang walla walla bing bang ...Then the witch doctor told me what to do.... Ah ah ting tang walla walla bing bang, a song by David Seville.* The coupe was almost jumping with the music and their very piercing voices. Finally, the song was over and they were all laughing and gasping for breath.

The small troupe was on their way to the Warwood First Presbyterian Church for a Youth Fellowship Sunday evening worship and dinner. The Ohio River was off to the right side of route two and the left was dominated by the high steep rock pocketed embankments. Driving through Follansbee and Wellsburg past steel mill gray mammoth structures, the blue collar nature of the region was unmistakable. The homes, store fronts, dreary green lawns, sidewalks, and even utility poles were covered in a gray dust. The environment was moon-like—but not to this group. This was home, their habitat, even to Jamie who had lived in the same atmosphere in Birmingham.

"What side dish did you bring Ron?" Amanda asked with her finger pulling at the back of his neatly brushed hair.

"Hey, watch that. It hurts when you pull on it."

"Oh, the poor baby says it hurts."

"Well it does," Ronnie responded playfully.

"You two are like an old couple, just like my grandparents, Niki teased."

"What do you mean?" Amanda retorted. "We just know each other very well."

"Well I hope not that well, if you get my meaning," Niki added.

"Thanks a lot. We are just good friends," Amanda piped up. She was around five feet four of sparkle, mystery and underlying intelligence. Her rich caramel-brown hair was long, shiny and seemed to bounce with her every movement. She portrayed a nun-like personality, but had her own version of "waywardness." The smile on her face was constant and caused her cheeks to puff-up with dimples, highlighting her deep brown eyes.

"Yeah, that's what she always says to me when things start to get interesting," Ronnie popped in mischievously from the front seat.

"That's what you say now, but you are the one who always says 'Oh no, let's slow down.' It's not me." Amanda set the record straight quickly.

The car filled with laughter and clownish behavior continued between the close friends, with Marc getting involved in even more kidding and foxy insinuations. Jamie seemed to be along for the ride, just listening to all the jesting between the four friends who had been together all throughout their school years.

Warwood was only a thirty minute drive from Weirton. The church was located directly on route two, next to the town park, along a small stream running through the town to the Ohio River. As they pulled up to the church, the parking lot was nearly full. The attendance was going to be sizable. Marc parked at the far end of the blacktopped lot. Amanda reminded everyone to bring the covered dish that they brought, while hounding Ronnie again with the question of his offering. "I don't know, something about beans and a salad," was his answer. "It's your mother's three bean salad," Amanda said triumphantly. "Told you," she winked at Niki.

"Well that's what I said, an old odd couple," Niki blabbed.

Marc and Jamie winked at each other and fought hard not to laugh out loud.

"I missed not being with you Friday night," Marc finally opened the conversation that he had been thinking about since their unexpected separation at the post game dance more than a week ago. He had wanted to share the victory over Steubenville with her. It was an important night for him, the team and the school—one that he wanted to celebrate with her. Everyone had been asking about her, wondering why she wasn't with Marc. They said she had been at the game with the Cheerleaders near the bench. He had wandered around the victory dance at the center looking for her. He searched for her in the teen room, even at the church next door and even at Di-Carlo's Pizza, anywhere he could think of. No Jamie. She had told him that she would see him at the dance after the game. He joined a late party at Niki's, but that was mostly couples, and he had felt out of place. This was the second week-end in a row that he was all alone. What happened? Charleston had been such a great time. The last two week-ends had been more than disappointing.

Marc and Jamie had seen each other during the week at school right before the Steubenville game. They crossed paths in the hall changing classes and had eaten lunch together a couple of times. However, these encounters were only short conversations with classmates all around them. The game with Steubenville was foremost on Marc's mind, though he was also very anxious to spend some alone time with Jamie after the game. He thought that was also true for Jamie.

Following the game, posing for pictures in the locker room, celebrating with his team mates and coaches, taking a quick shower, driving quickly to the Community Center, Marc was eager to be with Jamie and celebrate. But Jamie was nowhere to be found. His mood went from cheerful to miserable as he searched. He wanted to call her, maybe drive by her house, or even stop in, but he had lost confidence about their relationship.

The Sunday Youth Conference was his salvation and unknown to him, hers also. She knew she had upset him. Niki had given her all the details of his disappointment. If she could just talk to him, he would understand her dilemma. It was not him; it was her family, mostly her father and his concern for her safety. He was very sheltering, concerned about her acclimation to the American way.

The five stayed close to each other at the opening worship service and ceremony. Marc and Amanda had small parts in the proceedings, as they were each an officer. The dinner was an opportunity to be together, perhaps sit next to each other, but the meal at a table for eight provided no real prospect of any personal conversation. Finally, with dinner over, and the main worship program in the sanctuary, Marc took her hand and they slipped away into the basement of the church where they could be alone.

"Ah'm sorry, Ah'm always saying, sorry. Ah cried all Friday night. My Mum n Da went to the game n said Ah had to go home with them. Ah tried to tell them that Ah could get home by bus or with Niki, but they wouldn't let me. They didn't want me by myself out that late." Her English accent was deep in her excitement. She had been losing the Birmmie twang from being in school and hearing nothing but American English. But in her hassled sulk, she was pure British. Her eyes watered, her voice was shallow, and she was fighting back tears and shaking.

"Please don't cry. I didn't want to upset you. I understand, and we will find a better…some other way to see each other. I don't blame you. I was just so happy with the win, and I wanted to be with you. Then, I couldn't find you," Marc wrapped his arms around her and tried to comfort her by rubbing her back and holding her hand. She leaned into him, put her head on his shoulder, and sniffled a little as she tried to relax and compose herself.

"Ah know. It's my fault," she stammered.

"You're not at fault. It's just parents. They don't understand."

"Ah will talk to them this week. Especially my Mum, she is easy to chat-up. She will understand."

"Can I kiss you, please?"

"Right, brilliant!" She leaned in and tilted her head. They kissed, softly at first, with more passion as time passed.

They separated far enough to see the smile on each other's face, then joined lips again.

"What are you doing? Don't you realize this is a church?" Came a gruff voice from someone standing in the dark hallway.

Chapter 5

Beginning

"Mum can we talk about something that is very…very important to me? It wíll only take a few minutes."

"Why…of course Jamie, but can it wait? Ah'm about to put this meat in the cooker for dinner."

"Right…but not too long Ah want to do it in private before Harry n Da get home. It's very private n personal."

"Oh, dear…if it's that kind of a discussion we can start right now. You talk n Ah'll listen."

"Brilliant …yes, but please let me tell you everything before you say anything… please."

"Right Jamie…are you sick or something? Oh Jamie is there something wrong?" Jamie's mother now had concern in her voice. She stepped back from the kitchen counter, leaving the roast sitting in the oven pan. She quickly sat at the kitchen table wiping her hands on the multi-colored towel.

"No Mum, nothing is wrong with me. Ah'm well. It has nothing to do with how Ah feel. It's about someone Ah met n want to be with," Jamie responded quickly realizing that she had scared her mother.

"Be with? What does that mean? You want to leave home?"

"No, oh no, that's not what Ah want. Ah've to explain everything to you. Let me start with what Ah want to say," Jamie bellowed out in exasperation and frustration.

"Okay dear, tell me. Ah'm listening n sitting waiting. Take your time. You can tell me what you want." Ellen Toliver adjusted her chair and glanced around the sun filled westward facing kitchen. The sun was setting in full view through the window over the sink and she wanted to give her daughter an opportunity to catch her breath so she stared into space. "Fair enough, Ah'm very interested, so tell me. Ah'm listening...; take your time hon."

Jamie took a deep breath, attempted to gather her thoughts, her confidence. All of a sudden, what she thought would be an easy conversation became a stressful moment. She pulled a chair out from under the kitchen table and sat next to her mother. The moments of silence set an awkward atmosphere.

"Well, Ah've my ears open!" Ellen sputtered as her face softened.

Finally a reply, "Yeah...well, Ah met someone that Ah really like. A boy! He goes to school with me n is a footballer, a player. He's a good friend of Niki's, Amanda's n everyone you know. He goes to Cove Church n sings in the choir. We want to see each other." Jamie paused, waiting to see if there was a reaction.

With a deep breath, Jamie continued her animated elaboration of her new friendship, "he wants to date me n Ah need for you n Da to understand that n let me see n meet him after school n football games. Ah can't keep having you pick me up all the time. Niki n everyone else go to the dances n parties on their own or with their mate n find their own way home. Ah need a little freedom. He wants to be with me n bring me home in his car," finally a breath.

"Well! Are you going to tell me his name? Or should Ah tell you!"

"Marc Floreau!" was spoken simultaneously by Jamie and her mum. They looked at each other. Mum smiled and Jamie's face turned flush red.

"How...how did you know? Who told you?"

"No one told me or your father. At church you are always looking for him n making sure he sees you. You ask everyone you talk to if they know where he is, n you always go in his direction. When you talk with Niki or Amanda, his name is always in the conversation. We are parents n parents pay attention to what is going on with their daughter."

"Why didn't you say something? You should've let me know, or asked me about him. What does Da say? Is he okay with Marc?"

"You need to talk with your father. Ask him."

"Is there a problem? What's the problem?" Jamie asked as she closed her eyes and swallowed hard.

"There is no problem. We've no problem with Marc, but your Da wants to talk with you."

"Did he say that? Did he say he wants to talk with me about Marc?"

"Don't get all ruddy about it. He just wants you to understand some things."

"Understand what? That Ah need to keep my knickers up! Bummer!"

"Now Ah didn't say that. You're annoyed, so don't go potty about it."

"Can't you talk with him about my having someone Ah fancy?"

"You need to talk with your Da yourself. Ah can be there, but…"

"Mum, what's for dinner?" Harry raced into the kitchen, charging in without even saying hi and slamming his book down directly in front of Jamie. "Where is my football?" Harry was five feet tall, skinny, freckled, with his reddish-brown hair short on the side and back and long enough on top to resemble a porcupine. He was more legs than body, as he was experiencing a twelve year old growth spurt.

"Harry get out. Get out of here," Jamie yelled, now very annoyed. "Go away. Can't you see we are talking," Jamie shouted, threw a book at Harry, stood straight up, and stomped out of the kitchen and out the back door to the deck.

"We'll talk later dear," her mother said in a soft voice and slowly stood and went back to her waiting roast.

The auditorium was crowded. Everyone was looking for a seat so they could eat quickly, and then maybe get outside for a few minutes and a little fresh air. There was no cafeteria in the school so the freshman and sophomores had lunch in their homerooms while the juniors and seniors ate in the main floor of the auditorium. Unless you had someone saving seats for a group, it was everyone for themselves in finding a seat in the large theater to have lunch.

Marc, with his brown bag made his way to his "reserved" spot. Athletes had a few privileges; they usually congregated in the very back left corner of the forty year old facility. He always sat in the next to last row, well under the overhang of the balcony. It was the quietest and darkest location.

The main high school building was completed in the nineteen twenty's and was considered one of the gems of the blossoming steel mill town. The auditorium, which was part of the then new high school, was a main attraction in the early years with its two story theater seating, large stage with a spacious back stage area, extensive show lights and a state of the art sound system. Marc's mother and father told detailed stories about stage plays, musical performances, movies, community meetings, political rallies, union organizational meetings, and even special religious holiday pageants that took place within the four walls of the assembly hall before and during the war.

The five hundred seat chamber had, since its high water point, served many different purposes for the school and the community. With the growing population of Weirton and the high school during and since the war, the hall served as part classroom, luncheonette, study hall, temporary library, theater, storage room, rest area, romantic hideaway, indoor cheerleader practice facility and also as detention hall. The black, hard wood rickety theater seats had lasted for four decades, however, they were anything but comfortable. The large windows on the outside wall had long ago been painted black, making the entire hall seem to be blacked out from reality.

The balcony hung over about a third of the main seating area. It creaked and swayed with every occupant's foot step and movement. The safety of this second floor seating had been in question by students, faculty, and administrators for years, but each structural study by the higher ups had declared it safe and sound. However, the number that was allowed in the balcony at one time was only half of the former capacity. To ensure safety, half of the theater seats had been removed and the space was used mainly for small seminar classes. A major joke around the school was that the "policy and limited seating was to keep the injury rate low."

The back corner regulars, mostly athletic team members and their sweethearts were all in their usual seats around Marc, but he was still goose necking to find Jamie. They had agreed to meet for lunch as they passed each other this morning in the hall. She was late as usual. Since she had become involved in those special selective courses, her schedule seemed unpredictable. Finally, he spotted her coming through the main doorway, half running and half skipping. Her smile was broad and even at a distance her eyes were mesmerizing. Just seeing her, his breath hitched deep in his throat.

She was wearing an outfit that he had not seen before. The white poodle skirt was matched to a powder blue short sleeved blouse. Boy, did she look sharp and foxy. She had become the poster child for Vogue and her trendsetting was the talk of all the girls and guys. As she reached his row, slid past the first two seats in the row, one of which was broken, and sat down next to Marc, he couldn't keep his eyes off her.

"Blimey, what a day. There's this bloke in our European history class that never stops asking questions n the professor tries to answer them all. This bloke is a real funny chap. It takes forever for class to end."

"You don't have a 'professor,' you have a 'teacher' running the class. Your class is late as usual, lunch period is half over and I've already eaten mine," Marc said grumpily, showing his disappointment in having so little time to be together.

"Right, so you 've, it's not my fault," Jamie said with a bite out of her sandwich already half eaten. "Ah'm starved," as she searched through her cute cloth lunch sack. "This is a good brolly with meat n cheese."

"What's a 'brookie'?"

"Not a 'brookie.' Ah said a brolly. It's your sandwich, or my sandwich."

"I still don't understand all your British words. They are so funny and different. I'm not sure you are speaking English or just making up words, but you really are losing your accent more each day."

Jamie flashed a big smile and made a quick tilt of her head that caused her raspberry hair to flutter. He smiled back wanting to hug and kiss her, but turned his blushing face away. "Don't make me wait too long," he kidded.

"Wait for what?" She responded with smirk.

"Use your British imagination and dictionary."

He kept staring directly at her, questioning her about tomorrow night and plans for the football game." You going to the Steubenville Central game tomorrow night? It's over in Steubenville, up on the hill behind the town."

"Yea, Ah'm going with Niki n the cheerers. Ah'll be there, but Ah hear there is no dance or party after. Ah'll 've to go home with Niki and Amanda."

"Yeah, the away games are always too late to have a dance. We won't be able to see each other unless you wait for me at the school. The team bus comes back to the school so we can shower and get dressed. I could take you home..."

"Ah can't; Ah just can't. It would be too late. Ah've to go straight home n so does Niki n the others. They say it will be close to eleven before we get back n my Da said that Ah 've to be home by eleven."

"You told me what your dad and mother said, but we would be only a few minutes late if you wait for me. That shouldn't be a problem if you tell them. I think you're trying to snooker me; you turn your British brogue on and off at you whim. Now you sound very British and before you sounded very American."

"Some words are natural in American n others are better in British. No matter what accent Ah 've, Ah can't meet you after the game at the school, Mrs. Stewart is driving us n she will not want to take me to the school and the others home. Ah can't do it, no, not tomorrow," Jamie said firmly but softly.

"Okay, I understand. By the way, I like your British voice best! Now, if we can't see each other on Friday, can you come to the teen room in the Community Center on Saturday? Or, maybe I could come to get you and we could go together to the center. You said your father wanted to meet me and talk. This could be the chance."

She smiled at his British voice comment, but held her ground. "No, oh no, not yet. We will make some arrangement later for you to talk with my Da. Not this Saturday. Ah can get to the center with Niki n meet you. You can take me home if Niki n Willy could ride with us," emotion was running high in her voice.

"Why do we...why do they have to ride with us? Willy has his own car. He doesn't need me to drive him around. I don't understand. Why?"

"Because that is one of my Da's rules. He doesn't want..."

"Rules. You never said there were rules."

"Remember what my Da told me."

"I know, we can date, but you never mentioned all his rules. I don't know all his rules. My parents don't give me rules."

"Yes they do. You've told me they want you to come home earlier n you've to go to church every Sunday n graduate from school. They've a lot of rules. They are just different from mine. Ah'm a girl, n we are living in a strange place, n he doesn't really know you so he gives me rules."

"Okay, you win or he wins."

"Right. Remember, eleven on Friday n Saturday. No week-day dating except at my house. No drinking."

"I don't drink. I'm an athlete; I don't drink beer or anything else," Marc started to get riled.

"Ah know, but it is also a rule from my Da n Ah've to let them know where Ah am going n who Ah'll be with. Also he doesn't want me to ride with you alone. He says it is too tempting."

"Tempting for what?"

"You know. Don't act dumb!"

"Yeah, yeah, you told me. I know. With all these rules, he won't have anything to worry about."

The bell rang, ending the lunch period and the auditorium erupted into a mass rat-like exit with Jamie and Marc taking a last, longing look at each other, letting their hands slip apart, going their own way.

"Hey! Are we here to play football, or to watch the fans? What was so important that you were looking at on that last kickoff? Everybody on the right side was five to ten yards behind the kicker. Damn it! Stay awake out there. We are winning, but there is another half to play. This game is not won. Steubenville Central would like nothing more than to knock us off so they could have the bragging rights in Steubenville. We are the better team, but not if we lose focus out there. Everyone, and I mean everyone, needs to pay attention."

"What is he talking about?" Marc leaned over to ask Ronnie as they sat in the shoebox size visitor's locker room at halftime. They sat in the far corner on the cold, wet cement floor because of the limited bench seating. The paint on the concrete block walls was peeling off in strips, and the strips and paint flecks were scattered everywhere. As usual, the visiting team was exposed to the worst conditions. That was certainly the case at Harding Stadium.

Ron's whispered answer didn't make much sense to Marc. "They were watching the fight."

Coach Warren continued to try to get everyone's attention in the crowded odor-filled room. The first half had gone the Red Riders way, but they were not at their best. The team was sluggish, did not have the spunk that they had shown in the first three games. A 12 – 0 score was okay; however, they had missed two other good opportunities to score, fumbled twice and Marc had missed one extra point. The second one was not even tried because of a bad snap. To make things worse, Will had seemed to be confused on a few plays and sloppy in handling the ball. "Poor execution," was the termed used by Coach Warren and the coaching staff. The entire team seemed to be experiencing a letdown after the high emotional victory over the Big Red last week.

As the half time ended, the coaches gathered the team in to a tight circle in the confined space and gave them one last bit of instructions and encouragement. Out the lone doorway they stampeded almost knocking each other down. Marc and Ronnie let the rush go by and were two of the last players to leave the room. "What fight?"

"The fight in the stands on the student side," Ron grunted and seemed to be irritated by the question.

"Who was fighting? Could you see?"

"Hell no, it was on the other side of the field!"

"Was it near the cheerleaders?"

"Hell, I don't know. What's wrong with you?" Ron sputtered as they ran onto the field, headed for the team circle for calisthenics to warm up for the second half. Ron stopped and stared at Marc through his helmet face guard and finally said, "You're thinking of that British redhead aren't you? Boy, she has you by a nose ring."

Marc wanted to protest, but Ron ran off toward the middle of the circle, leaving Marc standing alone in the end zone, looking at the student stands. "Are you alright, Dash?" came the deep voice of Sage. "Hey you better wake-up. We have a second half to play. Come on, let's go, romeo."

"Huh. Yeah, I know, I'm coming…I'm coming."

The second half was a different story for the Red Riders. They demonstrated the depth of their talent. They were almost barbaric in their blocking and tackling. Marc had a couple of blocks that would bring high praise during the Monday night viewing of the game film. One was a blind side come back block that flipped two Crusaders head over heels. It was set up by Kenny Washington, a speedy sophomore halfback who cut back across the field on his way to a touchdown. Both of the defenders did not see Marc coming from the other side of the field, giving him a perfect target. They somersaulted on the turf and had to be assisted in getting up. Marc could almost hear the "ooh's" and "aah's" from the stands. It was one of those football contacts that a split second before it happens, you can see it happening; one that you could take pride in, and also one that you are thankful that you could walk away from—a full speed collusion.

The game ended 33 – 0 and the ride back across the Ohio River to Weirton triggered a party atmosphere in the bus. Marc was still on a high when they finally dressed and left the high school. He, Ron and Sage, the big lineman, were starving, so off they went to Big Boy's and a couple of hamburgers. It seemed that the entire team had the same idea. The Freedom Way hamburger joint was filled with players, fans and even a couple of coaches.

Finally, a booth was free and the three rushed to make it theirs. The diner was noisy, loud, cheerful and just jumping. They ordered, rehashed the game and some of funny things that happen at all games. The speculation about the fight in the stands seemed to be on everyone's mind. Playing away games was always more risky for the band and the fans. The team was somewhat protected by the administration, the coaches and the very fact that they were on the field. They would have to wait until tomorrow to find out what the fight was all about.

Everyone was busy eating when Bobby asked in his deep base voice, "You really like that Jamie?"

"Well, I don't really know."

"Don't bullshit us," Ron sounded off. "I've never seen you so lost in your thoughts as you were tonight. You would still be standing on the field if I hadn't yelled at you. You were totally in left field watching the cheerleaders and looking for her."

"Maybe," Marc answered with infectious laughter in his voice.

"Yeah, maybe, buzz. It was so obvious!" Ron responded to Marc attempt to avoid the question.

The music being played in the restaurant caught Marc's attention as it blasted: "*Could this be magic," by The Dubs: Could this be magic my dear, my heart all a glow … loving you so … having your love … my prayers were answered …*

"When did you redo your room? It looks so bright and the cream color of the bed and dresser match the wallpaper. Wow, you sure have redecorated. I love it!"

"Well Ah didn't do it. Mum n Marietta did the bedrooms about two weeks ago. Ah've never had such a completely coordinated room. It is cute, just brilliant. Ah love it too. All this new furniture is so different from that old second hand stuff that was in the house when we moved in."

"Things sure have changed over the last few months for you and your family. I can remember when you got here. You were so out of it," Niki observed as she walked around the room examining all the new knickknacks and the English keepsakes scattered on the new desk, dresser and bookshelves that added to the accented décor.

Jamie turned her head from the closet and looked at Niki with some discontent and responded with a snap, "It was hard coming to a new country n meeting new people. We moved into a house that was filled with someone else's furniture. Nothing in the house belonged to us. We…Ah, me, all by myself, had to start over. Ah had to find my way n it was really a difficult thing to do."

"I know. Don't get upset. I didn't mean anything bad. You are a real cool girl. Everyone loves you and you dress better than any of us. Please don't get upset!"

"It's hard not to get mad. Ah keep thinking of home, all my friends, my grannies, just being in our flat. Ah would like to show all of them our new home, my room, 've them meet you, Amanda, Marc—you know, everyone. Even though Ah've friends here, they are not the same. Ah grew up with everyone in Birmingham, and our neighbors were wonderful. People still laugh at me when Ah say the wrong thing, or when they can't understand my English. That's hard to..."

"Oh, don't worry about them; anyone who laughs is just jealous. They see you with all your new friends, great clothes, and they want to be you. Tell them to buzz off!"

"Well it's still hard to be the new person. It isn't quite as bad as it was, and your friendship did help."

"This room, all that is new in your home, tells me things are going well for your family," Niki walked around Jamie's bedroom impressed with the new decorum. Everything was new, and it looked like the bedroom was put together by a decorator from one of the trendsetting magazines.

Jamie started to feel a little contemptible; in truth Niki was right, Jamie's world had changed over the last few months significantly, and her Birmingham friends would not recognize her. Mum had been encouraged by da to make Weirton their home. That translated into redecorating, refurnishing, repainting and Americanizing their new home. Life's possessions overnight came without limits. The move to the states had improved their lot; they no longer lived in the past but were moving into a new era.

Mum and Marietta were shopping almost every day and coming home with clothes, home furnishings and remodeling ideas. Da seemed to accept her spending spree, usually reacting with phases; "as long as you are staying with the allowance budget," or "if it makes you happy," even "I'm sure it will be very nice when it's finished." Finally, "just don't do too much, too fast, and remember to stay within the allocation."

Contemplation ended and Jamie turned her attention to picking out an outfit for going to the Community Center with Niki and the others. She would be meeting Marc and wanted everything to be perfect. Out of her closet three new ensembles were thrown on the bed. She wanted Niki to react to each, her advice was critical; she was the only one in town who really understood teen fashion.

Niki was sitting on the pink, white, and blue bedspread marveling at all the exceptionally beautiful apparel. She held each in the air to totally see it, and "aahed, my-my-ed, boy-o-boy-ed" each one. "I like them all. Where did you find these? They are so unique and the colors are great,"

Niki also realized that she was losing her perch as the best dresser in the school. "Wow, I'm not kidding, where did you get all these new threads?"

"Right, they are brilliant, right. Well Mum n Marietta, you know her, she is the one who knows all about new clothes n fashion n stuff like that," Jamie was feeling a little self conscious, as if she was telling Niki some tightly kept secret, "She takes my Mum to all these fashion stores n shows. She is great, just brilliant at picking out the right things."

"Yes, I know Mrs. Branden. My mom goes with her some times, but she never comes home with so much. Well, we have to go in a few minutes. Anyone of the three would be great. Hurry we need to go…pick one. Marc will be amazed when he sees you. I hope he wears something other than an old plaid wool shirt."

They both giggled, with Jamie's face blushing as usual when someone mentioned Marc.

"Where are they? Marc said he would be here at seven n it's almost eight."

"I don't know, but standing around here waiting for them makes me mad. Will is always late, every time we have a date. I don't think he can tell time, but Marc is different; he is usually early. Something must have come up. He was real excited about tonight."

"How do you know that? How do you know that he was excited about tonight?" Jamie's frustration was evident and she was jealous.

"Oh, don't get upset. He calls me about everything. We are friends and have shared a lot, about just, I don't know, just things.

Jamie had turned away and had her back to Niki and her face was starting to redden. "Please Jamie don't take that comment in a bad way. He and I are just good, long time friends. Like a brother and sister," Niki said as she put her arm lightly on Jamie's shoulder, trying to ease the sting of her comment.

"Talking to you about his date with me? Boy, that is some friendship the two of you 've," was the sobbing reply as Jamie looked at her friend.

"Well you talk to me all the time about Marc, and I guess he knows that and wants everything to go real good between you two. That's all he talks about when he calls. He talks about you and asks if you like him, stuff like that."

"What do you tell him?

"I say yes. And he says he likes you a lot. He called a few nights ago and was excited about tonight, wanted to make sure you came to the center. He was excited…very excited."

"Haw, there you are," Will's bubbling voice broke in on their conversation as he came down the stairs two steps at a time.

"Where have you been, we have been waiting for you and Marc for an hour," was Niki's snappy response as she turned away from Jamie and quickly placed a hand on her hip to signal Will that she was upset by his tardiness.

Jamie and Niki had taken the Marland Height's bus to the Community Center and had been waiting for ages for Will and Marc to show. The teen room was part of the ground floor of the center, separated by its corner location, the restricted entrance and the snack bar that buffered it from the main hallway.

One of the side rooms was a game room, with a ping pong table, a shuffleboard game, card tables and chairs, and a variety of books and puzzles. The room did not get a lot of use on Friday and Saturday nights, except as a make-out spot.

The main room for the teens was a very large open-floored dance hall. There were chairs, benches and a few lounge chairs along the sides, but, they were rarely used, as most of the teens preferred to stand. There was an unofficial designated spot for the girls to stand, and in the other corner, a spot for most of the boys. The middle was reserved for couples or for pairs that were courting. Most dancing took place in the middle under a glittering ballroom chandelier that sparkled as it turned.

The large juke box in the corner near the entrance blasted out the latest rock and roll hits. All that was need was a dime or three songs for a quarter. The music was loud and varied from a very fast tempo to a slow romantic ballet. If you had a favorite song, you could spend your ten cents or wait for someone else to push your song's button.

"Hi, sorry I am so late. I am really…really sorry. I had to..."

"Late, we thought you were dead or something. Boy, are you in trouble! Not just with Jamie, but with me too," Niki expounded in a voice loud enough that everyone could hear even over the loud music.

"Give me a chance to…"

"We don't want to hear your excuses. We have been hanging around this entrance all night," again Niki cut Marc off before he could finish a full sentence.

"Explain," Marc, in a delayed mode, finished his sentence. "I can explain."

"It's too late to explain. You are both real airheads. Both of you," Niki responded looking back and forth between Will and Marc.

"Ah want to hear the explanation," Jamie spoke up sheepishly.

"You can listen to his excuse, I'm going to dance," and off Niki went to the middle of the dance floor with Will following.

"I am sorry. I had to work two more hours at the pool, I couldn't get away. Sorry… Mary didn't show again. She is always late or doesn't come to work. I don't know what her problem is. She did the same thing…"

"Who are you talking about?" Jamie, staring with a questioning tilt of her head and lips that quivered responded quickly, "Ah don't know any Mary."

"Mary Nellson. She was a Life Guard at the pool this summer. She goes to…"

"Ah don't care who she is. What are you talking about 'working more at the pool' …what pool? What working are you talking about?"

"I'm a Lifeguard…here at the Community Center. There's a pool here!"

"Ah know about the pool here. Ah've seen it. You work there?" Jamie responded emotionally.

"Yes, I work at the pool. I'm a Lifeguard," Marc snapped.

"Blimey, you never told me!"

"Well I thought I did or maybe I thought you knew."

"You never told me…never…not…ever. Ah thought you had cut out on me. Ah was really cranked."

"Why is it so important? What makes it such a big deal? What is cranked?"

"We are together every day…almost every day. Ah thought we could talk about anything. Ah tell you everything n you talk with Niki about everything," the conversation was getting a little testy and a crowd was starting to stare.

Marc looked around and stepped closer to Jamie and said in a quiet voice, "I'm sorry. Let's not fight. I work as a Lifeguard on the weekends, and I work at a gas station when I can fit it into my schedule. I work there about ten hours a week and here as a Lifeguard about the same."

"Why? You're in school! You're a footballer! Why do you 've to work during the school year?" The questions exploded into the conversation. "Why…why?"

"Well, because I have to. I have to buy gas and other things. I like to have my own money. My parents give me some money, but I like to have my own, a nice car and the gas for it," Marc started to explain. But Jamie had lost interest.

"You are right, Ah don't want to've a cow over this." Let's dance or just go in. Ok?" She took his hand and Marc followed her onto the dance floor, his flat top hair cut still damp with water droplets from his recent shower, his face reddish from his racing to get to Jamie and their mini-emotional exchange.

From the Jukebox, *Little Anthony and the Imperials sang, "Tears on my Pillow:" You don't remember me, but I remember you... You broke my heart in two… Tears on my pillow, pain in my heart, caused by you...*

Once, the little tiff ended, Marc and Jamie began to enjoy each other's company again, dancing, laughing at each other and everyone else. Jamie tried to give Marc some pointers on his dance steps, but he was too embarrassed to be much of a student. They sat in the corner for awhile watching others and talking about nothing. Finally, Will and Niki came over and said they were hungry and wanted to go across the street to Di Carlo's Pizza for a couple of slices. It sounded like a good idea, especially to Marc as he had not eaten all day.

Di Carlo's was a new experience for Jamie. Pizza was not new to her, but buying the hot snack by the slice was very different. She compared it to buying "fish and Chips" from a street vendor in Birmingham. Each of them had two slices with pepperoni and a coke. At a quarter a slice and each coke only thirty cents, the grand bill came to three dollars and twenty-three cents, with taxes. Will and Marc made a big deal out of splitting the bill since it was "their" treat.

It was after ten when they partially ran across Main Street and back to the Community Center in a light rain. The teen center was starting to empty. The girls said they had to get home and quickly. Marc said he would drive so the group jumped in his black Chrysler Windsor coupe for the five minute journey to Marland Heights.

"I'll be back for you in about ten minutes" Marc called over the back seat towards Will.

"What am I supposed to do while I am waiting for you…it's raining you know," Will uttered in a saintly voice, with his arm around Niki in the back seat, as if to register an official complaint.

"Come on," Niki said with a trace of disgust as she pushed the folding back of the half front seat forward pushing Jamie into Marc and the front dash. She reached for the latch to open the passenger's door. "We'll find something to do or you can just stand in the rain."

"It has been raining off and on all day and it's cold," was Will's response as he still sat in the back seat.

"Get out Will, he will get back for you in a few minutes and you can stand on the back porch!" Niki was already out of the car and partially running towards the back of her house.

"I'm coming, don't be too long or forget me," Will vented, "I don't want to get stuck here or have to walk all the way back downtown to get my car." In one motion Will was out of the car, running after Niki and the cover of the back porch. The rain was coming down a little harder and some was getting into the car.

"Close the door quickly before he decides to come back," Marc barked out instructions, quickly followed by Jamie. "He does not like this idea of you needing Niki as your chaperone."

"Ah know, Ah know, but right now we've to if we are going to've any time together," Jamie slid over closer to Marc and once again cuddled on his shoulder.

Marc drove away slowly and they both listened to *Jimmy Clanton singing on* WEIR AM," *Just a dream:" Why – Why do I love you … I can still hear that same mournful song … Just a dream … Just a dream."*

Even driving slowly, in five minutes they were in the drive way at Jamie's house. The rain was slowing and Marc turned off the engine. They cuddled even closer and finally they had their arms wrapped around each other. Jamie looked up into Marc's deep blue eyes as he leaned down and kissed her on the lips. The kiss was tender and followed by another. They lingered in the embrace and kissed on and on, until finally they broke away and were now holding each other cheek to cheek.

They both took a deep breath and started kissing again, this time with more passion. Marc's arm encircled her back and squeezed her closer and kissed her in earnest.

Jamie was excited at first as the kissing became intense and Marc's hands seem to hold her in a claw like grip, but suddenly she felt uncomfortable and pulled away in a jerk. They separated and Jamie said apologetically, "Ah've to go in…later. Ah'm flipped… later."

Marc had a shocked and disappointed look. "Why? Why now, we have only been sitting here a minute or two. It is only about ten-thirty."

"Yes, yes Ah know but Ah've'to go in…Ah've'to go in now."

"But, not right away. We can sit here. We don't have to kiss. I was…"

"No, no Ah've'to go now." And she slid over to the door and was out of the car immediately.

"Wait, please wait. I'm sorry! I'm really sorry for whatever. Please wait," Marc nearly fell as he jumped out of the driver's side door; he raced around the front of the car and then ran, trying to catch-up with Jamie as she was prancing toward the front door. They reached the front door just as the rain stopped, and under the overhang a few remaining droplets fell on them as they stood looking at each other.

"What? What's wrong? What did I do?" Marc begged to know.

"Nothing… everything is fine, it's just me. Ah don't. Ah mean, Ah can't make my parents upset or mad. They trust me. They…well they…"

"We were just kissing. It didn't mean anything. I just wanted to kiss and hold you…"

"Ah know…so did Ah but not so much, n not in front of our home."

"Okay, okay," Marc was trying to see her face but she had turned away and was facing the door. "I understand, but don't be mad. Not tonight."

"Ah'm not mad," was Jamie's nearly muted reply. "Ah've to go in," she added still facing the door.

"Now! Right now?"

Jamie turned sharply and looked straight at Marc and soothingly said. "Yes, n you need to pick-up Will. He will be mad if you are too long."

"Can we kiss good night?"

"We already 've," and she opened the door, stepped partway in, turned and whispered, "Goodnight, Ah had a nice time." The door closed, she was gone.

Marc stood at the closed door for a moment or maybe more. He was confused, and bewildered. He turned to walk away, stopped, looked at the door, wondering if she was just standing inside. He heard voices, walked slowly back to the car as the rain returned. He sat in the car for a few minutes drifting in his thoughts from disappointment, gloominess, anger and adoration and back again.

Finally, he started the engine of the "black widower." It was raining hard again and he had to get Will.

"Hi hon, did you have a nice time?"

"Yeah, it was right smashing," Jamie's reply was uncommitted as she could be. She tried to hide the forsaken feeling deep inside and the eyes that were tearing.

"How did you get home?" Came another question from the kitchen and her mum.

"Marc brought Niki n Ah home, because of the rain. Ah think Ah'll go to bed, Ah'm tired," was Jamie's unembellished answer as she turned quickly to go up the stairs. Her face was rosy with streaks of tears and her lips felt as though they were pressed, twisted and colorless. She couldn't let anyone see her, "Good night."

Her mother appeared in the hallway with a dish cloth in her hand, a blank but questioning look on her face, "Come tell us about your night. What did you n Niki do?"

Jamie could feel her face becoming ashen, her voice feeling weak and unsteady as she quickened her pace, reaching the top of the stairs before her mother could really see her face. "Not tonight, we were dancing a lot n Ah am really bushed." She turned and was gone from her mother's sight.

"Okay, Jamie dear. You get a good night's sleep. Remember church in the morning," Ellen Toliver replied in a slow and inquiring tone. She shook her head, trying not to over react to the snub.

"Yes, Ah know church in the morning. Good night Mum," partially crying, Jamie went in her room and closed the door.

The bright color of the bedspread, curtains, walls and clothes lying about did not seem as uplifting as when she had left earlier in the evening. Jamie sat on her bed, feeling some clouding foreboding settling over her. She could not understand her sadness. It had been a fun evening, even if the boys were late. She and Marc had danced, laughed, had pizza and had a romantic ride home. The kissing was great, even if a little scary when it turned more intense than ever before. Maybe that was it. She wasn't ready for a fast paced affair. Or maybe she was ready and offended with herself because she was ready.

She lay back on her bed, closed her eyes, tried to recall all that happened that evening, all that was said between her and Marc and how she had cut off the making out with him. She needed to apologize to him, talk with Niki about her feelings and mixed emotions. Niki would understand what she was experiencing. She was tired, her eyes heavy, and she fell asleep with all her clothes on and the lights still ablaze.

"HI FRIEND—Hope you had a nice time?" was Will's somewhat distressed greeting. "That was longer than ten minutes old buddy. Niki had to go in after her father came to the door the second time. And then the rain started again and I had to stand on the porch all alone. What kept you?" Will got in the coupe and tried to get the rain off his gray plaid flannel shirt and his brush cut hair.

"Nothing, nothing special, it just took longer than I thought. It takes almost ten minutes to just get to Jamie's house from here. Sorry, sorry bud."

"Well old bud," Will replied in an irked voice, "I'm not going to do that again. I'll drive my own car and take Niki home myself!"

"Okay, don't get all heated, cool it. I get it, we will work something out," Marc answered remembering Jamie's father's rule of not being in the car "alone." "We will do something different next week. If there is a next week," he added.

"What do you mean…IF?"

"Well, everything was going really well for a few minutes, but it just… well…"

"Okay lover boy, what happened?"

The two friends and teammates talked about the girls, dating and making out, as Marc drove them down off of Marland Heights, into the nearly empty parking lot in the back of the community center soWill could get his own car.

Getting out of Marc's car, Will asked if Marc wanted to go to Big Boy for something to eat.

"No," was the answer, "I have been up since early morning. I worked the morning shift at the gas station, then a double shift at the pool. I'm bushed. I'm going home and sleep. Besides church is tomorrow and my mom will be waking me up early. She will never let me sleep in. No, see you."

"See you Monday. Don't forget, Wellsburg this week, Friday."

"Right, Wellsburg…for five in a row."

"Five this season, I think it will be number twenty-three for the past three seasons," Will yelled back as got into his bright blue Chevy coupe.

"Wow, twenty three! See you on Monday."

The rain was only intermittent as Marc drove home the back way. He took it slow, trying to understand all that had happened today, especially tonight with Jamie's reaction to kissing. He didn't think he was too pushy, or had done anything out-of-line; at least he didn't think so. But, this was somewhat all new to him; he had never been this romantic with a girl. Maybe she didn't like him that much or in a romantic way. Marc was confused, but also very tired. He needed sleep and just time to think.

The rain continued, the window wipers "swished" clearing the windshield and streaking it at the same time. *This is WEIR for all you boppers in the Valley and here are The Drifters with that sweet sound of "Honey Love:" Love me, love me, love me…when the moon is bright…when you hold me…in the middle of the night… I need your honey love…let's kiss, kiss, kiss… That's a honey love.*

Chapter 6

Disappointment

With yesterday's all day rain now continuing on Sunday morning, the parking for church was surprisingly very crowded. Church on Sunday was full every week, but inclement weather usually reduced the attendance. Marc was late as usual, but even more so this Sunday since his mother had actually let him sleep in and miss Sunday school.

He parked the car as close as he could to church, jumped out, ran across the grass between the Community Center, into the back cellar door of the church, getting only semi-wet. With the Cove Church and Community Center adjacent to each other they shared the large city parking lot, a nice grassy lawn, which served as a picnic ground on nice sunny summer days as well as a short-cut from the car to the church.

As he entered the basement hallway, cut through the kitchen, past women cleaning up from an early Sunday morning bible class that his mother probably had attended, the organ prelude was already beginning above him in the sanctuary. He was really late. His mom, dad and his two sisters were surely in their pew, and with limited main sanctuary seating, there was probably no room for him. That was alright with Marc, the pew was too confining for him, and he liked room to wiggle, gawk, and change his location if he wanted to. His mother, Beth Floreau, called it his "vagabond nature." She was a God-fearing woman, with a strong sense of responsibility to her family and her children, but she also recognized that her son was a tumble-weed with his own agenda. Getting Marc to church was one of her successes.

Sure enough, to Marc's satisfaction, when he got to the main floor, the ushers were already seating parishioners in the annex meeting room adjacent to the main sanctuary. Cove Church had a unique feature. In between the sanctuary and the Sunday school/congregational meeting room was a floor to ceiling accordion wall, that when opened, doubled the worship space. The added space was a flat surface, higher than the sanctuary pews, so those worshipers sitting in the rows of folding chairs could not see the pew dwellers; but had a bird's eye view of the minister in his high perch and also of the full choir.

Oh, the choir, Marc thought, almost out loud. He had missed the last two weeks of Wednesday night choir practice and was unprepared to sing in the choir today.

Marc would have to avoid Mr. Abbot, the choir director or else he would be shanghaied into the morning's choir, even not knowing the hymn. Mr. Abbot and Reverend Ness liked a full choir loft, regardless of the sound. But Marc was so late that the choir was already in place, seated in the choir gallery and the service started. Mr. Abbot would not impress him today.

From his seat in back of the rows of chairs, Marc rubber-necked to try to find two particular families in the pews; his and Jamie's. His family typically sat in a pew about four or five rows from the front on the right side, while the Tolivers were usually seated on the left side almost at the very top of the sloping sanctuary.

Sure enough, there was his mother in her usual spot with his sisters, Betty and Barbara, but no dad. Dad must be working a Sunday seven to three shift. Sidney Floreau was a hot steel-mill roller at the Weirton Steel Company, where the schedule was a rotating shift. When Marc was young, he knew his father's complicated work schedule by memory, better than his mother. But with his busy schedule, Marc was out of touch with the day to day family activities, and had lost track of dad's working hours.

Looking past his family, Marc tried to locate Jamie on the far side. Reverend Ness had already finished the opening announcements, the doxology, and was into the opening prayer. As the service continued, Marc took every opportunity to stand and canvas the far pews for Jamie. Finally, while the choir was singing the offering hymn, he spotted her, towards the back, close to her family's normal spot. They were crowded in the corner with just enough room for all four. He kept watching her at each standing opportunity.

The sermon seemed to go on forever, exactly what the message was, escaped Marc as his attention was on Jamie. He had to find a chance to talk with her. They needed to talk about last night and how they had parted. Finding her after the service should be easy; he typically would watch both of the normal exits from church. That was his plan. They would talk after the service.

Marc waited at the side door entrance, the normal exit for the parishioners who did not want to wait in line to greet and have a few words with the minister. Most families used this side exit because of the convenient wide solid wood doors and the semi-circlular stone steps that allowed a quick and easy pathway to the sidewalk between the Community Center and the Church. The coat closet was also close by and those that had brought umbrellas usually set them against the wall in the atrium. Marc was reasonably sure Jamie would come this way. He would normally stand outside and watch both exit doors, but with the rain even heavier than when he arrived, this was his best chance to see her.

He waited, waited, and waited. Finally, she was in the hallway wearing a deep blue dress with white piping on the sleeve and white collar. She had a little blue rain jacket barely zipped. Her reddish hair was very flowing and bouncing with a white ribbon holding it in place near her forehead. She was adorable. He took a deep breath as she drew near.

"Cheers, Ah was hoping to see you. You must've been late, you didn't sit with your Mum," Jamie spoke first, quietly so only he could hear, smiling with a twinkle in her blue eyes. She was so close that Marc could smell the flowery scent of her hair.

"Eh, eh yeah," he stumbled for words. "I slept in and almost missed coming. Wow, boy you look great. I wanted to…well you know. I wanted to…"

She whispered, "Can't talk now, my parents want to get home, right away, sorry."

"Okay, that's fine, but can we …"

"Come Jamie, Get under the umbrella so we can get to the car in this downpour," her mother beckoned as she stood in the doorway with the opened black umbrella sticking out the doorway into the rain.

"Right. Ah'm coming in a minute."

"Now Jamie, Ah'm half in n half out in the rain. We 've to go, say good-by dear …now."

"Attendez une moment."

"Maintenant," came her mother's French reply.

"Oui."

"Ah 've to go, pip pip" Jamie mouthed towards Marc, with her head tilted and eyes wide; happy as she turned, joining her mother under the umbrella.

"What? What did you say? I'll call you tonight," Marc said, not sure she heard him as they were already half way down the steps.

He stepped outside as the rain coated the shoulders of his light brown corduroy sport coat. Others had to step around him as he blocked part of the steps. He stood back out of the way still watching Jamie and her mother dash around the corner and disappear. They were sprinting to their car as was everyone. He stood for a moment in the rain, not caring if he were getting wet.

"You'll get soaked out here Marc, without a coat or umbrella," a voice broke his trance, it was Mr. Abbot. "See you Wednesday night at choir practice?" a question raised by the choir director as he stepped lively down the stairs.

"I'll try. I'll try," Marc responded and stepped back inside the church and out of the rain. He needed to find his mother and sisters. This morning had not been what he expected. Last night remained an unsettled blunder, and he was concerned about Jamie and what her feelings might really be. She seemed distant this morning. She was speaking French; he did not understand French.

"Hello."

"Hi, Jamie? Is that you?"

"Hi, yes, yes it's me. Ah've been waiting for you to call. It's late, why…"

"I was, eh, I was working at the gas station."

"On Sunday? I thought stores were closed on Sunday."

"Well, the station's only open in the afternoon until six."

"You must be knackered. Right tired."

"No, no, I slept in late and we didn't have much business. Boy, I'm glad you answered the phone. I wanted to talk with you at church this morning. I was…"

"Right, Ah wanted to talk to with you. But Ah had to go home with my parents. Ah couldn't wait or say much."

"Well, I was hoping ...I just …I don't know what to say."

"Right, but we couldn't talk there anyhow…you know…not at church…"

"I know, but where are we going to talk about last night? I don't want you to be mad at me. We are…we seem to like each other and I…"

"Blimey, Ah do fancy you a great deal. You are my chap, you're an ace. We had a nice time at the center. Ah just didn't feel good about gallivanting…"

"What was that? I don't understand…"

"Ah'm just saying it was too much…Ah was afraid that we were going to do some hanky panky…"

"Hanky pan…what?"

"Hanky panky, you know, make out."

"Oh, oh I see. Well …"

"It was too fast, too soon, too major…"

"Yeah, I understand, I think. All we were doing was kissing."

Jamie tried to calm Marc. His voice was getting high pitched and loud. "We don't need to've a row. Ah like you, very, very much. We need to talk about last night, but not at church or on a dial-up. Please don't worry. We are…well we 've a nice friendship, you're my mate."

"I hope it's more than just a friendship and something more than a mate," Marc interrupted with a stronger voice.

"It is more, but we can't talk about our…our feelings on the bell," Jamie's voice was now in whisper mode, as if someone was in the room or close by.

"Yes, I know…you are right. Buzz, I get it."

A long pause in the conversation was finally broken by Jamie. "We will talk at school or find someplace to chat about this…right?"

"Right, right. We'll discuss everything some other time. Maybe in school tomorrow?"

"Oh, not tomorrow. Ah won't be around most of tomorrow or Tuesday," was her quick response.

"Why not?"

"Our advanced biology class is going to the hospital to see their research department."

"To the hospital? What for?"

"The doctors n nurses are going to tell us about why biology is so important in medicine. We will get to use their equipment n do our own experiments. It should be really exciting."

"Eh …real exciting. But when will I see you?" Marc voice sounded dismayed.

"Well, probably Wednesday. We can 've lunch together."

"Okay, Wednesday. We can talk and I'll call you."

"Call…maybe! Ah don't like to talk too much on the bell. My brother is always around n everyone can hear what Ah say. Ah'll see you Wednesday. Ah need to go."

"Yeah, right. See you on Wednesday."

"Wednesday, right, brilliant!" Jamie ended the conversation with "Cheerio."

For Marc the conversation was less than satisfying. They didn't talk about much that was on his mind. What did she mean about "making out." He was confused more now than when the day started. He had only kissed her.

For Jamie the phone call was odd. She had said some things that she had not even thought much about. She was right about their relationship going too fast. But, she did like Marc a great deal and wanted to be with him and even kiss him more and more. But where does it go from there. So much had happened over the last six months that she going in circles. She was a Brit and he was a Yank. Was that okay or was that daft?

Do you want to dance and hold my hand? Tell me baby… Oh baby do you want to dance…Do you want to dance under the moonlight? Hold me baby all through… It was *Bobby Freeman on American Band Stand singing: "Do you want to dance."*

Jamie was singing along and dancing solo around her bedroom. She was watching, or more like really listening to her favorite TV show,

American Band Stand, on a small portable nine inch screen on top of her dresser. Built-in rabbit ears were extending completely out of the small gray metal box in a twisted configuration in an attempt to get a reasonable picture. The picture on the post card screen was very fuzzy, with shadows in the corners. She could barely see the performer or the couples dancing, but the sound was reasonable and she enjoyed this song and the beat. Dancing, especially American style, frisky and free spirited, was, as Jamie thought about it, a dog's bollocks. If only her mates from Birmingham could be here, dancing with her. She missed all her chums. With the song ending, Jamie flopped on her bed, head on her pillow, and bare feet on the two stuffed animals at the far end.

It was late Friday afternoon; she had just had supper and was waiting for time to pass before she was off to the Friday night football game. Her mind wandered, thinking how excited the American Band Stand program always made her feel. The music was always the most current Rock and Roll hits, the stars were live, the couples danced so smoothly. They were on live Television, the audience was national. If she lived in Philadelphia, she would be at the show every day—that is, if her parents would let her.

Tonight should be great. The game, the cheering, the band, the majorettes, the teams running up and down the field, she knew most of them by their numbers and their names. Marc would be playing, and she would be with all her new American friends, everything under the bright lights. Then the dance party, a great do, at the Community Center. Marc was really excited at lunch about the game and the dance. They would meet at the center, the first time they were together since last Saturday.

Jamie had been very busy this week, so she and Marc had only talked briefly in school. She had spent two exciting days at the hospital research laboratory with her bio class, and then she was told by the Principal she would be initiated into the National Honor Society because of her academic achievements in the British school system. She and her parents were excited with the recognition.

On top of the National Honor Society, Jamie was appointed to the Weirite Year Book Staff, another unexpected honor. Then to put icing on the cake she, Niki and Amanda had been elected to the homecoming court. Jamie was shocked, enraptured and high as a kite for the last two days.

All these kudos for Jamie were just part of the elation the Toliver family were experiencing. Jamie's father was officially offered the opportunity to become a Vice President with Weirton Steel, and to make their move to the states and Weirton permanent. This was a major decision for her parents, Harry and especially Jamie. With the family's future now tied to Weirton, Jamie and her parents had also decided that they would stay here through the foreseeable future and that Jamie should plan to attend an American college. Her home in the states was now more settled, and she could plan with certainty for next year. At school she met with the Assistant Principal, Mr. Alexander, to make arrangements to take the SAT College Entrance Examination in Wheeling. Jamie was eager to start her search for a college, in America.

Everything was coming together for Jamie. Suddenly, she was feeling very much at home in Weirton High School and the United States. However all of this did not dismiss the fact that she was still missing Birmingham, her long time friends, her grandparents, uncles, aunts, cousins, and everything that was British. She would visit England as soon as should could. Maybe some of the family would visit from England. This week had been "off the trolley."

Band Stand was starting to sign off. The closing was an oldie: "*Let the good times roll," by Shirley and Lee: Come on baby, let the good times roll… Come on baby, let me thrill your soul…Come on baby, let the good time roll… Roll all night long…*

Jamie started to get ready for the game and her night out. She picked a red turtle neck sweater, a black full skirt and a pair of red tights underneath. Fall was in full swing and temperatures were falling lower each day. It had been raining all week so she would have to wear some kind of boots, which would not be very fashionable, but would keep her feet dry and warm. Niki would pick her up about six fifteen and they would get an early start. Niki would be driving her mother's car, a new first, and Amanda and Sarah would be with her. It was going to be a girl's night out, with football, cheering, dancing and, best of all, Marc.

The high school gym floor was cool and the tile-covered wall hard on his back. He was braced against the wall under the half moon metal basketball backboard perched overhead. The gym was a beehive of activity as the team dressed and readied itself for their game against Wellsburg. The scene was repeated for each home game. The thirty year old gym was run-down and had long passed its prime purpose as the high school's home court for basketball. The gym was a subfloor, well below the basement floor of the deteriorating high school. From where Marc sat in his all red, black accented, football uniform, the facility looked like a narrow tunnel, with its sides rising from a canal setting on a forty-five degree or even a greater angle. The nearly perpendicular stairs leading to the floor above at the basement level appeared dangerous from the sub-basement gym floor. Hard to believe that just five years ago the high school was still playing basketball in such a constricted space.

As he looked towards the other end of the burrow span, it narrowed into the two dungeon cut outs that once served as team benches during games. *Those are nothing but dark holes in the wall,* thought Marc. *Thank-goodness we don't play our basketball games here anymore and can use the new facilities at the Community Center.*

Finally, Marc focused on tonight's game, the sixth game of the season. They should win, but he was still nervous, anxious to get on the field and get the game started. Once the game was underway, the nerves would settle, concerns would be forgotten, and the excitement and fun could begin. Marc always enjoyed game night; being on the field under the lights, hearing the noise of seven thousand or more fans, hearing music from the band directly behind the bench, the cheerleaders, the majorettes, and the feel of the pads, uniforms and even the smell of the grass. What a high, especially this week, which for him had been nothing but lows. Marc needed something uplifting.

Last Saturday night with Jamie had been a real downer, Sunday was not much better. It had rained most of the week; football practices had been in the mud. He and Jamie had not fully sorted out Saturday's disaster, and actually, he had only talked with Jamie twice all week because of her many activities in school.

Marc went to choir practice at church thinking that Jamie would be there. She did not show, and he ended up being the only young person there with all the adult regulars. His attendance pleased Mr. Abbot, but he had wasted the entire evening. On top of all these problems, he found out that he was flunking Algebra II and would not be eligible for football or basketball unless he did something about it. So he dropped the class, to the anger of Mr. Joyner, the student counselor. Marc still had enough credits to graduate; however, any thoughts of college were slipping away. Although he was in the College Preparatory Curriculum, he had avoided or dropped out of most of the courses that were required to get into college. Soon Mr. Joyner would tell Marc's parents and that would cause even more unrest, especially for his father. But Marc felt good; at least he would still be able to play sports. He wasn't really planning to go to college; was he?

Marc rested his head on his helmet as he lay on the cold floor. The gym was quiet now as everyone waited for the pre-game ritual. The coaches would give a pep talk; the team would leave for the stadium walking through the alley and part of the parking lot. Their cleats would make a din of music on the bricks, cement and gravel trail. Fans would yell and pat them on their back and butts rooting them on. The lights would get brighter as they entered the stadium. It would be time to play football.

After the game he would see Jamie at the dance, take her home and maybe settle his misunderstanding from last Saturday. Go - Go - Go.

She noticed him coming through the door way with Ron and Will. She started over towards him as he moved her way. They reached out to each other, held hands as they stared at each other for a second or two."Great game, you were smashing out there, we won," was Jamie's greeting.

"We were brightly good tonight as you Brits would say," Jamie smiled at his remarks embarrassingly, with a turn of her face. "They were not that tough. No sweat. Easy game for us," Marc added.

"You were doing so much, a real ace, catching the ball, running, kicking those extra point things."

"Well, they finally threw me the ball. I have been the number one decoy for half the season. I should have scored on the second reception, but I..."

"You were limping n holding your leg. Now you are even standing funny. What happened? You are blatantly hurt."

"I got hit, by my own man. Sage ran into me at full speed, that big kook. My leg is bruised somehow."

"Oh, you poor thing, does it hurt now, are you in shambles?" Jamie asked playfully, but with real concern. Marc had walked into the post game dance limping slightly as he tried to downplay the soreness in his right thigh. But the discomfort was noticeable. He was standing tilted on one leg, the left leg, so he could take his weight off the right one.

"Yes, I have to admit it does hurt. It is all tight and feels like the knot in the muscles are getting tighter. Its real bad news," Marc touched his right leg.

"We can sit, let's sit for a few minutes, over there," Jamie motioned towards the corner near the entrance to the dance. A few chairs were scattered about and no one else was around. Sitting at a dance was not cool, but Marc nodded yes. They walked over to the darkened corner, with Marc limping, Jamie holding his hand and arm, and gazing at him with wonder.

The corner chairs were perfect. For nearly a half hour they talked about the past week, all her news about her da agreeing to stay in Weirton, and the game. Jamie did most of the talking, asking some uninformed questions about football, which was still a strange game to her; then changing the topic, describing everything that had taken place at school. She recounted the week, her excitement with becoming a member of the National Honor Society, the appointment to the Weirite Staff, but most of all her parents' decision to remain in the United States. Finally, she told him of her new quest to find the right American College, although she referred to college as "Uni."

Marc listened, barely able to slow her spiel, long enough to acknowledge her lengthy oration. All this was great, for Jamie, but it left Marc a little cold since his world revolved around football, work and trying to win Jamie's favor. The National Honor Society was in never-never land for Marc. He knew it existed and many of his friends were members, but it was inaccessible to him, from his world. Being on the Weirite Staff was cool, but what one did on the Staff was a mystery to him.

Marc was glad Jamie would be staying in Weirton. It had the sound of permanency and would, or could, impact his future. Now, maybe he could see the possibility of something long-lasting for the two of them. College for her, that sounded logical, but for him that type of a future was out of his reach. He had thought about college, but the reality was, that his just graduating from high school would be a family first. No one in his entire family had even completed that many grades, let alone thought about attending college. Last year he had a conversation with Mr. Joyner about attempting to go to the Army Military Academy at West Point, a real stretch for anyone from Weir High. Mr. Joyner left no doubt that his academics, which were nothing but C's and some 'D's, left that possibility, impossible. The best that Mr. Joyner saw for Marc was attending some state school, an athletic scholarship at a small college, which would require not only strong coaching support, but higher senior grades. Better yet, enlisting in some military service might be an option. Of course the final drop back position was the mill, or worse, coal mining. After that disappointing conversation, college of any kind or means seemed to Marc to be out of reach. His thought now was the Army or the Mill.

Marc continued to acquiesce to Jamie's chronicle of the past week and her grand tactics for the next few weeks and beyond. Marc was part of the conversation only sparingly, laughing, joking, longing for her touch, but distant. His leg was very sore. He was uncomfortable even sitting and he was concerned. He had been ill with Rheumatic Fever during his freshman year. That resulted in weeks in the hospital, months of restrictions of all physical exertion, lost work possibilities, and no social life. This was his first real athletic injury and he was starting to get alarmed. What he thought was a charley-horse on the field was starting to feel like something more significant. He did not want another hospital experience.

Sage was running at full speed in the third quarter trying to make a tackle when he hit Marc instead, and even worse, rolled up on top of Marc with his two hundred-plus pound body. It was a nasty hit; Marc was slow to get up and tried to walk and run the soreness off. He continued to play, but as the game got into the fourth quarter, he started to limp noticeably and was forced to slow down.

Finally a sub came in as Coach Warren waved him to the sideline. He went to the bench, was checked by Coach Romeo and the team physician, Doctor Grecoski. Other than a cramp, he seemed all right, was told to keep it loose and was permitted to return to the game. He went in and out of the game, but less and less as the game went deep into the fourth quarter. He tried to kick an extra point, but missed as he could not get any power behind the kick. Finally, the Red Riders were five scores ahead, the outcome was settled, second and third teams were getting some playing time and he was out of the game. He sat on the bench until the end, in great discomfort.

After the game, back in the locker room, his limp was even more evident; Dr Grecoski checked his leg again. The thigh was black and blue, warm, very taut and sore to the touch. The doctor confirmed that nothing was broken, but the bruise was deep. "You need to keep hot moist compresses on the leg over the weekend. And stay off it. If it continues to give you problems, call your coach or see me on Monday," was Dr. Grecoski's advice. And now, just sitting with Jamie, it was sore, very sore.

"Can we dance, or are you feeling beastly," Jamie asked delicately. He wanted to answer "no" but he wanted to keep her happy. She looked so sharp, so cute and cuddly. He just couldn't say "no;" she had bewitched him again. They danced a few romantic, huggable, dreamy, melancholy ballads. While he limped through the dancing, he enjoyed having her embrace him, having her sweet smelling hair intoxicate his good senses, having his arms around the small of her back, the feel of her cheek on his, and hear her whispers in his ear.

Jamie danced the up-beat tunes with friends, returning to Marc's side as he sat quietly in isolation. His dancing had caused spasms throughout his leg, so he was more comfortable just sitting and watching—a very unusual posture for him. All of a sudden: *The Diamonds came blasting over the jukebox system;" The Stroll:" Come let's stroll, stroll across the floor, come let's stroll across the floor, now turn around baby...I feel so good…baby let's go strolling by the candy store…strollin', oh yeah.* Jamie rushed over and grabbed Marc's hand. He started to follow her into the stroll line, but stopped short of joining. "Can't, this leg is hurting too much. I hate to be a drag."

"It's okay, quite, Ah'll be back," and off Jamie went to stroll. Marc went back to his corner seat with his concern growing, but not enough that he was willing to leave Jamie.

The evening went by quickly; all too soon it was ten-thirty and the dance was ending. Everyone was leaving the community center gym to start for home, De Carlo's Pizza, Bob's Big Boy, The Diner, or some other party spot.

"We 've to go. Ah still need to be home by eleven."

"Right on," Marc responded immediately. Finally, they would be alone. "I'll take you home. It's time to cut out."

"Oh ducky, Ah've to go home with Niki. Sorry!" Jamie said sheepishly. "Ah came with her and she has her Mum's car. Amanda, Sarah n Ah rode with her to the game n then to the dance."

"Crazy, wow, this is crazy. I was planning on us being together tonight at least for the ride home. You said this afternoon ..."

"Ah can't. Ah just can't tonight. Ah told my parents, Ah'd be with Niki n the others. You know the rules of riding alone with you!"

"Yeah I know your dad's rules. They are stupid. You were going to talk to your ..."

"My Da is not stupid," Jamie cried angrily.

"No, no, I didn't mean..."

"Ah can't, Ah just can't tonight. Ah need to go with Niki. You can walk to her car." Jamie's response was a little more controlled but still firm.

"I don't want...we ...I..." Marc was almost tongue-tied with disappointment and Jamie's aggressive come back.

"Come on, Ron n Will are going to walk us all to the car. Come on," She took his hand; together, they limped towards the parking lot.

With that disappointing outcome, Marc joined the others, the seven, Sarah being the lone ranger in the crowd without a hand to hold, and, as usual, complaining about her solo walk all the way to the new nineteen fifty-nine Plymouth Fury, with its long, pointy back fins. The couples held hands, cuddled, occasionally kissing while Sarah and other passer-bys "Oh, oh, oh, oohed" at their passion. The mood was upbeat, joking, laughing, with everyone having a good time in the shadowy light. Finally, the car was reached. The guys all had to fully examine the stylish new car inside and out. The four girls slid in after one final peck. Will grabbed and kissed Sarah playfully to make the love fest complete. The white and green heavily chromed Plymouth was off. The guys stood in the dim parking lot talking about the girls, the makeshift dates and especially, the shortened evening with no make-out time.

"Let's get a hamburger at Bob's," Will suggested.

Ron was quick to answer, "You're the boss."

"Me too," said Marc. "If this leg doesn't fall off, damn that Sage, couldn't he have hit someone from Wellsburg instead of me?"

"Come on, I'll drive. Just leave your cars," Will mumbled as he headed to his blue coupe.

As they got to the top of Marland Heights hill, everyone remained quiet. Amanda popped out with: "I miss not going home with Ron. It's our special time to be together. It is our time to talk about us and the future... and just talk about little things."

"And make-out until your father turns on the front light," Sarah chimed in.

"Well yes," Amanda answered giggling. "But it is our time. That's the only time we really have to be alone. You know what I mean."

"Yeah, I know what you mean, but all Will wants to do is really make-out. After a few kisses, I'm through," was Niki's quick reply from behind the steering wheel.

"That's a bunch of hay. We all know you're the make-out queen," Sarah interjected with a sharp tone.

"What? What is s bunch of hay?" Jamie asked from the front seat as an extension to Sarah's comment.

"Oh, she means B.S., but doesn't want to use the swear words," Niki answered and then elaborated, trying not to show her irritation. "I'm <u>not</u> the make-out queen, you just think so. I like to kiss good night, but that is enough for me right now. One or two kisses are my thing. Why do you think Danny Groves and I broke up? He wanted more."

"Boy, that's news to me," Sarah said faintly.

"News to me, too," Amanda chimed in.

Jamie sat pondering Niki's and Amanda's comments, taking it all in, talking about the future with boy friends, making-out or not making-out, Sarah going solo while the others have mates. It gave her pause.

Sarah was the first to be dropped off at home, then Amanda. The next stop was Jamie's house and she sat silently until Niki backed out of Amanda's driveway and started towards her last drop off. "Do you really not make-out with Will or your other boyfriends?" Jamie's question pierced the silence.

"Well, er, no, I don't do a lot, or any petting or necking or whatever you want to call making-out. Kissing can be nice and great sometime, but not all the squeezing, and touching ...well you know. I just don't want to right now. Some day when I feel like it, I might, but not now. When I really like or really love someone, not with Will or the others or anyone I know now."

"What about Marc? You dated him."

"Well, yes. But that was more as a friend, not a boyfriend. We've know each other a long time, almost like a brother-sister thing. Don't tell Marc that I said that. We were just hanging out together, that's all."

"But you did kiss him? Right?"

"Yes, you know I did. We talked about this before… few times. We didn't make-out," the last few words emphasized with tone and intensity. "We kissed a few times playing spin the bottle as kids, a few times at my back door. Don't get the idea that we were a tight couple. Jamie, I have never been fast or raunchy with anyone, certainly not Marc." Niki's answer to the personal, probing question became more perturbed as she ended.

"Oh Niki, Ah am sorry. Ah know you don't, you don't, well, you know what Ah mean. Ah really cocked up n you're my friend. Please don't get all fagged? Ah don't want you to be mad at me," Jamie was almost crying with regret.

"I'm not mad, but some people think I'm fast and I'm not! What does 'cocked up' or whatever you said, mean? It sounds rather foul, like some unspeakable language. What are you talking about?"

"Bloody no, no…it is just another Birmingham word…it doesn't mean anything, nothing, just nothing."

They were now stopped in Jamie's driveway, with Niki waiting for Jamie to open the door when Jamie turned towards her. "You are my best friend n Ah learn a lot when we talk. You helped me fit in," Jamie's voice was cracking with compassion. "Ah like Marc. Ah like him very much. We kiss n hug, but, Ah'm not sure what Ah want next. Ah want to keep liking him, n dating him, well you know."

Smiling they looked at each other. Jamie opened the door and started to get out, turned her head. "Thanks friend. Thanks. Pip pip till Monday," she dashed for the front door when she saw her mother standing in the open doorway.

Room 210 was Coach Warren's home room and he was sitting at his desk going through a stack of paper. He raised his head to see Marc limping in about ten minutes before first bell. The limp was obvious even though Marc attempted to minimize the pain. "You don't look too good. Leg still sore? Your limp is bad."

As Marc reached the side of the desk, he looked at his coach sheepishly. "It is really sore coach. I tried to stay off the leg, but it continues to hurt."

"I talked to your dad at church and he told me you were home in bed most of the weekend. He was concerned about the deep dark blue color of the bruise and so am I. We need you Friday night for Follansbee."

"And I want to be ready, I want to play."

"Well, let's get you to Dr. Grecoski. Go down and see Coach Baker. He will get you to Doc and have him look at that leg. We need to do that first thing today. Coach Baker is expecting you and may have already called Grecoski. We'll get you taken care of. Go now; keep me informed of what is happening with the Doc. I'll see you at practice if the Doc lets you move around…"

"Okay, Coach, I'll go right now. Thanks."

The home room crowd was starting to fill in their seats as school was about to start. Marc moved slowly to the door saying "Hi" to most of students rushing to get seated before the bell. Once he was in the hall, he headed towards the stairs and the Dean of Students office.

The weekend had been a difficult one for Marc. The leg was uncomfortable; he stayed home on Saturday and Sunday, not even going to the Community Center Pool for his Life Guard shift or the gas station for work on Sunday. More unusual, he stayed home Saturday evening, even though Jamie was going to the center to dance and hang-out. Phone calls from Ron, Will, Sage, and Niki checking on his condition only made staying home more depressing. When he called Jamie, twice, and found out that she was going to the Teen room with Niki, it made him more upset. An opportunity to spend the evening with Jamie was lost to a "damn" hit by Sage, his own teammate. "Damn it and damn Sage, the big spastic." But, he could not even walk around the house without holding on to the walls. On Saturday night, home was his only choice!

He told his mother that his leg was too painful to go church. His parents were very concerned about him and the injury. His staying on the living room couch, watching TV, or lying in bed with hot water compresses on the leg was something for their son to commit himself to. He was never at home longer than he had to be; seldom could be found in his room except to sleep. It was obvious that he was hurting. The bruise, if that's what it was, had turned a deep blue/black, had become warm to the touch, and caused Marc to wobble around the house, taking only small and guarded steps.

Marc considered calling Coach Warren or even Dr. Grecoski, but decided to wait to see how the leg was on Monday—a decision that his mother and father disagreed with, but one that they left up to him. "It was his leg, it's his decision." Marc was also concerned that if he complained too much, he would not get to play in Friday's night against Follansbee.

Upon returning from church, his father told him about the conversation with Coach Warren. The coach was concerned, wanted to make certain Marc came to see him first thing on Monday morning. So the die was cast before he even talked to Coach. First Coach Warren, then Coach Baker, then the hospital and Dr. Grecoski. Now everything was out of Marc's hand. All he wanted to do was to get the leg fixed and play football, and of course see Jamie.

Dr. Grecoski was waiting at his hospital office for Marc. The fiftyish, short, plump doctor examined the leg in more detail than he had following the game Friday night. Ex-rays were taken, even blood samples, and a leg specialist, along with an orthopedic doctor did a second examination. A physical therapist conducted a third exam, and finally they told Marc to wait while they conferred. After about half an hour, he met with all three. The news was good, nothing broken, nothing pulled, nothing torn, but the bruise was deep into the Quad and Hamstring muscles. It would take days to get relief and that could only be done through hot tub therapy at the hospital, supervised by Dr. Kowand, the Hospital Physical Therapist. It could be done on an "out-patient" basis, twice each day for a week or more.

Marc was relieved that it was nothing permanent, but he was concerned about all the back and forth to the hospital, school, and home. He wanted to know if he could practice, and the answer was "not right-away." Could he play on Friday night? "We don't know, we will tell you on Thursday." Could he go to work at the pool and gas station, "not if he wanted to play Friday." Did he have to go to school, "yes." The treatment would start immediately. Then he needed to report back to Coach Warren and call his parents.

As Marc sat in the hot tub with water bubbling all around him, he watched the other patients, all older and a few elderly, doing all kinds of exercises, even calisthenics. Marc was not happy to be in a hospital setting. The last time he was here was in his freshman year for almost two months, recovering from Rheumatic Fever. He missed almost half a year of school and when he returned, he was limited in his activities, especially sports. He was not permitted by the doctors to play any sport until well into his sophomore year. Just being in the hospital reminded him of that catastrophic epoch. Marc did not want a repeat of that experience.

Marc was not at his normal lunch spot under the balcony in the dark shadows. No one had seen him or talked to him since Sunday afternoon. Jamie was worried. Someone had mentioned that Marc had been in Coach Warren's homeroom before school started. That was all the information Jamie had.

She had spent the weekend getting started on looking up colleges at the Weirton Library with the help of Niki and Amanda. They were both doing the same thing, except that they had already narrowed the field. Niki was sure she would go to the University of Pennsylvania where her father and mother had graduated from and where her older brother was attending. It was a big state university about an eight hour drive from Weirton. Amanda was considering small private schools closer to home. Jamie was not sure what the difference was between "state" and "private" schools. In England, colleges and universities are state schools run by the British government, and tuition for those that do well in the A-Level Exams is free. Private schools were very expensive Preparatory or Prep Schools that get students ready for University. All these different American options and terms had Jamie confused. It was going to take her time and a great deal of effort to focus on a selection on the American enrollment process.

On Saturday evening she had gone to the Community Center with Niki and the others, even though she was sure Marc wouldn't be there because of his injury. With Marc not there, she danced a number of the slow songs with different boys. She missed Marc, but it had given her a chance to enjoy meeting some of the other guys who had stayed on the fringes because of Marc. The girls left the boys in the parking lot, but Will had even kissed her softly goodnight. That was a first and a little flushing. At church, no Marc. Now, at school, no Marc.

As school ended, Jamie finally spotted Marc going down the stairs to the locker room and he saw her. He waited until she came down to the step that he was standing on. Their greeting was a little awkward, but they said longing "hi's," held hands and told each other how much they had missed the other, then finally Marc told her about his day, the doctor, the therapist, the treatment, what his week would be like going to and from the hospital, and the unknown prospect of playing in the Friday night game. He was all right, but sore and concerned. Jamie listened, tried to comfort him, and wanted him to "ring her up tonight." He said he would, and they went their separate ways after checking in all directions and stealing a short kiss.

Marc reported to the coaches in their cracker box of an office secreted behind the football equipment storage room. They were squeezed in like sardines, so that when you spoke with one you were really talking to all four. He told them what the doctors had said, what his treatment would be and that there was a chance that he could play on Friday. He emphasized the last point. They all seemed to be well aware of the diagnosis. Dr. Grecoski obviously had already called them as well as his mother. Coach Warren told him to do what the Dr. wanted, attend classes and be at practice each day so he was aware of anything special they were planning for Follansbee. The decision to let him play would be made on Friday.

Following every one's instructions was exactly what he did. He was busy going to hospital twice a day. Jamie was just as busy with the question of college, and getting to know what being on the Weirite staff was all about. They saw each other in the school hallways as they changed classes and a couple of times for lunch. A few evening phone calls enabled them to keep in touch, but for the most part they spent the week doing their own thing.

On Thursday he was permitted to run a little and on Friday was told by Dr. Grecoski that he could play. Coach Warren called him into the coach's office and told him to be ready to play offense, but he would not be on defense or do any of the kicking. He would also not be on any of the special teams; he would only play offense. Marc was both pleased and disappointed. He was going to play, but only part time. He took great pride and enjoyment in playing every play. He looked forward to playing defense where there was physical contact on almost every play. His biggest satisfaction was punting and kicking the extra points. His play would be limited to being the wide receiver on every play so that he would not be in any heavy contact. But at least he would play!

Follansbee was also undefeated; it could be a difficult game. It was the sixth game of the season and an away game. They would play home next week, followed by two away games, and then home for the last game of the schedule, which would be homecoming weekend. The Red Riders rolled to another lopsided score, mainly on their speed. Marc had almost no contact and finished the game sore but fine in regard to the injury. With it being an away game there was no post-game dance, no time with Jamie, no goodnight hug and kiss. That Saturday everyone seemed to be busy, so the Community Center was calm that evening. Marc worked a double shift at the pool just to have something to do. Jamie was involved in some family thing and everyone else was someplace else.

The next three weeks of the season were a repeat of the Follansbee week. For Marc it was light practice, some work at the Pool and a few extra hours at the gas station. He saw Jamie only briefly as they moved about the school halls, and sat together at lunch a few days. Friday evening they met after the Wheeling Central Catholic game, but Jamie was riding with Niki again, so it was a short, uneventful evening. Saturday evening that week was a bust as Jamie had a sleep over with the girls.

They arranged to meet at church a couple of times since both were going to be part of a Youth Sunday where Marc would deliver a third of the sermon and Jamie would handle one of the bible readings. Reverend Ness wanted everything to go off smoothly, so the meetings were practice sessions. Marc was the only one who was not completely prepared for the run through, which lead to some scolding from the good Reverend. He felt a little embarrassed, but, was glad to spend time with Jamie.

The eighth game of the season was a Friday night game at Clarksburg Victory High School. That was a four hour trip. The team made the trip by school bus, the cheerleaders by car, and there was a caravan of cars for fans, but no band. It was too far and expensive to take a one hundred fifty member band. The trip to and from Clarksburg was made in one day with the game played in between going and returning. Clarksburg Victory was also undefeated, a power house in the middle of the state. However, the nineteen fifty-seven reigning state champions were at the top of their game.

Weirton won easily. However, they did have two season ending injuries to the two starting guards, who also played defense. These two injuries along with the bumps and bruises of a long season were potentially a problem.

The night trip home from Clarksburg was long and uncomfortable. The two o'clock a.m. arrival at the high school had everyone a little testy. The winning streak was now at twenty-six consecutive victories, the longest in West Virginia High School history, a fact lost to the sleepy eyes.

As Marc drove to the Community Center for his life guard shift the next day, he remembered that just about all his buddies, as well as Jamie, Niki, Amanda and many of the others were in Pittsburgh to take a preparatory class for the new college entrance test, the SAT, the Scholastic Aptitude Test. The class was to get them ready to take the four hour test next Saturday in Wheeling. Marc was about the only one not taking the test. College was for them. He would do something else after graduation, maybe the Army or maybe just staying around Weirton. Maybe he would learn a trade, like barber, or carpenter, or whatever came along. At least he didn't have to take another class, just to take a test.

"Hi, how are you? I missed not seeing you last night. I thought you might come down to the teen room at the Center! Not one of the gang was there; where did you all go?"

"We didn't get back from Pittsburgh until almost nine," I went to bed and slept until noon."

"You weren't in Church either!" Marc said with disappointment in his voice

"I told you I slept until noon," was Niki's exasperated response. "After the Friday night game with the long trip home, then going to Pittsburgh all day Saturday, sitting in a class, and all that stuff, I was exhausted. So was everyone."

"I know. It was just that I was all by myself at the center. There was no one there! That's the second Saturday in a row that the place has been dead." The pause after his frustration outburst was extensive. "I called Jamie tonight but her mom said she couldn't come to the phone."

"She is all right, just tired like me and the others. I need to go. This week is going to be a killer, with the game in Wheeling on Friday, then the SAT's in Wheeling again on Saturday, then the Sunday Youth Day! You better be ready with your part of the sermon."

"I'm ready, yeah! I'll be ready."

"You better be. I'll see you in school tomorrow! If I can wake up. See ya."

Marc hung up the phone. He walked slowly up the flower rugged stairs holding on more to the solid cherry wood banister than usual as he tried to understand how things had changed over the past month. Everything seemed in order a few weeks ago, now everything was all confused. In his room he turned on the radio. WEIR 1400 was playing a country song: *By Don Gibson, "Oh Lonesome me:" Everybody's going out and having fun. I'm just a fool staying home and having none… I know that I should have some fun and paint the town… A lovesick fool is blind and just can't see. Oh lonesome me…*

Chapter 7

Potential

Church pews were quickly being occupied as the parishioners converged on the sanctuary entering from all three sides. Most were coming through the side doors from the Sunday school rooms as the ceiling-high folding doors were opened into the large fellowship hall. The majority knew exactly where they wanted to sit, their self-appointed pew claimed by habit. The less frequent Sunday attendees looked right, left, and even down front to find an open pew that no one had claimed.

Behind the pulpit, stationed on the raised dais, was Reverend Ness, seated in an over-sized high back ornate solid red oak chair. The chair was big enough to be a pew all by itself. He was looking through a dozen or more three by five index cards that would help him keep an orderly process to Youth Fellowship Sunday. He would serve as the master of ceremony. The worship service itself would be presented by the senior members of the youth fellowship. Each of the eight amateur parsons was prepared to do his or her part, either preach part of the sermon, read the scriptures, present the call to worship, accept the tithes and be the face of the church holiness.

Flower stands filled with Fall flowers; Mums, Asters, Asiatic Lilies, Bottom Poms, and Hydrangeas in enchanting colors of oranges, purples, reds, off-whites and assorted lush greens, bordered the alter. The banners, pulpit scarves, paramount and even the clergy tippet worn by Reverend Ness over his black robe were liturgically purple. With the red oak pews, flooring, furniture, woodwork, and ceiling planking, the vibrant colors set an angelic atmosphere.

The activity of finding seating was subsiding as Reverend Ness stood and strode toward the raised pulpit. His six foot three, full body frame added to the Godly scene. The congregation silenced quickly. He stopped just short of his target, turned to glance at the eight service participants and mouthed a silent "ready?" The minister stepped directly to the pulpit and raised his arms as an instruction for all present to stand. The congregation rose as one.

Everything went well. The readers, the service leaders and the preachers delivered a very solid performance. As the eight sat in the midst of the raised platform, the congregation was very attentive to the talent revealed by the maturing adolescents. Jamie read the scripture from *2nd Corinthians, Chapter 13: "... Finally, brethren, farewell. Be perfect, be of good comfort, be of one mind, live in peace: and the God of love and peace shall be with you..."* Will led the church in the Sunday prayer. Niki, Amanda and Marc shared the sermon directed at "Love God; Love Each Other."

It was easy to recognize the preparation that Niki and Amanda had made for their segment of the message. The structure was compact, with clear and simple current examples. Each was relaxed in her delivery as if this were a normal happening. Even their appearance, Sunday conservative dresses with just enough teenage color highlights, made them appear respectively cute. The bows in their flowing hair gave them an enchanting manner and they seemed to captivate the faithful.

Marc's comments, while appropriate, were not as polished. He had finished his sermonette about a week earlier and had not looked at it since. Just before they took their places, he re-read his efforts. He stumbled through a few points that he was trying to make and misread a few words. But the toughest part was his delivery. He had two coughing spells, his voice was nasal and crackly, and at the end, be became hoarse and lost volume.

Marc had started to come down with cold and sinus symptoms on the return trip from Wheeling after the game. The rain, sleet, snow and cold that descended on the game had left him and others with chills and discomfort. By Saturday evening he was not at all well. Even an early to bed night with some home remedies from his mother had not helped.

Awaking Sunday was difficult and just coming to church was an effort. If it had been any other Sunday, he would have stayed in bed. He could barely sit through the entire service, getting up and making a six to seven minute speech was very difficult. He knew he was struggling and so did the fellowship. He stumbled back to his seat grabbing for a handkerchief. At least he had thought ahead enough to bring one. He was wearing an un-creased pair of pants that needed to be dry- cleaned, a sport coat that did not match, scuffed brown shoes, and to top it off, he needed a haircut. Still, he had done his duty. Youth Day at Church was over; he could go home and crawl into bed.

However, first the reward for being part of the worship service was to stand in a receiving line to accept accolades from the congregation. As the last hymn was sung, the presenters and Reverend Ness made their way to the back of the sanctuary.

The singing was loud and enthusiastic. The choir, tucked in their screened off nook, led the congregation in a 19th century Protestant hymn: *Nearer, my God, to Thee, Nearer to Thee, E'en though it be a cross that raiseth me, Still all my song shall be, Nearer, my God, to Thee…Though like the wanderer, the sun gone down…Yet in my dreams I'd be, Nearer, my god, to Thee…There let the way appear, steps unto Heav'n… Angels to beckon me, Nearer, my God, to Thee. Nearer, my God, to Thee, Nearer to Thee.*

With the song's end and rumbling in the pews, everyone started to make their way to the exits. The line of well-wishers was long and the comments very encouraging, even though Marc knew his contribution was not top shelf. He shook hands, and said thank you mechanically and politely. When it was finally over, all eight of them headed for Fellowship Hall and a seat.

Marc was the first to collapse into one of the very hard and uncomfortable folding chairs that at this stage of his discomfort, served as a lounge chair. Niki, Jamie and a few others quickly surrounded him with their own chairs reliving the experience, and expressing satisfaction that it was over.

"Wow, boy, am I tired!" Niki announced over and over. Each of the others had a tale of woe about the hour of being in the spotlight, except Marc, who just sat drowsily, completely oblivious to everything.

"You are not well, are you?" Jamie observed, leaning in closer so that her voice did not carry. "Your face is almost white n your eyes are closing. The cold is getting worse, right?"

"He sure is sick. He needs to go home before we all get sick," Niki picked up the gloomy prognosis, her voice loud enough to grab everyone's attention so that the concentration was now on Marc and his poorly state. "Your voice sounds like a cricket, or maybe one of those croakers down by the river. You need something to help with your cold and nose."

"Buzz, no kidding," Marc's reply was fatigued and throaty. "I need to go home!"

"You certainly do, and right now! Hello girls: you had best stay some distance from him or you'll catch what he's got," Beth Floreau, Marc's mother broke in authoritatively. "I told you to go straight home when the service was over. You want everyone to get this bug?" she questioned him not expecting an answer.

"Yes, I'm going."

"Now! Not tomorrow, now. You girls let him get home, now."

"Yes Ma'am," Niki and Jamie answered in unison. "We will."

Marc's mother walked away, leaving them for a quiet moment or two.

"You'd better go Marc," Niki said, "We'll see you tomorrow or whenever."

"Right, whenever you're better, please call," Jamie stood and walked away followed by Niki and the others.

Marc stood wobbly and said in a croaky whisper, "OK, call."

"Ah haven't seen him. He usually is coming down the hall."

"Well, I haven't seen him either. He always stops in the library before home room. He was a no show this morning."

"Ah 'm really worried about him. He was so woeful on Sunday. Even his mother was about to 've a cow because he wasn't home in bed."

"Sounded terrible after the game on the bus. That damn rain and snow! And us with no heavy parkas, I could kill the managers, or whoever was responsible."

"Maybe he'll be at lunch, Ah so want to see him."

"Have'ta go. Algebra class is downstairs," Sage took off down the hall in his run, shift, hopping manner. He dodged the few stragglers still in the hall, turned the corner towards the stairs.

Jamie realized the time, checked the hallway one last time for Marc, and quickly trudged into her biology lab room, slightly ahead of Mr. Ginn shutting the door. She took her assigned seat at the lab table and heard the class bell.

Where was Marc? That question consumed her thoughts. He never called Sunday evening; he must have been really in bad shape once he got home. He always called when she asked him to. She would look for him at lunch; maybe, he slept in and will come in late today. Her mind raced like a roadster. All she could think about was Marc. In her mind, she relived the wet, cold Friday night trip to Wheeling for the game, followed by taking the SAT's most of the day Saturday, Sunday's Youth service, Marc working at the pool and always busy, busy, busy.

Sage looked fine and he had been in the rain, snow and mud. His week-end was just as busy. He did just about everything she did. Jamie liked Sage. He was always a blast to be around. He was funny, a comedian. He dressed better than most of the guys, always had on a sharp shirt or sweater. Certainly a better dresser than Marc or Will! Drove one of the best cars, a Ford something. He didn't seem to have a dolly on his arm. He played the field, which the girls liked because that meant they each still had a chance.

Sage was tall like Ronnie, maybe six feet two or three, a flat top haircut, and always a batch of books under his arm. A bookworm no; bookish, yes. He talked about books that he had read, and how much he enjoyed reading, learning new things, knowing history. His nickname with the girls was Classy Chassis, a hip person with an athletic body.

Jamie laughed under her breath as Mr. Ginn at the blackboard was talking about human genes and their ability to reproduce. She drifted back to thinking about Marc. Hopefully Sage, or someone else, would have some news, or best of all, Marc would show up for lunch.

The possibility of news about Marc was slim. He was still sick when he woke-up, maybe worse rather than better, yet he was determined to go to school. Not because of concern over his academics, but over being eligible to play against Parkersburg on Friday. His mother wanted him to see Dr. Grecoski now. Nevertheless, he was independent and told her he would go after school or practice, as soon as he could. She was upset with his disobedience, and the antagonism grew. Regardless, off he went to school.

He won the spat only because his dad was working the daylight shift, having left on the six thirty-five a.m. bus. Dad would have ended the back and forth immediately, and Marc would be on his way to see Dr. Grecoski.

Walking in the front door of the school, he was met by Coach Baker standing at his normal place at the start of the school day, the bottom of the main stairway. Coach Baker motioned him over to the side, asking him how he was feeling. A few words into this conversation about his condition ended with Coach sending Marc immediately to see Dr. Grecoski at his office in the hospital. Marc started to object, but Coach Baker cut him off, giving him two choices.

"Go directly to the hospital office. You know where it is. He will be expecting you, and I will call your parents. We don't want you in school in your condition. You are contagious, and can only cause problems for other students and staff. You are certainly not going to learn anything coughing, sneezing, and blowing your nose. You're no help to yourself, or the team. Now go straight there. I'll tell your teachers and Coach Warren. Or you can go home! Now get yourself to Dr. Grecoski. You and he are becoming good friends. Go, get out of here!"

He was not well and he knew it. Going to see the doctor was the only right thing to do. He left school, went down the extended cement stairway outside the main entrance to his car. He climbed in, sat for a moment, took a deep breath, and tried to clear his sinuses. Many thoughts flooded his mind: *boy, another lousy day, the hospital again, Dr. Grecoski for a second time this month, damn it.*

The car engine droned instantly with the turn of the key, the radio lit-up instantly blasting music from WEIR, too loud for his stuffed head. He turned the volume down, put the car in gear, drove out of the parking lot, down Virginia Avenue, turned left onto Main Street, headed toward the Carol Way Hospital and listened to the grand old oldies from 1957: *"Out In The Cold Again," by Frankie Lymon & the Teenagers; "Waitin In School," by Ricky Nelson; "Loving You," by Elvis Presley; "Teardrops," by Lee Andrews & the Hearts;* and just before he reached the hospital: *"Searchin'," by the Coasters: Yeah, I've been searchin', A-a searchin' Oh, yeah. Searchin' every which a-way…Now, if I have to swim a river…On a blueberry hill… Oh, yeah, Searchin'…"*

As he walked into the hospital, he kept reciting the lyrics *"I'm Searchin,"* to reduce his stress and try to lower his heart beat. He was certain that Dr. Grecoski would bring up his heart condition. The doctor was not comfortable with his playing sports after his Rheumatic Fever illness three years ago. Marc had been cleared medically for sports activities only reluctantly. That problem had started with a bad cold like this one. *Not again, not again,* he thought.

No one was at the reception desk so he walked over to the waiting area and sat down. Two minutes passed and a nurse in her white uniform, including a cap that was tipped to the side seeming ready to fall, asked his name, motioned him to follow her to an examination room. Dr. Grecoski was all business, none of his light hearted smile and small talk. The nurse took his temperature, blood pressure and pulse as the doctor simultaneously asked questions about his condition, symptoms, listened to his heart and chest, and examined his ears and throat. After all this medical attention, Marc sat on the exam table, the doctor sat at his desk, and the nurse with arms folded across her chest, stood between. The bad news, delivered by Dr. Grecoski while standing with his back to Marc writing on his chart, was not a surprise. Marc was to be admitted to the hospital, endure more medical tests, and simultaneously be started on an aggressive medication regiment.

Dr. Grecoski turned to face Marc while the nurse moved aside. "With your Rheumatic Heart history we can't take any chances. You have a high temperature, much higher than is safe for you. Your glands are all swollen, your throat is very irritated, and you probably have another strep infection. That is not a good combination of problems for you. You should have seen me yesterday or even better Saturday. You must like waiting until the last minute! You're just like your father."

Marc tried to smile, but just moved his head in a yes motion. What he feared had become reality.

"They have a bed ready for you upstairs. Go with the nurse and I will contact your mother, although we have already talked. She told me of your reluctance to come and see me. Not a smart move on your part or your mother's."

"It's not her fault..."

"Never mind whose fault it is. It is the hospital now for you. Go, get in bed." The doctor finished his lecture, rose, and exited.

"Come on, let's find a wheelchair and get you upstairs," were the nurse's first and last words.

Jamie got to the auditorium late as usual. Lunch was almost over when she reached Niki, Amanda, Will, Sage and the dark corner gang. Still no word about Marc, although one of his teachers had said he was in the hospital. Then Amanda told everyone that Ronnie and Carl Miner were also in the hospital because of injuries sustained during Friday's game. Both Ronnie and Carl had been in Wheeling on Saturday to take the SAT's, but dutifully went into the hospital on Sunday for x-rays and such. Sage reported a few more of the team members were either sick or injured. The list of incapacitated seemed to be growing hourly.

This was homecoming week, a big, maybe the biggest event of the year for the entire school and community. It was without a doubt the biggest football game of the season. A win would send the Red Riders to the state Championship game. Then Niki put the icing on the cake when she mentioned that Molly Bouchard, the head Cheerleader, was also sick at home. It seemed to the gathering that there were more people at home than in school. The bell rang, lunch was over, and classes would start in five minutes. They scattered.

A band of nurses marched around getting Marc ready for bed. One minute he was walking into a four bed ward, the next he was in a window view bed, under the covers in an open back hospital gown, a nurse sticking a thermometer under his tongue, another was inserting an IV needle in his arm. Marc was told he was in a sterile ward for contagious patients. He was not to get out of bed unless a nurse was present; he would be having tests throughout the day, and he was not permitted any visitors except his parents, especially not his sisters. The doctor would be in to see him about noon, and lastly, the IV meds would make him sleepy.

"Lay back now and go to sleep," were the last instructions. He lay back with his head on the pillow and looked up at the flat, ten foot high white celling.

Finally this whirlwind day was slowing to a crawl. Hell, he thought, what a day, no what a month, double hell, damn, what a senior year! Marc's mind was working overtime as he succumbed to his hospital bed. Everything started on Friday with the trip to Wheeling Island Stadium in the usual two school bus motorcade. At the start of the game, the temperature was cool, but not really cold; the field was solid, with some ruts, grooves and a few hollows caused by the heavy use during the long season. This was a municipal field, used by numerous city schools, and it was showing wear with almost no grass, bare ground throughout, with weaving white lines for yard markers.

From the very start, Weir High controlled the game. They scored two quick, long play touchdowns. Marc was part of the offense, catching two passes, one for long yardage, for the first time in the past three games. He was only playing offense, but at least he was busy when he was on the field. The game was going well, but yet, there was an uneasiness on the Weirton side as the first quarter came to an end. The weather turned, changing quickly as if someone had opened a northern facing door. It was suddenly colder, very cold. It started to rain, then started to pour, turned to sleet then turned to snow before finally turning to a sleety, rainy snow with arctic winds. The second quarter was miserable; the bare ground became mud, the grooves became paths for streams, the hollows into puddle-like lakes, the white yard line markings gone. Regardless of the weather, the Red Riders scored again off a Wheeling fumble and continued to outplay the hosts.

At half-time, in a dirty, dingy visitor's dressing room with limited seating, the team attempted to get warm. They were soaked. Everything on them was soaked, muddy and clinging skin tight. The winter down-hooded parkas, specifically for this weather change, had not been loaded on the buses. They were in boxes ready to go, still back in the hallway at school and somehow had not been moved to the buses. The players had no way to get warm on the sidelines or in the locker room. The coaches had their parkas, but there were no parkas for the team.

It would be a very cold, wet second half, both on the field and on the bench. Players had already noticed that the fans had brought winter jackets, the cheerleaders had heavy parkas, and even the band members had heavy parkas and protection for their instruments. Players grabbed their own coats and wore them on the sidelines. Marc had only a flimsy fall jacket with him. That would be of no help and he would need it to be dry after the game.

Rain, sleet and snow continued throughout the entire second half. Weirton scored again; however, so did the opponents. As the fourth quarter started, Wheeling scored a second time, changing the momentum. With Wheeling driving again, Marc was on the sidelines jumping up and down to keep warm. Suddenly at the end of a defensive play, the Red Riders had two players down. After a few minutes, Marc realized that it was Carl Miner, Weirton's Allstate halfback and Ronnie, an Allstate defensive back, offensive end. Both were down for a long time and when they did get up, each was helped off the field. Now, both defensive safeties were out of the game.

As Coach Mendel came off the field, he came directly over to Marc. "You have to play defensive safety. Don't let that big wide end get behind you. They will be throwing right at you first thing. Be ready. Keep them in front of you. Go, Go!" Marc ran out, took a position he had never played before, except maybe in eighth grade for the Weirton Colts. Somehow, with his luck, the precipitation stopped, the wind died down, and it was all of a sudden better passing weather.

The ball was thrown high and long over the middle. The big end, in his soaked white jersey, was streaking across the field tracking the ball's path. Marc had stayed back as he was told, then made a darting move toward the racing receiver and the dropping spiral. He crossed in front of the white blur, grabbed the ball from just over his helmet, and turned directly toward his distant goal. He slipped in the mud, regained his balance, and maneuvered the slippery ball under his left arm. Friend and foe were falling all around him trying to change direction. He stayed in the middle of the field for twenty yards or so, and then made a sharp cut to his left toward better footing along the sidelines. He picked up a couple of nice comeback blocks and rushed into the end zone!

Marc's defensive gem changed the momentum again, the Red Riders won their twenty-seventh consecutive game, and were nine and zero for the nineteen fifty-eight season. Only Parkersburg was left.

Everyone was freezing from the wet cold weather. The buses had heat, but not enough to compensate for damp bodies, even after temperate warm showers.

As he finished reliving the start of this disastrous weekend, he knew he had played well Friday and he reveled in that, but look where it got him—in the hospital, sick!

"Alright, everyone settle down. Settle please ...Can I get everyone's attention please? Ladies quiet please." Everyone in the back-stage room started to quiet down. A few took seats and others holding dresses or other items stopped where they were. "Quiet please! Thank you. Please be quiet so we can discuss what will happen on the field." Miss Darnie, the French teacher and the faculty advisor to the Homecoming Festival Committee, was trying to get everyone's attention as the Homecoming Court gathered in the large room in the back of the stage in the auditorium. There were evening gowns hanging from racks available throughout the space. "I know this back stage area is not the best place to change into your gowns, which are very beautiful, very much so. I love all the colors and the wide hooped bottoms. These dresses are like being in a fantasy story. You are all going to look beautiful. I even wish I could wear one. But not tonight, this is your night, do enjoy it."

"Even though the dresses are lovely, they cover a lot of space at your feet and will be difficult to manage as you get in and out of the cars, walk on the track or go up the steps to the raised platform after the queen is announced and crowned. Please be careful, hold onto your fathers or whoever is serving as your escort. They should help you move around with these wide dresses, so hold on to them as you move around. Take your time. Once you are in the cars, you need to ..."

Miss Darnie, a tiny, non-descript lady, in her late twenties, continued to give instructions and tips to the six homecoming court girls, their friends, helpers and mothers. It was an exciting night for the nominees and everyone celebrating homecoming. At half-time one of them would be announced as Homecoming Queen and wear the crown to the post-game dance at the Community Center. The Queen would also preside over a number of events during the year including being featured at all the City's holiday galas. Being Queen was both an honor and a responsibility.

"Where are we going to leave our gowns after we change for the dance?" Amanda asked Miss Darnie.

"Right here dear. They will be perfectly safe. A few of the ladies and some students will stay in this room to keep watch during the game. After the game when you change to your dancing clothes, everything will locked in the costume room, and we will be here Saturday afternoon if you want to pick up your dresses and any other personal things you wish to leave here overnight.

"That's all I have. Enjoy yourselves tonight. Be careful as you move around. You have a lot of time to get dressed. Thank you for your attention."

"I hope I can get around tonight better than I did at home," was Niki's comment to the five or six people around her. "I kept tripping on the hem and bumping into furniture."

"So did I," Amanda laughed. "So did I."

Jamie, part of the circle, sat quietly next to her mother and Mrs. Branden, who had been a tremendous help in finding a perfect Rose Red, white trimmed formal grown with a matching wrap. Aunt Marietta, as Jamie called her, helped find a seamstress so that the Hollywood style dress fit perfectly. While Jamie would only wear the dress for the half-time crowning ceremony, it was a perfect dual purpose dress, one that would set her off at the upcoming Christmas/New Year's Eve dance.

"Ah am really nervous. Ah've never been involved in such a big happening, this is such a bash it frightens me."

"You'll do fine Jamie, just fine. You are going to look beautiful," Aunt Marietta said, as both she and Jamie's mother rejoiced in the experience that they all were having.

"Girls, girls – please, quiet please, thank you, a few last points. If you are going to use one of the winter capes or stoles provided by Stone and Thomas, please, extra please, don't damage them and bring them back here at the end of the evening before you go to the dance. Enjoy them, let them keep you warm, but be careful with them. By the way, they will go on sale next week if you are interested. Now about …," and on she went.

The big night was starting for the Homecoming Court. But first, the game…

Girls were gathered on the landing and the steps leading to the main floor of the school. Some were sitting on the steps, others leaning with their backs against the wall or door with arms across their body as if cold or dejected. Cheeks were crimson from the crisp fall air they had been in for the past three hours. Each was waiting for her football hero so they could be off to the homecoming dance at the Community Center.

Marc and a few others exited the locker room in the basement, walked up the bottom rung of stairs to the landing at the front outside doors. They were the first to exit, so the girls stirred, checking to see whose hero was arriving. There were mostly guarded greetings, a few acknowledgements by name and even fewer comments about individual performances or the game.

Marc noticed the, more than usual, red eyes on some of the yearning faces. Cool temperatures, wind, mill soot could account for some of the cardinal peepers. Or maybe it was the disappointment in the Queen selection, or a disappointing band performance. On the contrary, he knew it was the results of the game. That was why his movement was pure drudgery, his head monitoring his feet and his eyes a matching blood-red.

Red Riders had lost, lost decisively. Their game winning streak had come to a passionate end. The football season was over, with a nine win, one loss record. A loss on the final Friday night of the season! For the first time in almost three years they had lost—been defeated—knocked out of the state championship game. The team, students, fans and entire community would have to live with this defeat for nine or ten months before they had a chance to redress the hurt.

Marc twisted his way through the cluster of girls and up the stairs to the main floor looking for Jamie. He spotted her next to the door of the principal's office. She saw him. As they approached each other, they both saw the watery eyes. She looked at him with sweet compassion and whispered silently, "sorry, so sorry!" They touched hands, she moved towards him, placed her head on his chest, both stood still and silent for a moment, stepped back, stared at the other, hugged again, and moved as one out of the center of the hall.

Marc ogled at her, finally kissed her gently on the check. She smiled, blushed. “You look very nice tonight. I’m sorry you weren’t elected queen, but you’re my queen.”

“Wow, blimey that was so nice of you. Wow! Actually, Ah was just happy being selected for the court. It was wonderful.”

“Well, you should have been queen. You had my vote.”

“Ah ’ve only been in the school two months. My Mum says it was a reward from the students n the school for being so nice.”

“Well, it was. You are nice, very, very nice.”

“Ah had a great time tonight. Ah got to ride in a convertible, sat on the back of it just like a queen. Ah got to wear a beautiful fluffy dress, like nothing Ah,’ve ever seen. My Mum said it was better than her wedding dress. People were cheering, yelling my name. It was awesome.”

“I haven’t seen you in that dress, at least not up close. I looked for you from across the field, you looked great,” Marc cut in.

“It’s a right proper dress, you will see it at the holiday dance.”

“You’re thinking that far ahead?”

“Blimey, yea, right. A dress like that needs to be worn more than once. You’ll see it. Ah look grand,” she said gleefully.

“You look wonderful right now!” Marc was admiring her as he stepped back to get a full view. She wore a silhouette type dress, the top scooped down away from her neck. It was royal blue, had lacey sleeves, a knee length pleated skirt, and it crinkled when it moved. She was a darling. She wore a winter jacket loosely pulled around her shoulders.

“You really, really look majestic. Is that a new coat?”

“Right, Ah had it on at the crowning of the queen n on the stage on the field. Mum bought it for me right after we got back in the school to change. Niki n Amanda also bought the ones they wore.”

It was getting crowded as the players were coming up from the locker room. Gals were matching up with their guys, and everyone was leaving the building, moving down the twenty cement steps leading to their cars. Marc and Jamie did the same, hands grasped together.

The Community Center gym was lavishly decorated, the dance was open to the community, although the crowd was certainly dominated by students. The atmosphere was gloomy. Most were huddled in small groups with only muffled voices controlling the conversation. The jukebox was loud enough to fill the huge space; nevertheless, the dance floor was almost empty. Over in a far corner the Queen, Lindsey Deville, was surrounded by a small party of friends, mostly still in their band uniforms since Lindsey was a majorette in the band.

Marc, Jamie, Niki, Will, Amanda and even Ronnie, with his shoulder and arm in a sling, gathered off to the side with mostly football players, their girls, cheerleaders and some band members. The conversation was stale, everyone avoiding the "elephant in the room" topic. As the evening progressed, the morbid tone seemed to be cast aside and some normalcy returned. The dance floor filled, chatter picked up, laughing got loud, and horse-play steered the jokesters.

As Jamie and Marc danced cheek to cheek, both relaxed. The tension of the evening, the bustling fall, the injuries, sicknesses, uncertainties, academics of the past two months faded away. Something of contentment ruled them. Towards the end of the evening, which had been extended to eleven due to the length of the game, dancing peaked. Everyone was on the dance floor, even some of the very shy guys joined in some line dancing. Football season was officially over. It ended on a sobering note, but the spirit was still there and enjoyment of the moment prevailed.

Eleven o'clock brought blinking lights, followed by all the lights coming on as the gym emptied quickly. Walking to cars was like a parade. People yelling, running in every direction, names being called out, car engines being started and reved, hugging, squeezing, a stolen kiss made fun of; upbeat moments prevailed after the initial tragedy. Jamie and Marc found Marc's coupe in the middle of the lot. She jumped in and scooted over next to him making sure they were shoulder to shoulder. With the turn of the key, the engine purred and the radio blared: *Ooh wah ooh wah, why do fools fall in love? Why do birds sing so gay and lovers await the break of day? Why do they fall in love? Why does the rain fall from up above: why do fools fall in love? Why do they fall in love?...*

"Why do they fall in love? Do you know?"

"I don't know. Are we falling in love?" Marc redirected the question.

"Ah don't know," Jamie whispered as she placed her head on his right arm. "Ah don't really know!"

Why does my heart skip a crazy beat? For I know not will reach defeat. Tell me why... Why do fools fall in love? The Diamonds finished with a question.

They rode silently to Jamie's home. When he stopped the car in the driveway, he turned and looked into her deep blue eyes. They beamed at each other, kissed and kissed for a second, then a third. Retreated a bit and kissed for a fourth time.

"Thanks for helping me get through this night. I was really sad. I feel good now; still sad, but good."

"You needed to be sad. But all is okay. We had a nice time, well, after the game, I meant, Sorry."

"That's alright. We did have a good time. It's a good time right now. You are too much, so classy and sweet."

"You're sugaring me?"

"No, I mean it, you are what … what Will calls a 'real dolly.' Do you know what that means?"

"Yes, Ah bloody know what Will means. Thanks," her reply adding to the flippant banter.

"You have lost something! You have lost your English pronunciation, your English/ English. Your words are American.

"Yeah, they 've been going away, probably because no one talks to me except in American, or Ah should say, United States English. My brother n father lost their English pronunciation long ago. It's only me n my Mum now."

"Who are you? You are speaking more American now. You still have your accent, but the words are ours. That is cool. I think?"

"All right. Sure, my words are more American." And they kissed and both moved slowly out the driver's door. Their pace was slow. They stopped on the stoop, looked at each other again, leaned in for a last kiss, and Jamie opened the door and was inside.

"Did you've a good time dear?" Mum asked Jamie from the living room where she and Francis sat.

"Yes, we rightly did. It was sad losing the game; we all cried a little, but we had a good time."

Jamie walked over to both of them for a hug and a good night kiss. "Thanks, thanks for this wonderful experience. Good night."

"Good night dear," her parents replied.

Following homecoming and the disappointing Parkersburg game, the pace became uneventful, almost sedate. There were no practices to attend after school, no game nights, no highs on victories, no SAT's for the college bound to take, no organizations to join. There was just a lot of nothing. School continued with Marc getting a bit more academics into his day. Jamie was developing a strong academic record at Weir High in addition to being immersed in the Weirite and the National Honor Society.

However uneventful November was regarding school activities, it was not a complete loss socially. Everyone had more time to enjoy a full lunch period in their covered cove in the back of the auditorium, more time to stay a little later after school and make a run to Big Boy's, Isaly's, even the Community Center Lounge to just be, or just hang out. It was a cool summer time atmosphere.

Weekends were entirely free. Friday everyone met at the Center's teen room. On Saturday there were usually one or more house parties to attend. The senior girls worked out an entire November Saturday evening schedule so that they shared the party duties. All the group had to do was show up. On Sunday evening Cove church tried to entice the Youth Fellowship to have an event at the church. One Sunday was a pizza party provided by Di Carlo's with board games; another was popcorn night and a scavenger hunt. November week-ends were filled with fun, couples parties, freedom and some down time.

Since homecoming, Jamie' parents had moderated their rules for socializing. She was still tied to curfew hours, but those could be adjusted to the evening's events. She was permitted to ride alone with Marc, have him pick her up at home, bring her home and even have him visit her at home. They made it clear that there was not to be any heavy making out, no "hanky-panky" as her father said using his favorite term when advising his daughter. Her constant response was, "Oh Da Ah wouldn't."

The Toliver family had reached a comfortable arrangement. Marc took the new rules as good news and was delighted with the relaxation. Jamie and her father reminded him of his responsibilities: to drive safely, treat Jamie with respect, and observe her dating restrictions. Frances Toliver made his thoughts known the first time Marc was invited into the Toliver home. Everyone was on board with a new social contract.

"He said what to you?"

"That I had to slow down. My car was carrying his little girl and he wanted her safe."

"Those are his actual words? Please!"

"Yep, close, He used some of those exact words."

"Boy, that's something," Will shook his head, seemed to disapprove, and went silent.

"It's not as bad as it sounds. Her father and mother are nice. I like them. Jamie and I are enjoying ourselves. They are just silly rules. At least we can date and have some fun. I'm good with what he said. It's okay," defensive words from Marc.

"Ok, if it doesn't bother you, I guess it's okay with me. At least you get more than a good night kiss."

"What's that mean? Don't you?"

"Well, we kiss goodnight most nights at the door, but that's it. You know Niki. She's great fun, not a real lover."

"Oh, yeah, I know Niki. That's just her way, Jamie is not much different. We kiss and hug some, maybe more than once, however that's the end. That's okay with me. We've been having a good time. I really like her."

"Good for you, hey are you going to Niki's tonight? Do you know what time it starts?" Will was dribbling away; Marc could hardly hear him with all the noise in the gym.

"What?"

"Niki's—when are you going to show up?" "SWISH" went the net. Will was on a hot streak.

Marc rebounded the ball, passed it back out. Another "SWISH" of the net. "About eight. I think that's when the party starts, that is, unless Jamie's going to help Niki set-up, get ready." "SWISH" "Boy you're on today!" Marc complemented Will's shooting prowess.

"That's me, always 'hot handed'."

"Aye, except on game day!" Marc kept the ball to take his own shot and made a funny face.

"Should we put the chips and stuff out now or wait? Don't want them to get stale."

"Chips don't get stale that fast. Empty one bag, keep the other two closed. Keep them at the end of the table by that big bag of cups."

"Uh-huh," Amanda answered Niki. She and Jamie had come over early to help get Niki's family game room ready for about two dozen friends, the Saturday night party pack.

Jamie was upstairs in the kitchen helping Mrs. Stewart prepare some hot snacks, hot dogs, Swedish meat balls with tooth picks in each, small bun things and warm cocoa. The pop and juice were already down stairs in an old steel wash tub filled with ice. Decorations were limited to a few balloons, hanging tissue balls, crepe paper, festive table cloths, and napkins all red, white or black Weir High colors. A record player, along with stacks of forty-five RPM records, filled one corner of the room and a few more chairs than usual had been placed around. The old pool table was ready; everyone always wanted to play pool, both guys and gals. These low key shindigs were vibrant and merry, everyone relaxed, just enjoying being with friends. Spirits would be high; being together was all the entertainment needed.

Well bless my soul, rock and roll, flyin' purple people eater. Pigeon toed, undergrowed, flyin' purple people eater. I like short shorts... By Sheb Wooley was ending.

"That's a stupid song. Really dumb. Why do people play it?"

"Just to feel good, to feel stupid, you do that sometime," Jamie noted.

With a wry smile, Marc answered, "Well, maybe some times. You're right, sometimes."

"Let's dance, then Ah have to go home. You know curfew is ten thirty tonight."

"Ten thirty, I know. This song is right on target."

Why must I meet you in a secret rendezvous?...Wish we didn't have to be afraid to show the world that we're in love...Till we have the right to kiss openly we'll just have to be content to be in love secretly... By Jimmie Rogers

As the song ended Marc kissed her quickly, "That song tells our story: kissing secretly."

"Don't be silly. People 've seen us kiss. Even my parents 've seen us kiss."

"They have not."

"Don't you think they look out the window when we are sitting in your car or when we stand at the front door for five minutes saying goodnight."

"Ah, well, maybe. I had hoped not," Marc expressed concern.

"Come on, we need to say good night n thank Niki n her mother for having the bash."

The car came to a stop and they both exited holding hands walking to the front door. "Do you think they are watching tonight?"

"If they are, then you don't want a good night kiss?"

"Yes I do," He leaned in and kissed her quickly and ran back to his car.

"Remember, tomorrow there is a youth meeting at church in the evening. You need to bring something to eat with chili."

Marc climbed into the big wide front seat, sat for a minute. *Nice night,* he thought, *Chili, what do you eat with Chili? Bread?*

"I have to say, that turkey was delicious. Everything was delicious. The bird was very moist, tender, tasty. Thanks to everyone," Sidney Floreau wiped his lips with a napkin. He sat back, gazed around the table, "You outdid yourself this year," his compliments continued as he reached out for his half-filled glass of wine and finished it.

"You have my vote. Yes sir, that was the best in years," Uncle Len chimed in, gave his wife Kar, short for Karen, a thumbs-up.

The two sisters, Beth Floreau and Karen Bouchard, had prepared a multi-course Thanksgiving meal for both families. They had a twenty-two pound turkey with all the family favorites: mashed potatoes, sweet potatoes, stuffing, gravy, bacon topped green beans, squash, cranberry sauce, two different dinner rolls, and of course, for dessert a couple of pumpkin pies, and even a coconut cream pie, Sidney's favorite. The dishes covered the Floreau's extended dining room table. The two closely knit families totaled eleven when you included Sara's, the oldest Bouchard daughter, fiancé, John. They would be married next summer.

"Does anyone want something else, a second piece of pie, maybe just a small one?" Kar asked sheepishly.

"Are you kidding," responded Len. "Sid and I have to go to work in another hour. We will already fall asleep on the bus, maybe even on the job."

"Not at work, please! Sleeping while standing at that rolling mill would send me to my final resting place."

"No one is talking about a final resting place, you'll have another piece of pie in your lunch buckets," Beth made a chilly response as she started to clear the table.

"Let the girls do that. I have something we need to talk about with Marc."

"With me, what about?" Marc began to feel some impending dread.

"You are never home or at the dinner table, so this is a good time to talk. Your senior year is half over and graduation will be here quickly. What happens after graduation? Do you go to college, or what choices are you thinking about?"

"Oh boy, here it comes, another one of those Uncle Sid discussions," Sara speculated.

"Well, that's a good question for your sister, too," uttered Sara's father, "Molly will be graduating at the same time, and she, also, has to set some goals for herself. All we ever hear about is cheerleading and dancing at the studio. It's time for her to plan for being a high school graduate, also."

Molly Bouchard sat stoically across from her dad. She said nothing, just looked at him and her mother.

"Marc, what do you plan to do?" Beth joined in.

"Well," he hesitated, "I haven't made any real plans, Mom. Graduation is a long way away. I have my senior year to finish, and then I can do something. I don't know what, yet. I am busy with school, and basketball is starting. I don't have the time to think about it, now."

"Now is the time, son." Sidney jumped back in wanting to pursue the issue. "If you're just going to stay in Weirton, I guess there is not much to think about. But your mother and I hoped you would be thinking about something other than just staying home. That's good for only a year or so. Eventually you have to go out on your own."

"Well, not right away. He can stay for a while," Beth set Sid straight.

"I know not right away, but at some time he will want to be on his own. If he stays in Weirton, he can live here as long as he wants to. There will come a time when he finds that he needs his own place."

"Yes, but not right away, dear. Not right away."

"Of course, of course. Your mother is right. Regardless of what we say or do, graduation will come, so will summer, and so will life after this summer. I'm just saying, planning ahead might be helpful," Marc's dad made his point.

"I don't know, Dad. Do we have to talk about it today? It's Thanksgiving."

"We have to discuss it sooner or later. As May approaches, you should have some ideas, some plans."

"Well, I do … somewhat. Maybe the army. A couple of the other guys are thinking about the army, maybe I will, too."

Uncle Len hypothesized, "the army could be good. You might find yourself there. It could get you started on a career. Teach you to do something."

"Yeah, that's what I was thinking; there's no war. I could learn a trade in the army, even the navy, and then come back to the valley after the service."

"I thought Marc was in the college prep classes at school?" Aunt Kar asked.

"I am, yes, I am, but I'm not interested in more school, or any of that kind of thing. I want to do something, not take more classes with books, that's not me, it's not…"

"You don't have any books now, what would…" Molly exclaimed!

"What does that mean, what is the 'no books' comment about?" Sidney Floreau's antennae's picked up something as he stopped Molly in mid-sentence.

"Nothing Uncle Sid, nothing, I should have kept my mouth shut," Molly could feel Marc's glare boring into her.

"Molly, we haven't heard your ideas yet. What do you want to do after graduation?" Her mother was changing the subject.

"Mom, you know I am staying around Weirton, living at home, getting some kind of a job and marrying Freddy soon."

"Oh are you? There's that Freddy talk again. You need to rethink that move dear," Uncle Len snapped at his seventeen year old daughter.

Sid stood, "Sorry I started this discussion. I need to change and get ready for work." Looking directly at Marc, he added, "We will have this conversation again—soon!" His comments finished, he walked away from the table.

"This has been a great day," Jamie exclaimed as she and Marc took seats at the opposite ends of the Toliver living room couch. "Thanksgiving dinner was the tops. Food, food, food. We had everything. Turkey is delicious, never had a real big turkey in England, we've these small, little birdy things call Hens. Most English hens are wild, n've a coarse taste. My grandpa always described the taste as bitter. Turkey is delectable, almost sweet, very yummy, especially the dark meat." Jamie went on for another five minutes describing the entire meal, from a crackers and cheese treat, to the pumpkin pie with whipped cream. She loved it all.

"You really enjoyed the food. Ours was great, too, but it's great every year. Wow, you had an enjoyable experience today. A new holiday for you, you are really funny. I have never heard someone talk so much about eating. Did you try everything?"

"Right, everything, delicious. You want some pie?"

"No, no, we had pie, still have a whole pie at home, no more pie for me."

The Toliver's had celebrated their first Thanksgiving. They had invited the Branden's, their adopted American Uncle Gus, Aunt Marietta and their two young boys to join them for Thanksgiving dinner. Jamie and her mother cooked the turkey, made the potatoes, beans and the hors d'oeuvres. Aunt Marietta brought all the other dishes. The two families had a festive meal and were still enjoying the day.

Harry had taken the boys up to his room after dinner, now they were running back and forth across the ceiling. Jamie had already tried to get them to quiet down, so far unsuccessfully. The adults were playing cards at the recently cleared dining room table. From all the discussion about bidding, taking tricks and setting the opponent, the game was probably

Bridge. Marc had just arrived and their only opportunity to be alone was the living room couch.

"How was your Thanksgiving dinner? You're always talking about your Mum's great cooking"

It was obvious that she hadn't been listening before when he had answered this question. "It was fine. She and my aunt had a great meal. My dad really liked the turkey. It was some new brand of turkey, 'Sugar Baked' or 'Butter Baked' or something like that. It was very good and big, too."

"Thanksgiving is a fun holiday, all this great food. Nothing to do but cook n eat. The turkey is called a 'Butter Ball;' we had one too. Mum says we will've one for Christmas. We also watched the parade on TV and some football. Well, I really didn't watch the football. Ah saw the parade from New York City, wish Ah could 've been there n seen the big balloons, especially in color."

"Butter Ball! That's the one! While we were eating, I was remembering that last year at that time we were playing in the state championship game. Sad not to be doing that today. But, that was last year."

"Right, that was last year. Other things are happening; you n Ah are happening this year," Jamie smiled brightly, moved an inch closer, and entwined her fingers in his.

"Other things are happening. We had a very funny conversation after dinner today, not 'ha ha' funny, but kind of testy, almost an argument."

"What do you mean?"

Marc's face turned serious, he looked towards the dining room to make certain no one was listening as he took hold of her hand. "Well, my dad had one of his 'let's talk moments,' and the discussion became very stressful, at least for me."

"About what? Ah 've met your Da n he doesn't seem to be stressful."

"Usually he isn't. He is strict, and he doesn't laugh much, but today he was very serious."

"About what? Tell me what it was about."

"He wanted to know what my plans were for after high school."

"What did you say? What was the answer?"

"I don't have an answer. I don't know. You know what you want, college. So do most of the others, but not me."

"You don't want to go to college? Why?"

"It's not for me. I want to, but, well, I just don't know what I want to or what I can do. I'm not smart like you, Niki, or Sage. I'm just me. What about you and me?"

"What about you n me?" Jamie asked pointedly.

"I don't know, I've been thinking maybe, well you know, maybe we'll want to be together after school."

Chapter 8

Future

"You need to keep the ball moving; find that open man. The ball has to move faster than the defense can move. Okay, try it again. Marc, you have to set the pace. Move the ball quickly. Sharp passes, crisp, quick. Try it again."

The Community Center gym was filled with nearly forty candidates involved in the final practice before the varsity and junior varsity teams were picked. Coach Warren would coach the varsity; Coach Romeo, the JV. The season would start at the end of the week so practice needed to become concentrated on game situations. More emphasis was needed for the fifteen or twenty players who would be counted on to be the major contributors. The coaches did not like cutting anyone, so everyone could stay and practice. However, only select players would dress for the games. So, the outcome of today's practice was important. Some would be happy, some sad.

Marc, Will, Ronnie and a few others had been through this final selection ordeal over the last few years. As starters in their junior year, now as seniors, their roster positions were set. They would be the core of this year's team. They were looking forward to a strong season. Basketball had a different atmosphere than football. There were only a few players; they were unmasked, visible to the proximity of the fans. Good or poor, play was seen by all and fans identified with a specific player. Each player had his personal score for each game. To win, you had to perform as a team.

Marc enjoyed basketball more than any other sport. Finally, the season was about to start.

As the whistle blew, the players gathered around the coaches in the middle of the gym. The few that had participated in the final drill were breathing hard and paced around to cool down. Coach Warren thanked everyone for trying out for the team and congratulated them for their efforts. He encouraged those who were not selected for the two teams to continue to attend practices because they may improve to a point of being added to one of the squads; someone might quit or get hurt and a spot could open up. He reminded those who were selected that nothing was permanent and they would need to continue to play well and improve. He told the mid-court gathering that the roster selections would be posted the next day in the locker room. With that, practice ended. Coach then called six or seven names to sit in the bleachers. Marc, Will and Ronnie were part of that group.

"You are the core of this year's team. You have all played for me last year or in some other sport. You know what to expect from me and Coach Romeo. We will be fair but demanding. We expect you to give your all at practice and in the game. We expect you to be competitive in wanting to win, but most importantly, to show sportsmanship, win or lose. Co-captains will be Willy, Ronnie, and Marc. If the officials need to talk with a captain and all three of you are on the court, Ronnie, you are the spokesman. Do you understand that arrangement?" Coach looked at the three.

"Yes, yes Sir," were their responses.

"Good, any questions?"

No one spoke up. They were dismissed.

As the group jogged to the locker room, Ronnie grudgingly said, "Boy, Coach seemed a little up-tight."

"He sure did. His face was tense and his voice very, very mad or stern would be better," Will chimed in. "He even called me Willy, he never does that."

"I didn't see anything at practice that upset him," Ronnie observed. "We had a good practice. Everyone seemed to work hard, even some of the drop-outs."

As they pushed into the locker room, Marc stopped and looked at Will and Ronnie. "Coach was upset because he has to choose the final roster. He doesn't like to reduce the number, even if they can still practice. He likes to keep everyone who wants to play. It bothers him to cut someone, or even tell him he is not going to dress for the games. At least in football everyone can dress and sit on the bench. But, not in basketball."

"Never thought about that," Will replied. "Never even considered how he felt."

"As leaders, he was trying to tell us that we need to be grateful of our opportunity to play, and that we will need to lead," Marc finished and went off to his locker.

"When is he going to go?"

"In a fortnight, or maybe earlier, once everything is sorted out. He will be flying over, so it will not be the long trip like it was for us. Once he leaves, he will be there in a day."

"Fancy that. Wish Ah could go. It would really be fun to see everyone in Birmmie. Ah could see the whole clan you know. Suppose Da would let me fly over with him?"

"You 've school, Ah need you here with me n your brother. Your dad has business there, that's why he is going. It is business, not a holiday."

"Ah know, but Ah so want to see everyone n tell them all about America, n our new home, tell them about all we've seen, my new clothes, my new friends, the car we 've, tell them everything."

"Well, not this time," she paused … Ah guess Ah should tell you that your father n Ah 've spoken about you, Harry n me going to England in the summer n maybe staying for a long holiday."

"Oh, oh Mum, can we, can we really go back? A long visit would be great! It would be brilliant. That would be aces!"

"Well, it is only a maybe. It is very expensive for all of us to go. It is something we will need to chat up with your dad."

"Ah will, Ah will. Ah'll talk to him every day about going."

"Now, don't go bloody bonkers about it. We'll just need to keep it on his mind."

"Right, Ah understand, right."

"Another thing," Jamie's mother had held this back because it was not a sure thing. "Your father is going to try n bring the Grannies Tolivers back with him to spend the holidays."

Jamie's face brightened like a candle's flame. Her mouth opened wide, her head turned back and forth like it was on a ninety degree swivel. "Oh my, fancy that! That will be … it will be just so wonderful."

"Calm down. It is only maybe. Your father will talk to them over there, so nothing is set for certain. It would be a very dear expense for them to come."

"Oh, Ah just know they will, Ah know they will," Jamie's excitement was over-flowing.

Mother and daughter continued the conversation about what the grannies' visit would be like while preparing dinner in their "so very modern" American kitchen that would be such a delight for granny to see. Frances Tolliver would be home from work soon completely unaware that he would be bombarded with questions the second he opened the door. Harry was upstairs in his room so he would hear about all of this at dinner. It would be an exciting evening at the Toliver's.

She was running at nearly full speed when she came into the side door of the auditorium. The aisle was crowded so she zig-zagged her way to the back and towards the corner bunch. Jamie slithered past the broken seat, plopped herself down next to Marc and took a deep breath. She was drained from her long run to lunch, Marc and her friends.

"Slow down. You're all wiped out. What are you running from?" Marc tried to calm her.

She struggled to catch her breath and blurted out, "My granny and grandpa are coming to visit, or we think so," she panted, gasping for more oxygen. "We don't know for sure as yet, but my Da is going to bring them back with him."

"Slow down. Talk slowly so I can keep up. Your grandmother or father is going to what?"

She sat back, gulped more air, took her time and explained, "My father is going back to England in a couple of days. He has some business over there, in Birmingham where we are from. That's where we live, or did live."

"Yes, I know you're from England and Birmingham. Slowly!" Marc lectured.

"Right, Ah know you know. Let me tell you."

"Okay, okay, tell me."

"Marc, shut up. Let her talk," Niki butted in. Marc held up his arms indicating he was through.

"Well, the Company is sending my Da back to Birmingham. While he is there, he will see all of our family which will be brilliant for him. He is going to ask my Grannies Toliver to come here for Christmas. Ah haven't seen them for almost a year, or really about nine months ago. Won't that be wonderful? Ah can't wait!"

"When will they be here?" someone sitting behind her asked her.

"Ah don't know. We are not even sure they will come or even can come because of the sterling."

"She means money, sterling is money," Marc clarified.

"They know its money. Let me finish. We just don't know if they can come, but Ah do hope so, it would be so brilliant. Ah miss them so much."

Jamie and the gals around her kept up their lively conversation about grandparents, lost friends, Christmas gifts, holiday food and more. The guys just sat, ate their lunch, tried to interrupt when they got a chance, but ended up just waiting until the end of lunch bell. As it rang, the group in the secluded corner disbanded.

Marc and Jamie walked out of the theater setting holding hands, "I'll call you tonight, okay?"

"Yeah, okay, about eight."

"You are really excited about your grandparents visiting."

"Right, Ah am. It will be so wonderful to see them."

"I am glad for you. Talk to you about eight." They took a long look at each other and went in different directions.

"You will be with Niki for the game tomorrow?"

"Yes, we are going to take the bus. My first basketball game! Another first."

"It is exciting, a new season. You will really like basketball. It's fast, constant action, a lot of yelling, just what you enjoy."

"Niki says it is fun n we get to see all you boys running around in little shorts."

"They are just like swimming trunks. There is nothing sexy or cute about them."

Jamie giggled, "Alright, Ah'll see you tomorrow." She knew she had caught him off guard.

"You'll see. What about your grandparents? Are they really coming?"

"We don't know yet. We are hoping they will come back with my Da. Ah'm really excited. My granny is almost my best friend. Ah spent a lot of time with her during my summers. They live in a small town about an hour from Birmmie. It is really a farm, but my grandpa works as a post deliverer. He does some small farming with sheep, a couple of cows n chickens. But, Ah don't think you would like their home."

"Why would you say that? I love animals; we have two dogs."

"Well, that isn't the point. They don't 've electricity or… inside plumbing."

"What? That's not true. You're kidding me!" Marc exclaimed.

"It's true, no electricity or water, that is, except a hand pump n a well."

"Wow, that's terrible. No, I would not want to live there, visit perhaps, but not have to stay there."

"It is difficult sometimes. There is electricity in the town now n they are about to get it in their house. Also plumbing is being put in. Maybe it has already happened."

"At least you have grandparents. I never knew any of mine. They were dead before I was born. One granddad was still alive I guess, but he died when I was just a baby so I never knew him."

"That is so sad. Grandparents are great. They tell all kinds of stories about England before the war n during it. They were all a part of the Home Guard."

"Really? I hope they can come here. I will look forward to meeting them and catching some of those stories," Marc sounded wistful.

"Me, too. Ah've to go now. See you tomorrow at lunch, goodnight."

"Yeah, goodnight," he said as her phone clicked.

"That was fun, much more so than football. Everything is inside, nice n warm. You run a lot and the ball moves so quickly. Ah was not sure what was happening."

"It is a fast game and we do run all the time. Good feeling to win the first game. Winning is always a good feeling...Was everyone happy with a win?"

"Well, the cheerleaders were happy. Everyone was yelling so much it was hard to talk during the game. America is full of excitement n fun. Ah really enjoy everything n now basketball."

"It's my favorite sport, the best of all of them. I like the action."

Marc and Jamie were getting close to Jamie's house. The game against Wheeling Central Catholic was on a school night, so everyone was headed home early after only a few dances in the teen room.

Marc pulled into the driveway and turned the car off. They sat for a few minutes and kissed. Jamie sat back, smiled, "Well, Ah need to go in. Tomorrow is the day my father flies to England and then we will know if the grannies will be coming. Ah really 've to go … goodnight." She opened the passenger door and leaped out and ran to the front door.

"Goodnight, see you tomorrow at school," Marc yelled. Well, he thought, no walk to the front door or even a last kiss. Nevertheless, he smiled, started his coupe and was on his way home.

WEIR blared the *Bobby Freeman hit*: *Do you want to dance and hold my hand, tell me baby I'm your lover man…under the moonlight. Hold me baby all through the night…*

"What college are you visiting this week?"

"My father and I are going to Kent, The University."

"Where is that?"

"Kent, Ohio, near Akron. It's a state school with about 10,000 students," Ronnie answered.

"Damn, how many schools have you gone to? You seem to be going someplace every weekend," Marc continued to pursue the issue.

"Well, I've seen two schools already. Kent State will be the third."

"You ready to make a choice?"

"Not yet, all these schools want me to play football. I'm not sure I want to. I really want to play basketball and baseball in college. I would have to play end or someplace on defense. I don't want to do that, so I'm not sure any if these three schools are right for me."

"Boy, I wish some school was asking me to play any sport for them, but not one college has said anything to me. You, Will and Carl, maybe even Sage, have all kinds of recruiters calling you, but not me."

"Well, you keep saying you don't want to go to college!" snapped Ronnie. "Why would they be calling you if you don't want to go to college?"

"Well, I don't, but maybe I would if someone asked me. They could ask, couldn't they?"

"It doesn't work that way. You have to show an interest. You need to tell Coach Warren you're interested so he can give your name to the recruiters. You have to initiate this yourself!"

"I still don't want to go to college. I'll be happy staying here, in Weirton, working—getting a new car, settling down."

"Settling down!" Ronnie exploded. "Who are you going to settle down with? Jamie? She is going to go to college. You know that."

"Well maybe, but maybe not. She's interested in college and probably would be able to get into whatever college she chooses. But she is also not sure about going to an American school. She might decide to go back to England or not go to college at all."

"And her uncertainty is what you are basing your decision on? That doesn't seem very logical," Ronnie ventured. He turned his head towards the bus window. It was starting to get dark and the countryside was an overcast gray. He could see houses silhouetted against the foothills with barns scattered close by. The sun was setting and would be gone during the next hour bringing an early evening winter night.

They sat quietly for a few minutes. Ronnie turned back, "You should talk to Coach. He could help you. He knows how this recruiting thing works. He could set you on the right course…help you decide to consider going to college."

"I… I am," Marc floundered, searching for the words. "It's easy for you. You have the grades and have been all state in two sports as a junior.

My grades are terrible. My Dad has been mad at me for the last two years because of my grades."

"Grades are important, but first you have to let the schools know you are interested in going to college. You have to talk with Coach Warren so he can help."

"Yeah, maybe, but I can't see myself in college. Going to all those classes and studying. I never study, not even in the library."

"Suit yourself Marc, but do yourself a favor and rethink everything you have just said," Ronnie ended the discussion.

Sitting quietly for a few minutes, Marc jumped to another subject, "You're not going to play tonight?"

"No, this shoulder is sore again. Doc and Coach want me to sit out the next couple games and rest it until after Christmas. I got knocked down a couple of times in the Madonna game and bruised that muscle again."

"Ouch! We will need you tonight. They have a big guy in the middle."

"I heard Coach say he was going to use you underneath and replace you at guard."

"What, again? That's what he did last year a couple of times. I hate that. I'm a guard. I want to control the ball, control the action."

"That's what he told Coach Romeo last night at the end of practice."

"Well, he never said a word to me," Marc was upset with this new revelation. "I'm only six feet-one maybe six feet-two if I stand on my toes. Everyone inside is bigger than I am."

"You play big inside. You block out, rebound well, and you're our best defensive guy."

"But I'm not an inside guy. That's my problem. I get stuck playing every position and not enough time playing my position. How is a college going to know how good I am at guard if I have to play center every time you get hurt."

"Hey, don't get mad at me. Talk with Coach; maybe that's not what he is planning."

"Well, you know it is and so do I. That's what he did last time even when we had a couple of big guys on the bench."

Ronnie just turned and looked out the window again as the bus went through the streets of Little Washington, Pennsylvania on their way to

Morgantown, West Virginia and their third game of the season. Marc shriveled down into the hard bench seat and fumed alone.

The parade route was lined with Weirton families, in various scatterings of folding webbed chairs. All the scouts were marching by: Boy Scouts, Girl Scouts and Brownies and Cub scouts waving to their families as they passed. Their numbers were large, at least a hundred marchers and their leaders. Behind them came fire trucks, yellow and white, but the red trucks with whirring sirens were the ones that attracted the youngsters.

The parade this last weekend before Christmas had been passing by Jamie, Harry, two of his friends and Marc for forty-five minutes. Most of the parade units had been groups of military veterans, various churches, lodges, police units, dance schools, youth groups, but had also included specialized horse riding ensembles and even a group of trained dogs. So far three bands had performed; two from local high schools and the Weirton Steel Company band. Then, of course, there were the politicians riding on the back of a convertible in the twenty five degree weather.

Harry and his friends loved it when the public service vehicles went by as they threw candy to the crowd, and the boys raced into the street to gather as much as they could. Jamie and Marc were sitting on a high brick fence surrounding a funeral home watching the procession, laughing, yelling a little and just plain enjoying the very chilly winter morning.

"Ah'm glad my grannies didn't come with us, this cold n all this commotion would've been too much for them."

"What do they say about America so far?"

"Not much, they 've only been in the states for about five days n at our house for only two n are still taking it all in. They love our home, can't believe how big n beautiful it is with all the modern things, new furniture n such. It is just wonderful to be with them. It had been way too long."

"What did they say about flying across the ocean, what about New York City?"

"All they said about flying was that it was a very long time to sit in one place n that it was very loud on the plane. They didn't really see much of New York, but were glad to spend almost two days there resting after their long flight."

"Boy! If I were in New York City, I wouldn't be sleeping."

"But, you're not sixty or maybe seventy years old; Ah forget. My mother's parents, my other grannies, are in their seventies n just can't make the trip, they 've health problems n also can't afford it."

Just then, Marc could hear more band music and started to see the flag bearers leading the procession in the front row of the Weirton High band. Behind the band, he could see another big red fire truck, probably with Santa Claus sitting high on the back of the big ladder as was usually the case. The band was playing Christmas tunes and the closer they came, the louder the music. Conversation died away, and Harry and all his friends began jumping up and down cheering and waving as the band marched by, followed by the long awaited Santa.

"That was great, just brilliant," a rosy, cheeked Harry roared over the last of the music. He and his friends rushed into the street to follow Santa and search for any unclaimed candy.

Jamie added her own assessment, "That was really great, not as good as the parade on the telly, no big floats or balloons, but still lots of fun."

"But cold, I'm freezing. Can I drive you home? Let's get out of the cold. It's starting to snow. You'll have a long wait for the bus and that Marland Heights bus will be packed."

"Well, maybe. My parents told me to catch the bus, but they didn't know you would be here. Yes, where is your car? It is cold and it will be faster riding with you."

"I parked behind the Community Center. Come on boys, let's run," he shouted at the three young boys who were cramming candy into their pockets as well as their mouths. Marc pointed the direction, and it felt good to race each other for the car. Harry and his friends jumped in the back of the coupe. Jamie slid in the passenger side, sliding over a bit to be nearer Marc. He started the car and *Bing Crosby's* voice crooned, *I'm dreaming of a White Christmas, just like the one's I...* "Just give the car a few seconds to warm up, then I'll put the heater on."

May your days be merry and bright, and may all your Christmases be white...

"What are you going to do on Christmas day?' Marc asked as he inched the car forward into what was now a steady snowfall.

"Ah'm going to 've to spend Christmas Day with my parents n grandparents. It's a family day for us n we need to be together."

"Me, too. My family always has all the relatives over. They come in and out all day long and everyone eats and eats. My mother cooks for days before Christmas so she has tons on the table."

"Sounds like fun," Jamie chimed in. "We'll 've lots of food too, but probably not as much as your mum."

"Hey, why don't we get together the day after. That's the day we visit my aunts' homes. All the aunts demand, and I mean demand, that everyone comes to their homes as well. They even have more food than my mom," Marc ventured a smile.

Jamie, laughed, "That might work. It is Boxing Day for us, but with no family here … I'll ask my mum."

"Right on, that's a good idea. Ask your mum." Then Marc went quiet and softly said, "I have a present for you and I'll give it to you then."

"Brilliant, Ah've one for you, too."

They both smiled and Jamie laid her hand on his arm. Marc tried to concentrate on the snow covered roads as they neared Jamie's house. "Hope I don't have to put chains on. I hate to fuss with chains."

"What are you talking about, what are chains?"

"Oh, they are a bunch of steel chains that go around the tires so the tire can get some traction in the snow."

"Whoa, Ah never heard of anything like them. Where do you get them?"

"We keep them in the back of the car, in the trunk," Marc explained as he pulled into the driveway worried about the snow that seemed to be piling up faster by the minute.

"We will follow my mother and sisters to my Aunt Mimi's. There will be most of my cousins and other relatives there, great food—more than you and I could eat in a month."

"Excellent," Jamie paused, "Ah'm anxious, so stay close to me."

"I always do, don't I?"

Jamie smiled and moved closer to him in the front of the black Chrysler. The last storm had piled six or more inches of snow on the ground, but Marc's driveway was clear and dry, as were the roads. It had been a white Christmas, perfect for Jamie's first Christmas in this booming steel mill town. She and Marc had exchanged presents just an hour before at Marc's home, and now they were going to meet his extended family who mostly lived on Marland Heights. This was a part of Marc's family holiday ritual: round robin visits to family. Tomorrow, Marc would have dinner at the Toliver's, meet Jamie's grandparents, see their gifts, and enjoy a piece of an English holiday.

"My Granny is finally feeling comfortable with being here. The trip was hard. She had never been away from the Midlands n lived all her life in two little towns close to Birmingham. Now, she has been to London, been on a cross country train ride, been in a plane flying across the Atlantic, been in New York City, n now is staying in the middle of the United States. She keeps saying 'so much to see; such a big land.' She is so sweet, everything is new to her. She is surprised by the telly n all the shows."

"What about your grandpa? How does he see America? Does he say anything? You never mention him."

"He is very quiet. He does say that Weirton looks like an English mill town. My father agrees; although, they both think people here in the U.S. live better. You ve much more than the English people, Ah agree."

"Well, we have a reasonably good life. I want more in my future, but we have many things." Marc had driven about half way to Aunt Mimi's and he wondered how Jamie would react to the clamor and boisterousness of his relatives.

"My mother is missing her family, especially her mum. She is planning for Harry n me to go home with her next summer."

"When would you go?"

"Ah think right after graduation; probably stay for a month or longer."

"Gee, in the summer? I thought you and I would spend the summer having fun, at the pool, go to some lakes and amusement parks. It was going to be our summer."

"It still can be. Ah'll be here for part of it, until Ah leave for university."

"That's what I mean. You will be gone most of the summer; you will just come home and then have to head right off to school. I'll be here all by myself."

"No you won't. Everyone will be here."

"But not you, not you!" Marc was upset and his voice expressed it.

"It's not set yet."

"Sounds like it is."

They both sat back and listened to: *I'm dreaming tonight of a place I love. Even more than I usually do…I'll be home for Christmas. You can count on me, please have snow and mistletoe and presents round the tree, sang Nat King Cole.*

"I'm sorry. I didn't mean to get upset. It's just that I was looking forward to the summer with you around," Marc apologized.

"Right, me, too. Ah'm sorry. Ah don't know what is going to happen, n summer is a long way off. So let's not get our knickers in a twist."

"Well, I guess that means we are not mad at each other, not at Christmas."

"Blimey, no!"

As they pulled into Aunt Mimi's street, it was obvious that a small family reunion was underway as cars were parked along both sides of the street. Marc's mother, his two sisters, and a few others were walking up the sidewalk towards the house. Her neighborhood, near the Marland Heights pool, consisted of small modest homes that sat above the street level. Most of the homes had holiday decorations and lights outlining their structures, although at this time of day they were unlit.

Marc and Jamie parked, walked across the street, up the front steps, and directly inside without knocking. The amazing aroma of food had greeted them even on the sidewalk and was smothering when they stepped inside the cramped home. People were everywhere. When you entered the home, you were standing in the living room and the tiny kitchen was off to the left. The living room was like a postage stamp with a silver Christmas tree with blue flashing lights, only about three feet tall, sitting on an end table in one corner. All the chairs were taken and the back hallway was filled. Marc led Jamie into the kitchen cubbyhole, introduced Jamie to Aunt Mimi; then to Aunt someone else, Uncle so and so, cousin whoever and her new husband, and so on.

"EAT, get a plate, EAT," Mimi ordered constantly. She was a robust, short statured woman in her late sixties, or maybe seventies. Her appearance had not changed in Marc's lifetime. She had a deep voice, a European accent, a vocabulary that was a mixture of Hungarian, Serbian and American, and a heart big enough to feed an entire neighborhood.

So with a large plate in hand, Jamie was taken by Marc's mother through the kitchen, explaining each food offering. Huge electric ovens of fried chicken, pigs in a blanket or cabbage rolls, Kielbasa by the pounds, roast beef and noodles, turkey and stuffing were scattered about. Along with the main courses were all the sides: potatoes, vegetables, salads, breads, rolls, and of course, pies. Everyone was walking around with overflowing plates of food. Jamie tried to take a little of everything to taste dishes she had never heard of before, and ended up having seconds of many of them. After a couple of hours at Aunt Mimi's, they moved to another cousin's home eating even more. By the time she was ready to go home, she had been given an entire apple pie to take home to the Toliver's.

"Thank you for including me today. Ah had a great time. Everyone was brilliant, and the food—it was bloody great," Jamie enthused.

"It's always fun, and I agree, the food is unbelievable. Everyone liked you."

"Now, tomorrow you are coming for dinner here. Not as much food, but good food. Plus, you'll get to meet my grannies."

"Right, I'll be here. Did you say four o'clock?"

"Yes, four."

They kissed a few times as they stood at her front door, then kissed for the last time. Jamie went in with her pie as Marc walked back to his car.

The conversation was slow at the start. Jamie's grandparents seemed a little distant until her grandfather asked about American football. He had only seen the game played on television and had compared it to rugby. Once he started with questions, it seemed as though he would never stop: "What do you talk about when you are in a huddle? Why do only some players run with the ball? Why can you only throw the ball forward?" And on and on.

Marc attempted to answer his questions; however, Grandpa Toliver's comparison was always rugby. Marc knew absolutely nothing about rugby and had never even heard about rugby until Jamie mentioned it and Harry had tried to explain the rules to him.

Just when Marc thought the conversation was over, grandpa asked about basketball. England had no such game. Grandpa Toliver had seen some American soldiers during the war play what he thought was basketball. Marc, with the help of Harry, tried to explain the game, but felt they were only partially successful. Dribbling seemed to be the most difficult concept for him to understand. He kept comparing basketball to English football or American soccer. Holding the ball or throwing it confused him.

Marc invited him to come and see one of his high school games. There was a game tomorrow in Pittsburgh, an eight team holiday tournament, to be played at the University of Pittsburgh. Well, he could not get to that game, but he would definitely be interested in seeing one and was delighted when Jamie's father offered to take him and Harry to a game early in January.

The conversation slowed, but then Jamie's granny began asking questions about food. Jamie had told them about the varieties of food offered at Aunt Mimi's and everyone was jealous, wanting to know the taste, ingredients, and nationality of the dishes. Marc had few answers. All he knew was that the menu was a combination of Hungarian, Polish, and German, actually a hodge-podge of recipes from the various nationalities represented here in Weirton.

It was a fun time for all. America seemed to be a big surprise to Jamie's grandparents. Everything seemed big and fast. There were more cars, more stores, more room in homes, more food and more activities of just about everything. In meeting more and more Americans, they found to their surprise, they liked them.

The family sat down to a very nice meal of English roast beef with some kind of an odd tasting sauce, boiled potatoes and greens of some kind. It was good, not as tasty as yesterday's smorgasbord, but good. The dessert was a jelly-like pudding, with a special name that Marc did not understand, perhaps they had said trifle? Both Jamie and Marc agreed later they would have preferred pie. The one given to Jamie had vanished quickly last night as soon as it was placed on the kitchen table.

Following dinner, Marc knew he had to go home. It had been a full day of basketball practice, life guard duty in the Community Center and now, this evening at Jamie's. The team would be leaving early tomorrow morning for the tournament. Marc said his thanks and farewells; then he and Jamie stood at the front door, for a few moments.

"You're not coming with Niki and the cheerleaders tomorrow?"

"No, Aunt Marietta is taking Mum, Granny n me shopping at the Hub. But don't worry; Ah'll see you New Year's Eve. Don't forget, we are going to the big dance at the Country Club."

"I even bought a new dark suit for it."

"Great, we will both 've new clothes. Remember, Ah'm going to wear my homecoming dress that you never saw."

"Oh, I remember, I've been thinking about it," Marc whispered. "Can I kiss you here?"

"Step outside," Jamie opened the door.

New Year's Eve was a mild, lazy evening as Mr. Toliver drove his wife, Jamie and Marc along the half mile entrance to Williams Country Club. The entire length of it was brightly lit with ornamental street lights. Large bulb Christmas lights were strung from each light to the next. As snow still covered the ground, it seemed like a wonderland. Spot lights saturated the two story pillared white colonial club house. Colorful Christmas lights outlined the entire structure, Fir trees, spotted throughout the grounds, were lit lining the two major entrances. Even the porches had Christmas bells hanging from the ceilings.

Once inside, coats and wraps were checked, as the orchestral music reached their ears. They could see the dining room tables elaborately decorated and an enormous Christmas tree reached to the ceiling in one corner of the room. The group walked around greeting those they knew, meeting some unknowns, and finally finding their assigned dinner table. This was a first for Marc. He had never been to such a high brow party. When he mentioned this to Jamie, she reminded him that this was also a first for her and her mum. Her father had attended a few such events, but even for him, this was pretentious. Nevertheless, all were relaxed as they approached the dance floor.

Marc marveled at Jamie's stunning appearance. She was beguiling, yet cute. The dress was everything she had said it would be, and she wore it gracefully. As they moved into the center of the floor, they were relieved to find they were not the only young couple there. Niki and Will appeared, along with Ronnie and Amanda. The three couples decided to form their own little group, switching a few nameplace tags so they could form their own "young people's" table.

It was a bewitching night; a night to love, to be loved and to fall in love. It was the end of a very dramatic year; one that had held many new adventures for this group of friends with the prospects of even more to come. Their lives were full of such enjoyable times, a combination of youthfulness and the awareness that a new world awaited them in the not too distant future. They would remember nineteen fifty-eight for all that had occured, their friends, their adventures, this night and the dreams they each sheltered.

With dinner over, the adults sat quietly sipping after dinner drinks or just coffee. The youth had the dance floor more to themselves, and as a result the band changed generations to some slow rock and roll mood music.

The lead vocalist began to sing an *Andy Williams* hit: *Are you sincere when you say, I love you? Are you sincere when you say I'll be true? Do you mean* every *word that my ears have heard? I'd like to know which way to go, will our love grow?*

They danced to half a dozen current love songs, and the parents joined in, filling the dance floor as the magic midnight hour approached. Everyone started to search for their New Year's hats and noise makers as the band began counting down the end of the year in five minute increments until it finally reached single seconds…ten, nine…five, four, three, two, one: cries of "Happy New Year" filled the building along with horns tooting, crackers snapping and popping sounding like fire crackers. Everyone was kissing their partners, wives, sweethearts and everyone else within reaching distance. The entire room was overcome with merriment as the band struck up *"Auld Lang Syne."*

The haunting tune was played and sung three or four times. Marc and Jamie were off to the side of the dance floor, hugging each other, pretending to dance. They faced the large picture windows that overlooked the deep, black horizon that, during daylight, encompassed the gorge of the Ohio River and distant flat land. Always a breathtaking view, tonight it was a wonderland of shadows, deep purple clusters, and silvery fog winding its way between the trees that clung to the precipice and the span of sparkling lights that twinkled far off, indicating distant societies.

"This view is enchanting and disturbing all at the same time. It makes me feel thrilled and dejected, maybe even insignificant. It is so beautiful on this night filled with magic."

"Blimey, you are a romantic," Jamie responded as she continued to lay her head on Marc's shoulder and cuddle against him as they swayed to the music.

"I wish this could last forever. This has to be the best, the best ever."

"Blimey, it surely has been."

"That is two blimey's in a row. Are you going for a record?"

She playfully punched his arm. "It's my word. Ah can say blimey n use it as much as Ah want."

They swayed more, and then separated their hold on each other.

"Blimey, Ah don't want anyone, especially my parents, to get the wrong idea about us. We should 've space between us."

"You're bloody right," Marc moved back and they laughed at each other.

Still grinning, Marc asked, "Do you understand that New Year's song, *Auld Lang Syne*? The words don't make sense to me?

"Well, Ah know it is Scottish. It meant something in the past, but Ah don't really understand either. It's just a sentimental song about better times in the past, or maybe better times in the future."

As they enjoyed the moment, Jamie's mother searched them out to let them know it was time to leave. The grannies had been home alone with Harry and now that it was past midnight, it was time for the evening to end.

After thanking her parents for such a fabulous evening, kissing Jamie one last time at the front door, Marc went out to his own car. The one o'clock in the morning drive home on the first day of the year was carefree as he sang along with just about every record on WEIR radio.

It was a new year and a new beginning; he had a very pretty, sweet, foxy girlfriend. He was in high school with his entire life ahead of him, and he was happy. Bring on nineteen fifty-nine.

Chapter 9

Setback

"Please find a seat so we can get this assembly started. Everyone to a seat please. Teachers, let's make sure everyone takes a seat." Principal Paige continued to get the Senior Class Assembly to quiet down so the program could start. For the most part, the three hundred plus class members had settled in the auditorium seats. A few stragglers were being rushed into the back rows under the balcony.

"A reminder, this is a Senior Assembly, senior class members only. If you are not a senior, you are in the wrong place." Most people looked around to see if anyone, and who, was out of place. Everyone seemed to be in the right place, so Dr. Paige continued.

"I know that this is only the second day back from Christmas holidays and as seniors you have five months left of high school, but you need to be aware of the important events that will take place over the next few months. These activities, dates, opportunities are important so that you will be ready to go from high school to the adult world." He stopped for a few moments while the words settled across the audience causing some moans and groans. Dr. Paige was a short, well dressed man who would tolerate some discontent, but very little.

"All right, that's enough. We understand your feelings, but graduation will come sooner than you think and we are preparing you for the inevitable. Now to run the program, I will turn it over to our Dean of Students, Mr. Baker. Coach, it's yours. Dean Baker stepped in from the side to the podium and began by reading the schedule, and identifying the speakers.

The assembly would last two hours and cover events that would occur over the next four months during the school hours or after. The students settled in for a rather long morning.

It seemed that everything that was on the school's mind was discussed. The topics were not those at the top of the list for most students. The presentations involved qualifications needed for graduation, number of credits, specific courses, grade averages, attendance and personal conduct. College information nights were announced where students would have the opportunity to hear about specific colleges and universities. Career information nights had been planned with local employers who would describe jobs and the employment process. Recruiters from the various military services would be on hand. Union leader visits for trade co-op programs and career testing opportunities would be held.

After all the discussions of post graduation possibilities, there were presentations of graduation dates, ceremonies, requirements, family roles, etc. This was followed by a lengthy discussion about prom, the preparations, committees, rules, post-prom events, behavior, dress codes, and finally the consequences of senior pranks and horse play.

While the mass of stone-faced youths sat silently, their fidgety movement in the dilapidated wooden seats kept up a constant hum of creaking wood and metal. At times the corrugated sound was so lusty it disturbed the speaker. Interest faded as time expanded. At last the lunch bell rang and the assembly was dismissed.

The lunch bunch moved to their isolated corner their self-appointed seats. Initially, the gathering concentrated on their lunch bags as, by this time, everyone was starved. As appetites were appeased, the group began to discuss the two hours of chatter they had just endured.

"It was way too much information for me to absorb. I got lost with all the dates and times. Hopefully, the documentation they gave us will have more details in it," Mandy Gates, one of the cheerleaders bemoaned. "I'm only interested in getting into college and going to prom… if anyone asks me," she hinted as a couple of the guys kidded her about the last comment.

"College! That is all anyone talks about. I'm tired of hearing about going to college. Go if you want to go. I'm through with school. I wanted to quit two years ago, but my parents said, 'no'," Rick Schild uttered impulsively. "I'm going to work with my father building houses. I don't need all these people to talk to, and I don't need college!"

"Hell, Rick, you're lucky. Most of us don't have a dad with his own company," a voice from a few rows down challenged.

"So what? You all have your own ideas of what you want after school. You don't need all these special days or nights to listen to someone tell you what to do."

"Oh, I don't think it's that. These nights are an opportunity to hear about options. There are lots of options out there," Ronnie turned to Rick with his two cents worth.

The conversation started to become more localized to those sitting in the immediate area. Amanda, Ronnie, Will and Niki sat in front of Marc and Jamie.

"That was a lot to digest in one long morning. I want to go to college, but the question is where?" Amanda pondered. "I don't think I would like a big school. Our size here is just about right. You can know everyone and enjoy what goes on. A small school is for me."

"I'll go anywhere that will pay my way," Will insisted.

Ronnie had a big smile, "You'll go anywhere, if someone else pays."

Will laughed, "You know me well, Ron."

"Everyone knows you," was Niki's speculation.

"I wish I knew what to do. I'm going to talk to some of these recruiters, even some of the employers, but the mill is the only good place to work. They have the best paying jobs and they do some good training, too," Marc said sheepishly. He knew that the others already had their ideas. He was still uncertain; nothing sounded good to him.

Jamie, speaking just to Marc, retorted, "You have many possibilities."

"Yeah, a lot of possibilities, but no certainties. A hitch in the service might be a certainty. I'm interested in talking to those guys when they come."

"Ah picture you someplace else, not in the Army, but someplace..."

"What's wrong with the army? I could do a lot in the Army. Maybe if I went in the regular army, I might end up at West Point."

"Maybe...it just means you n Ah will be going in different directions."

"I know. I don't want that. We need to work something out. Maybe you go to college and I go to the service and we get, well, we can be together after that."

"Blimey, that could be a bloody long time!"

"You're right, but that would be one way that we both get what we want."

"Oh sh…there's the bell, classes."

"Okay, I'll call you tonight." Marc started to end the conversation.

"Ah don't think Ah'll be home until late, something my Mum's going to do with my granny and grandpa. Better not call me tonight."

"Buzz, I'll call you tomorrow, no, see you at lunch tomorrow."

Off they went in separate directions.

"What is wrong with your car?" Marc asked.

"My dad ain't sure, something with the ignition. We got it over to the place my dad takes his car in King's Creek, so it should be fixed in the next few days," answered Will. "You don't realize how much you depend on a car until you don't have one."

"You're right. What did we do before we could drive? I used my bike a lot and rode the bus. It took all day to get to and from practice. You forget how helpless you were then," Marc proclaimed.

"Well, we certainly didn't have the freedom we have now. I had to catch the school bus home this afternoon. Boy what a drag. It was like watching Howdy Doody, all the freshmen and sophomores," Will complained.

They were headed to an unusual evening basketball practice at Dunbar gym. Dunbar had been the high school for only black students, before the West Virginia schools were integrated in nineteen fifty-five. Dunbar High School was no more. The building was now a part of an elementary school.

Cleaning and refinishing the gym floor at the Community Center meant that the varsity would be practicing during the evenings for the next few days at the Dunbar gym. Neither Marc nor Will, nor any of their white teammates, had ever been inside the Dunbar facilities. It was located on Weir Avenue, which ran behind a major part of the Weirton Steel Mill. The avenue was on a ridge midway between the main city cove and the plain of Weirton Heights. Its location made it one of the sootiest and dustiest environments in Weirton, much like Weir High School and the Municipal Stadium sitting on the other side of the mill.

They were at the top of Weirton Heights road headed down the steep five percent grade hill that transversed the heights to the valley. Marc shifted into second gear so he could control his descent speed at least past the Wheeling-Pittsburgh bus garage. It was a driving technique his dad taught him. It saved the brakes and was safer. Marc looked off to the left and watched a couple of ten ton slag trucks emptying their loads in a valley being filled with mill slag for the past eight or ten years.

"I can't believe that valley is almost full. I can remember when it was a deep forest valley. When you were in a bus going up or down, you could see almost to the bottom and the road was right on the edge of the cliff."

"Yeah, I remember. It was scary, just going up or down," Will countered.

"Now it is almost bursting. There is no valley anymore, just a lot of junk from the mill. They have already started to fill another valley between the hills in King's Creek."

"What happens when they run out of valleys?"

"I guess that's the end of the mill and the steel," was Will's half serious comment as they drove past another slag truck crawling about ten miles per hour up the sharp climb.

WEIR was playing: *"Get a Job," by the Silhouettes: Well every morning about this time, she gets me out of my bed cryin' Get a Job…Preaching and cryin' tellin' me I'm lyin' about a job that I never could find. Get a Job…* "Get a job, I already have two!" Marc shouted at the radio.

"Why do you work so much?"

"Well, I need to. I have a car and I like my freedom to do what I want to. That means my own money, and I like to work."

Will glanced over at Marc as they reached the bottom of the hill, and rounded the curve at the bus garage. "You like to work? Come on, no one likes to work."

"Well, I like to stay busy and have some place to go and something to do," Marc professed.

"You are an odd duck. You really are."

"So are you, we all are in some ways. You treat your car like you love it. You are constantly polishing it, adding chrome tail pipes, new upholstery and now you have a mechanic working on the engine. I do all my own car things, or I should say, with my dad."

"I do most of that with my dad, more so with my uncle; he is the sales manager for Di Novo's. If my college things get canned, he said he will hire me to sell used cars."

Marc looked away from the road and glanced at Will, "what college things are you talking about, do you have a scholarship?"

"Not yet, but Marshall has contacted me, invited me to their campus in a couple of weeks. It's for football."

"Gee, when did that happen?"

"Right after Christmas. Coach Baker called me and talked with my Dad and me."

They both remained quiet as they turned into Weir Avenue and climbed the hill to the top of the street. As they drove along the ridge in the fading evening light, spread before them as far as they could see, was a massive smoky structure. The mill was black, gray, filthy charcoal and slate covered with sprinkling light scattered like stars throughout the scowling scene. The only bright spots were the super heated blast furnaces that showered the darkness with sun bursts of blue, red, white hot masses with golden yellow streamers flickering about in the murky twilight.

As they moved down Weir Avenue, the continuous row of clapboard houses perched at the end of long steep stairs was almost invisible. The darkening night with the grizzled sooty gray covering made them appear to be unoccupied and dilapidated. Marc knew that both those conditions were not true. These homes sat at the crux of the mill's grimy discharge. All the cleaning, sweeping, painting and even bright lighting could not overcome the dust of the mill. They passed a few small stores, bars, car repair garages and finally pulled into the parking lot of the Dunbar gym.

As Marc edged out of the car, he directed a comment to Will, "I don't know how everyone gets schools interested in them and I get diddly-squat." Marc was obviously upset.

"Well, you don't want to go to college, do you? You keep saying no."

"No, I don't, but no college even asks."

"Because you have told the coaches that you did not want to go."

"I never told them that, hell, I don't want to go anyhow."

They walked into the gym, found the locker room and joined the others shooting around waiting for practice to start. The gym was about two-thirds the size of the Community Center floor. It was shorter and narrower, but it was in good shape. The wooden floor gleamed; the painted lines bright and the lighting bold. Each side had a group of six level portable steel bleachers. The only drawback for the gym was the size of the backboards. Rather than the usually rectangle-shaped boards, these were much smaller in a half moon shape. They were glass, but much smaller, the area to kiss the ball off the backboard into the hoop appeared tiny. This would take some getting used to. However, they would use this court only for a few practices.

Coaches Warren and Romeo appeared at the far end of the gym, blew their whistles and motioned everyone to one side of the court and told them to sit. Both men had baseball caps on, wore short sleeved sweatshirts and sweat pants. They had their stern coaches' faces on. They looked around at the twelve varsity players and the two student equipment assistants.

"Hope everyone enjoyed your few days off over Christmas and New Year's. We played very well in Pittsburgh those two games. We had a good win in the first tournament game. You beat a very sound team. You controlled the tempo and had good defense. You earned a nice victory.

The second game against Pittsburgh St. Joseph was a real education for not only you, but for Coach Romeo and me. St. Joe's is one of the top high school teams in the country and they showed all their talent. We played very well against a top team so you have nothing to be upset about. It was a good effort for a loss. That's all we ask—that you give your all.

By the way, if you didn't follow the sports news, St. Joe's won that holiday tournament by beating the Cleveland team by eighteen points. Remember, they only beat us by twenty-three points. It would have been even closer if the game ended with the third quarter. But, a game is four quarters!

I know some of you had never seen someone in high school dunk the ball. Even I had not seen anyone in high school able to do that. So, we had a treat to see five or six who could jump that high. The tournament was a good experience for us. We have five victories and one loss. Great start, great start. Now we are into the real schedule. We play at least one game a week and most weeks, two games. You will need to be in the best shape possible, especially you first seven or eight players. That means hard practices—lots of drills—lots of running. Alright, let's start with five laps," Coach Warren finished his comments and practice started with running, and would end with more running after an hour and a half of game situation drills.

As everyone left the Dunbar gym, Marc and Will returned to Marc's Chrysler. As they sank into the cushioned seats, Marc turned over the ignition and the radio spun: *"Whole lot of shaking going on," by Jerry Lee Lewis: Come on over baby, whole lot of shaking going on, Yes I said come on over baby, baby you can't go wrong. We ain't fakin—whole lot of shaking goin on…shake it, Baby shake.*

WEIR was playing: *"A Boy Like Me, A Girl Like You," by Elvis Presley: When a boy like me meets a girl like you, then I must believe wishes come true. I just look at you and I touch your hand, and this ordinary world becomes a wonderland…there are many girls I have met before…One to last a life time through…When a boy like me meets a girl like you…*

Jamie was in the middle of the front seat as Marc drove up Marland Heights hill. The rain was subsiding; but the steep climb seemed a little glassy as the run-off water was rushing down both sides of the road. The road had a shine that made it appear slippery and treacherous. Jamie could sense that Marc was very attentive to the driving conditions so she sat quietly, riveted on her own nervousness. It was an extremely haunting night with visibility limited to just the distance of the headlights. A sheer ninety degree stone slate wall rose on their left creating the notion of a black hole. It was so dark that Marc and Jamie could not see the cliff structure, but only visualize it from memory. They had been at the Community Center teen room dancing and enjoying the party atmosphere. From the basement room they did not realize that the heavy rain had turned to snow. With the change in the weather, Marc was concerned about the curvy and sheer nature of the hill. Finally, the car crept to the top of the towering drive and they both relaxed.

"Damn, that was scary. That road looked like ice. The sleet and heavy mist must be coating the headlights, everything was frosty. It gave me the willies, still does. Boy, I'm glad nothing happened. Hate to think about the trip down off this hill."

"You can stay at our house over night."

"Oh yeah, your parents are going to let me stay…maybe sleep with you?"

Jamie punched his arm, "Well, Ah won't let you in my room, now."

"I'm sure you won't. You never do."

Jamie hit him again several times. "You never even try. You're as inexperienced as Ah am."

"You hope so."

"Ah know so," Jamie snapped, hitting him again, moving closer to the passenger window.

"Okay, I'm only kidding," Marc took her hand, using just one hand on the steering wheel spinner knob navigated the coupe into her driveway. Jamie slithered back over to his side. They hugged and kissed a few more times and cuddled even more.

"You feel so nice and warm. You feel so good in my arms, "Marc whispered.

"Ah like to be in your arms," was her whisper back. In that few minutes of cuddling, the snow had enveloped the windows creating a cozy igloo effect inside. Wrapped in each other's arms, they snuggled even closer relishing their togetherness. At last, pulling apart, they exited the car, and reluctantly walked to the front door.

"Wow, this snow is getting heavy. I need to get home while I can."

"Don't you want to kiss me good night?"

"Well, you are always telling me that your parents are watching."

"If they are, so what?" Jamie put her arms around his shoulders and the kiss was long and passionate. "Ah hope they saw that one. Please be careful going home, unless you want to sleep on the floor."

"No floor for me."

"Remember tomorrow at Church, and remember the youth meeting in Charles Town or wherever we are going."

Marc returned to his car, scraped the snow from the windows before entering. *Wonder what this all means,* he thought. *That youth meeting is in Chester. Jamie doesn't always get things right.*

They climbed out of the black coupe, two from the front seat, four from the back, unwinding their cramped legs, arms and bodies. The back seat was very comfortable for three, but for four, not so much.

"I told you we should have taken two cars," Will complained.

"Oh, you enjoyed my sitting on your lap. Don't make a big deal about it. You will want me back on your lap again on the way home," Niki cut him short. Ronnie and Amanda were the last to twist around the back of the front seat and out the door. Finally they were standing straight, Ronnie stretching his six foot-four frame. "Someone has to sit up front on the way back," was his only comment.

"Come on, we are late and need to go in," Niki took charge, leading the way up the steps into the Chester Presbyterian Church. The sanctuary was filled with youth from all over the West Virginia panhandle. It was a somber group, sitting like church mice; the sanctuary small, the décor centered around chestnut oak pews, lighting was dingy and bronzed etched glass windows allowed only a muddy-type of sunshine to pervade the room.

The girls took their covered dish offerings to the basement kitchen. The guys located enough seats down in the front. The three girls returned just seconds before the service was to start, laughing about something. That caught a scorned glance from their minister, Reverend Ness.

With the final amen at the end of the worship service, the packed house started towards the basement stairway where the food awaited. The Weirton bunch sent Will ahead through the crowd to find them an isolated table. He was successful in converting a set table for eight in a distant corner into a roomier table for the six of them. After their cramped ride and the elongated service, everyone was anxious to eat, and eat they did. As usual, with such an event, the home cooked food was plentiful and delicious. Reverend Ness sitting at a neighboring table kept glancing over to check the decorum of his young parishioners. So far, all was well.

"Would you get me some more chicken and mashed potatoes?" Ronnie asked stretching his plate towards Amanda.

"I thought you injured your arm and shoulder, not your legs," was Will's quick quip.

"Oh, the poor boy is hungry. Of course, dear, anything else I can get you? Don't answer that!" Amanda responded playfully and dramatically, "Your wish is my command." She took the outstretched plate and slithered through the closely placed tables toward the food tables.

"Well, I am hungry," Ronnie answered the staring faces, "and my arm does hurt a little, but I do keep playing."

"Well, your arm wasn't hurting you Friday night. You did enough shooting in that game for all of us," Marc said jokingly, but also half seriously. Ronnie had scored twenty seven points against Wheeling, the most points for anyone this entire season.

Will quipped, "Ron did everything on Friday, except pass the ball," He and Marc laughed loud enough that everyone in the dining room turned to look at them.

The reply was a whispered mumble, "Go to Hell."

They laughed even louder when Niki scolded them with, "Will you three grow up? This is a church, you know. You can't go to Hell from here." Unfortunately, she said it loud enough for the surrounding tables to hear. As a consequence, Reverend Ness, who was sitting behind them said, "you can still get to hell from here, and I can arrange it."

With that whimsical comment, half the room burst out in tee-hees, some giggles and a few loud roars. A few faces were crimson and Ron tried to duck down under the table.

"What is going on here?" Amanda asked as she returned with an overflowing dinner plate for Ronnie. She had missed the short exchange and the clerical response. The table was still snickering, and it took a few minutes for composure to be restored. When they finally quieted down, everyone's attention turned to Reverend Ness's large frame and his staring deep set eyes standing over them.

"Enjoying the evening are we?"

"Yes, yes, sorry, hi Reverend Ness," were the stuttered responses from the chastised group.

"Well, enjoy yourselves, but remember this is a house of God, so don't overdo it."

"No sir, we won't," Amanda was the only one who seemed able to answer while trying to speak respectfully for her friends.

Reverend Ness turned and walked away. All six glanced around the table and then around the room, each laughing under their breath trying to gain control.

"That's enough fooling around for right now," Amanda had fallen into her good girl role.

"Easy for you to say that," was Ron's retort, "but what if Marc and Jamie decide, like they did at the Warwood Church, to go off to some janitor's room to have sex."

Jamie jumped straight up stamping both feet, and louder than she realized, burst out, "we weren't having sex! When you found us and scared us, we were just kissing!"

"Quiet, shh, hush, not so loud," her friends panicked as they reacted to her bluster. "He's joking Jamie! Relax," Niki grabbed her arm trying to settle her down. "He's joking." Again, everyone laughed, even Jamie.

Reverend Ness was again eyeing them from the far side of the room. This time his face was stern.

The constant joking, muffled giggles, and an occasional loud laugh continued throughout the evening. The six musketeers enjoyed themselves by ribbing each other. The ride back to Weirton had Ronnie in the front seat to enable him to extend his long legs, Jamie in the middle between Ron and Marc, her hip tight against Marc. Will was in the back with Amanda and Niki, his arms around both. They sang songs, told jokes; even a few raunchy ones from Will, talked about teachers, their funny parents, their classmates and just themselves. Their relationship was easy and smooth. They liked each other.

First stop was the Center parking lot so that Will and Ronnie could get their cars and take Niki and Amanda home. Jamie stayed put. Marc would take her home. The three cars left the lot, heading up Marland Heights hill.

Marc pulled into the driveway, turned off the car. They kissed softly, and then just sat back, talking about the coming week. School tomorrow, meeting for lunch, Honor Society meeting for Jamie, basketball practice for Marc, games on Tuesday and Friday nights, a college visitation trip on the weekend for Jamie, work for Marc and of course, church next Sunday. They would not see much of each other; the only sure togetherness would be after Tuesday's basketball game. However, even that might be changed because Jamie's father, Harry and her grandpa were planning to attend. They would have to wait and see how that worked out.

As they grew tired of talking, they walked to the door as was their custom, kissed again and parted. Both were tired but happy after a fun Sunday afternoon.

Marc started for home as WEIR played. *Many a tear has to fall, but it's all in the game. All in the wonderful game that we know as love... Soon he'll be there at your side with a sweet bouquet. Then he'll kiss your lips and caress your waiting fingertips. And your hearts will fly away... "It's all In the Game," by Tommy Edwards & the Four Tops.*

Only a dozen or so were in the pool as Marc sat watching in the high life guard's chair. Mary, the other life guard, was on the other side of the pool talking to someone in the visitor's balcony seating. The conversation had been going on for at least fifteen minutes; Mary was not much of a dedicated lifeguard.

It was almost seven p.m. and his double shift would soon be over. It had been a long day. Marc didn't know if he wanted to go home early, find someone to go to Donna's Hamburger's for something to eat, or go to the sock hop at the high school gym. It had been a quiet weekend with Jamie away with her parents visiting college campuses, West Virginia University today, and tomorrow Marshall University. Will and a couple other football players were also at Marshall visiting the football coach. So, Marc was on his own.

As he was getting dressed in the life guard's locker room, he decided to look into the teen room to see who might be in there. Glancing around the teen gathering area, it was obvious this was not the place to be. There were less than a dozen kids, all freshmen or at least no one he knew. He was hungry, but eating alone was not what he wanted. Surely he would find someone to join him at the sock hop.

Marc drove to the high school and it seemed like the right place to be. Had Jamie been home, they would have come together. The parking lot was full and a crowd gathered outside the front entrance even though it was an exceptionally cold night. Marc entered the school, went to the basement gym, which was darkly lit, packed with dancers, the chaperones sitting off to the side.

The sunken gym was the perfect place for an informal dance, not a good place for basketball, but an ideal place for loud rock and roll music, dim lighting, and secluded corners for romantic moments, and out of the way seating. Marc started down the steep stairs to get to the dance floor. He was stopped along the way to answer questions about Jamie and why she was not at his side. They were always together as a couple and he looked out of place without her. Finally he jumped down the final step, a double step to the wooden floor.

Scanning the congested dance area, he recognized Ronnie and Amanda. They were in a deep embrace and barely moving to the music. Behind them leaning up against the high bench that usually served as the scorer's table were a sizeable cluster of guys and girls. It was mostly the dark corner lunch gang and in the middle were Mandy, Sarah, Danielle, Darby and Niki. They seemed to be holding court and arguing about something. Marc walked over.

Marc, with a smirk, tried to be funny, "Ladies, you seem to be at each other's throats. What is wrong in paradise?"

"Nothing that we can't handle, Pinocchio," was Niki's quick come back.

"Pinocchio, why would you call me Pinocchio; I don't have a big nose. Do I?"

"No, just big ears," was another sharp retort from Niki as she turned and strode away.

Marc glanced at the group as most moved in different directions toward other friends. Sarah was the only one to stay. She looked neglected with her face tight, mouth askance, hair disheveled and eyes pleading. She started to speak, but all that came out was a whimper.

"Sarah, what is the problem here? You're crying … Niki's mad at me, and everyone is scattered to the four winds, what gives?"

"It was a girl thing. We had a disagreement about something, you don't want to know," Sarah replied with a cracking voice.

The conversation did not make any sense. Sarah was in a deep funk about something to do with dating. She was so depressed that what she told Marc was confusing. After five minutes of rambling, she decided she needed to find one of her friends. As quickly as she could, she was gone into the crowd leaving Marc utterly alone.

He glanced around for a comfortable spot or group. He felt very alone in a group of strangers realizing that he was lost socially without Jamie. He decided to leave for home and grab that hamburger he craved.

"You look lost," a voice behind him whispered. He turned around with a jerk and was staring into the face of Danni Taylor. "It's you," he stammered.

"Yes, it's me. Who did you think it was?"

"Sorry, you, you, I don't know. I was dreaming or something, so Hi," he finally said something lucid.

Danielle, or Danni, as everyone called her was a junior cheerleader, part of the Cove Church Westminster Youth group, a member of the church choir with an angelic voice. She was also one of Marc's oldest friends and his ex-girlfriend. They had been a couple during his sophomore and part of his junior year.

While they were dating in his mind, and in hers, that was not how her parents saw the situation. During the entire dating ritual, Danni was not allowed to attend school dances, go to a show, go to the Community Center teen room, have Marc to her home, ride in a car driven by Marc or any other teenager or even go to summer evening swimming parties at the pool. So, actually to say they were dating, was not quite the case. Everyone, including themselves thought they were together, but it was just an illusion.

The courtship ended right after the football team won the state championship last year, Marc's junior year. The celebratory dances and parties after the state game were off limits for Danni. Marc was left on his own to find fun without her. They never really ended the relationship, merely drifted apart. They had not talked much over the past year avoiding each other with simple "hellos" and "hi's." This was the first direct face to face conversation since that time.

After a five minute chat about nothing important, Danni suggested they dance. Marc could see no reason not to. They were a little stiff in each other's arms at first. As a string of ballads and love songs played, they began to get more comfortable with each other after a few minutes. On the crowded floor, others pushed them closer and closer together. Marc marveled at her beauty. Her face was darling with a perfect complexion, long silky blond hair, breasts that were more than exciting. She already possessed an entire womanly figure considered by Marc and everyone else, as jaw-dropping.

As they edged out of the dancing area, they made their way towards the sidelines, laughing together, smiling and rekindling some of their lost feelings. They leaned against the wall catching their breath when a group of friends joined them, spoiling the mood and hurried Danni off to another spot. Once again, Marc was on an island, alone. He noticed Niki making her way through the throngs of students, headed in his direction, eyes flashing. It seemed an omen of something looming.

"Still mad at me?" Niki opened the conversation.

"Mad, me mad at you, no, I'm not mad, but 'Pinocchio'?"

"I couldn't think of anything else to say, sorry."

"Do I have big ears?"

She turned her head to look away and giggle, "yuck, no, another one of my attempts to say something, say anything and escape that bunch."

"But you said I have large ears."

Niki snickered, "sorry, so sorry, come on let's dance," she reached out and took his hand and the two of them moved to the center of the room. He put his arm around her. *Connie Francis was singing "Who's Sorry Now:" I'm sorry I made you cry…Won't you forget. Don't let us say good bye…one little kiss won't you try…* As the song ended, Niki looked directly into Marc's eyes, "Will you do me a favor?"

"Sure, I guess, what is it?"

"Give me a ride home. I came with Amanda and Ronnie. They will want to be alone at the end of the dance, and I don't want to catch a ride with Sarah and the others. That's how this silly argument started."

"Over a ride in a car?"

"Never mind about the argument," Niki snapped rudely, "Can you drive me home?"

"Sure, absolutely," was his quick, concise answer.

"Can we go now? I've had enough dancing?"

"Sure, let's go."

"I'll just tell Amanda. Be right back. I need my coat and shoes."

After they both retrieved their shoes, Marc and Niki climbed the stairs out of the dance pit, walked down the hall, went out the ten foot high heavy oak wooden doors and ran to Marc's coupe.

Once in the car, Marc turned the key and as the eight cylinder engine purred, the radio blasted. "It will take a few minutes for the motor to warm and the heater to work."

"Buzz, I have been in your car before, you know!"

"Yeah, I know," was his laughing reply.

They sat for a few minutes waiting for the windows to clear. "I am really hungry, how about a hamburger, want one?" Marc glanced at Niki.

"Sure, I could eat a burger and maybe some fries."

"Good, let's go to Donna's Diner. I like their burgers."

"OK, go, go!" Niki encouraged him to get moving. Marc drove out of the parking lot, down Virginia Avenue, south on Main Street, past the Community Center, past the turn to Marland Heights, down the commercial strip and onto Freedom Way and the row of restaurants. He turned into Donna's Diner and into one of the car hop parking spots. The car was toasty by now and Marc and Niki agreed on their orders. Marc flashed his lights to signal the car hop girl to come out to the car. She ran out bundled for the weather including an aviator cap with the flaps buttoned down. After she took their order, they sat back in the warm car listening to WEIR, laughing about silly events from their past.

The burgers and fries were great and both of them devoured them quickly and slurped their double root beer floats. They left Donna's completely satisfied singing along with *Bobby Darin's "Queen of the Hop:" Well, I love my queen, do you know what I mean? Sweet Little Sixteen, Yes, that's my queen…Well, she wears short shorts and rock 'n roll shoes…Well, I love my queen, do you know who I mean. Sweet little sixteen, yes, that's my queen…*

As they headed up Marland Heights hill towards Niki's house, Niki moved closer to Marc. He looked at her. "Great night, lots of stars out, cold, but clear."

"Have you ever seen the view from the back of William's Country Club?" Niki asked as she leaned forward to get a better view of the night sky.

"Well, yes, on New Year's Eve. It was a clear night. We could see across the Ohio River Valley, off to the farm country behind Steubenville."

"Yes, that was a great view that night. I bet it's the same tonight. Let's go and take a look."

"Okay, but we can't get in the Club; what about your parents? It's almost eleven."

"My parents won't care; especially when they hear I was with you. Let's go see for a few minutes. There is a parking lot behind the club house a little lower on the hill, but it's still a great view. I've been there a lot of times with my parents and with my brother. It's easy to get to. Come on, let's go."

Marc drove for a moment and finally said, "Oh yeah, I know where that lot is. Good, here we go to see the stars."

Marc knew exactly where it was. He pulled behind the club house and went to the far end of the lot and pointed the car south. Exactly as predicted, the view was spectacular, and in looking around, Marc noticed they were the only ones in the lot to enjoy it. Niki sat against Marc and rested her head against his chest. She looked up at Marc and said tenderly, "This is wonderful, really wonderful. Thank you for bringing me here."

The stars numbered thousands. They were bright, twinkling, some silvery yellow, others golden blue, but mostly just bright, bright white. Far across the river gorge were just as many sprinkles of lights from homes, farms, and street lights. The night was clear, dark gray, but clear.

Marc looked down at Niki just as she tilted her head to see his face. Simultaneously they moved forward and kissed sweetly. They kissed again, again and again each time with more passion. Their bodies moved closer, they embraced each other as their kisses began to move beyond their lips to necks, face and back to their lips. Their arms wrapped around each other, they squeezed so tight that they were almost one. French kisses were heating their passion. Marc reached his hand under Niki's open coat and rubbed it over her firm pliable breast. She did not object, so he continued. They were both in a fanatical state of arousal, far beyond anything that either had ever experienced.

Suddenly, just as quickly as the sultry act had started, it stopped. They sat back, squared their shoulders against the bench seat and took deep breaths.

"I think that's enough," the silence was broken by Niki.

"Yeah, that's enough," Marc whispered quietly with a quavering voice, "awesome."

"Yeah, whoa! That's enough," Niki laughed. "I didn't see that coming! That was beyond anything, anything I thought about today."

"Buzz, you're right, beyond anything."

"Remember, we are just friends. This was only two friends, friends having a hamburger and getting a ride home."

“Yeah, you’re right, we are just two friends, getting friendly,” and he laughed.

“Oh, you! We are just friends and you bought me a hamburger and drove me home,” She giggled. “We have to stay with that story. Now take me home… please.”

“Right, friend…my best friend. I’ll take you home.”

Niki zipped her coat and snuggled next to Marc. “Home and no talking about our friendship to anyone, right?”

“Right… right.”

Chapter 10

Together

A noisy place every day, the auditorium was filling quickly with students eating lunch. The back corner was still rather empty as Marc, an early arrival, waited for his friends, more importantly for Jamie. He had not talked to her since last Friday at lunch before she left on her weekend campus visits.

He had waited for a phone call Sunday evening, but she never called. He wasn't sure what that silence meant: maybe she was home late from Huntington; maybe she was tired from her trip and went to bed early. Or, maybe she heard about the sock hop, his dancing with Danni and Niki, his taking Niki home, the hamburgers or more. He was anxiously concerned about what Jamie, Will and the others might be gossiping about what occurred Saturday night, mostly concerned about Jamie.

Amanda and Ronnie were walking along the back aisle headed for their seats in front of him. They said "Hi" and sat down with their books, coats, brown lunch bags. They turned and smiled sweetly at each other, opened their bags and took out their sandwiches. *Love, they are really in love,* thought Marc.

He spotted Jamie coming through the far side door with Niki, Will and the other members of the group. They all seemed to be in a jovial mood. As they entered the gray corner, Jamie crawled over the broken chair, sat next to him, leaned in and kissed him. Marc thought *good start.*

"Thought you would call me last night," he greeted her.

"Ah wanted to, but Ah was so tired. We got home late n Ah had to cook dinner with Mum. The trip was long n very tiring, Ah was zonked. The grannies went to bed by eight n Ah followed. Sorry, Ah did miss you."

"I missed you, too. It was a long weekend. What were the schools like?"

"They were great. West Virginia was great. The campus is in the town and set in the hills so you do a lot of up and down walking. We left the grannies at this downtown hotel n Da, Mum n Ah toured the campus n met with the admission director. We even were taken into a girl's dorm. It was really nice, not as nice my own room, but just fine."

"So, is that your choice or what?" Marc wanted to keep the conversation about her weekend, not his.

"Ah don't know, just not sure yet. Ah really liked the Marshall campus. We only had a self-guided tour though, so all we could do was walk in n out of buildings. Sunday, the admissions office was closed. So, Ah don't know what to think."

"Maybe you will have to go back during a week day, sit in a class and enter their dorms."

"Maybe. What did you do? Ah heard you were at the sock hop."

"Oh yeah, after working a double at the pool I went over to the school. There was a big group there, really crowded."

"You took Niki home?"

"She needed a ride. We got a hamburger at Donna's. I was really hungry, I had worked all day, starving really."

"You danced with Danni, too."

"Uh, yes, so what? It was a dance. She and I danced a couple of times. She is a just a good friend," Marc's response was rather defensive.

"Well, it better have been only been a dance," Jamie punched his arm with a smiling frown on her face.

"It was only a dance, don't get all bent out of shape."

"Right, Ah bloody well know you are good friends with Niki. But, Danni is an old love, don't start anything with her."

"Don't worry, you are my girl."

With that probe over, Jamie went into a more lengthy description of the weekend. She told him a great deal more about everything they saw, meals they ate, discussions the family had, etc. The grannies would be going back to England soon. That was saddening, but Jamie, along with her mum and Harry, was now making firm plans to return to Birmingham for the summer following her graduation from high school.

The big room began to empty again as lunches were finished. "Ah've to run now," Jamie called over her shoulder. "Ah need to talk to my counselor about the trip. Ring me tonight, ok?"

Marc was left sitting by himself. Everything between himself and Jamie seemed fine. Niki and Will were sitting a couple rows in front and appeared to be happy, joking and enjoying being together. Somehow, he and Niki had avoided eye contact so far. The concerns about some backfire from Saturday night were gone—at least for now. Marc started to leave as Ron stood and touched his arm, "Can you give me a ride to practice tonight? My dad's truck is not running and he took my car."

"Sure, I'm parked out front. I'll see you after class."

The radio was playing, wind was howling around the coupe as Marc sat waiting for Ron. He could see him taking two steps at a time as he ran down the front cement steps from the school. He was grabbing at the black steel pipe banister trying to keep from falling. Marc was not sure he wasn't going to fall face first onto the gravel parking lot. Somehow Ron kept his balance, ran to the coupe and hurried into the front seat. "Let's go! We're going to be late. Coach will give us hell, if we are, go, go!"

"I'm going. You're the one who is late, not me," Marc answered testily. "Where were you?"

"I was saying goodbye to Amanda."

"True love, eh, are you two really that much in love with each other?"

"Damn, I don't know. Yeah, I guess we are. We do love each other in our own way."

"What way is that? How can you love someone in 'your own way'?"

"Hell, I don't know. We really like each other and have for a couple of years. You know that." They were headed south on Main Street luckily making all the green lights. "I heard from two different colleges today. They want to consider me for basketball scholarships and invited me to visit," Ronnie ventured.

"Wow, great, which ones?"

"Tennessee and Maryland. Both are big state schools with really good basketball teams. They would offer basketball scholarships, not football, and maybe baseball, too. Coach said it sounds like both have a strong interest."

"Sounds like your bag."

"I hope so. That's what I was talking to Amanda about. It needs to be a joint decision."

Marc looked at him inquisitively, "What do you mean by a joint decision?"

"Well, you know, a decision we want to make together."

"I know what it means, but what does it mean or have to do with you and Amanda. It is your decision, your college."

"Well, we want to stay close, but go our own way. Go to the college that is best for each of us."

"I guess I still don't understand," Marc answered, like he was snooping.

"Well, she wants to go to a small college close to home. Her parents will pay for it. I want to go to a big school, maybe not close, but not too far from her. I want to study business and math."

"What does Amanda want from college?"

"I'm not sure. She likes music, church, maybe teaching. But, we know we want to stay close to each other and maybe marry after college."

"Cool, very cool. You have this all figured out, already talking marriage."

"Just talking. Just talking," Ron replied as Marc parked the car and they both took off running for the locker room and practice.

Tuesday night's game at Wellsburg was the last game in January. The Red Riders were awesome. They were on fire right from the start. Marc and Will served as the dispatchers sending the ball to Ron, Spider and Melvin. Marc, especially, kept furnishing the ball to Ron and Spider underneath the basket, in the paint, or to Melvin, out to the side. Between these two 6'4" dual centers, they scored forty points, with Ron getting twenty six. Spider was dominant under the boards. He was a senior, husky with a long reach. Melvin (everyone called him Melvin, his last name, as he did not use his given name of Thomas), was only a sophomore, but an accurate jump shooter, especially from the deep corner.

The starting five were really coming together. Four seniors who had played together last year and a talented sophomore who was happy in his role; three white, two black; two very good big men inside; three outside shooters; a very efficient point guard, all good rebounders and good, quick defensive players. As January, nineteen fifty-nine, came to an end, they were eleven and one.

Once seated in the bus, ready for the forty-five minutes ride from Wellsburg to Weir High, Coach Warren stood at the front of the bus, motioned for quiet, which happened immediately.

"Just a few words about tonight … You were at your best. Be proud of yourselves, and I mean the JV's as well as the varsity. The season is more than half over. It's been a very good season so far. Let's make sure not to waste it. The regular season is very tough from here to the end. We have Steubenville again this Friday. We beat them at home a couple of weeks ago, but playing at their place is different. We will need to be at our best, just like tonight. Then we have Farrell at their gym, another very good Pennsylvania team. Near the end of the month Charleston comes to our place. They are the number one team in the state. You know they will be ready for us, especially since we beat them in football. Be ready, stay ready. It was a good game tonight, let's go home." As Coach finished, everyone let out a yell.

"Is anyone coming tonight or not?" Marc asked the group of boys gathered at the front of the auditorium by the snack store that sold candy, pop, milk, chips, pretzels, etc., during lunch hour from the floor of the stage. Profits supposedly went to the Hi-Y groups.

"I'm going; I want to hear what they have to say. The Army may be the right thing for me. I can't do much else after school so I'm definitely going to talk to the Army and Navy recruiters," Jeff Malawus, the card shark of the senior class chimed.

"I'll see you there, about seven," Marc started to walk away. Sage grabbed his arm. "Are you sure you want to go to the Army, all those orders, uniforms, gee, the Army?"

"I don't know, but I… well, I don't want to stay here and work in the mill."

"Yeah, but the Army? You can leave Weirton and not go to the Army."

"You're right, but, and that is a big but, where would that be? I just can't leave Weirton and walk, or run around the country."

"Just don't commit to anything dumb, or sign some piece of paper that commits you to four years in the Army," Sage warned. They had been walking to the dark corner where the rest of their group was eating lunch.

"I'm not signing anything. I'm not stupid."

"Well, remember, I have seen you do some very jackass things. You can be very thickheaded."

"So can you, Jughead," Marc ended that conversation as he crawled over the broken chair and Jamie to get to his saved seat.

"What was that all about?" she asked. "You seemed to be fighting or arguing."

"Oh, nothing," Marc grumbled glumly. "He was telling me what to do or not to do when I talk to the Army recruiter tonight."

"That's tonight? Here at the school?"

"Yes, tonight. You want to tell me what to do, too?"

"No."

"Well, everyone else does, including my father. He doesn't want me to talk to them either. Well, right now I don't have many choices. Do I?"

"You have choices and they are your choices, yours alone," Jamie attempted to smooth things a bit.

"It is my choice, my choice alone. Well, maybe not completely alone. I want your input."

"What do you mean? Ah think Ah have made my choice. Ah am going to college."

"What about us?" Marc's voice lowered. "Are we going to stay, to stay together?"

"Blimey, that's a good question, Ah don't know. Ah think about it all the time, but Ah don't 've an answer."

"I think about it, too. I think it is an answer we need to make together. If I go to the Army, does that mean we are finished?" Marc was very serious and Jamie knew it.

"Ah, blimey, Ah can't say. You are my world right now. In the future, Ah, gee, don't ask me that," Jamie turned away with a tear in her eye.

"You're right, I can't answer it either," he whispered as he put his arm around her and pulled her close.

"You need to get the ball to Ron or Spider in under ten seconds. Can you see the clock when you are out front near the key?" Coach was yelling directly at Marc as the others with hands on their knees leaned in to hear.

"I think so; I'll find the clock."

Coach Warren turned his attention to Ron and Spider. "You two keep moving down low. Brush your man off of you or each other if they play man to man. If it is a zone, keep moving around under that basket. Let Marc find you."

Coach looked up at the clock. Everyone stood straight, ready to retake the court. The crowd that had settled during the time out suddenly became bold with loud yells, stomping of feet, shaking of the bleachers directly behind the Weirton bench. The entire gym was rumbling with sound and movement. The score was tied at fifty-two. There were twenty-three seconds left. Weirton had the ball and needed the last shot to occur just at the buzzer and go in.

It had been back and forth all night. Neither team could separate from the other by more than four points. The rivalry was just that; neither team was going to lose gracefully. The winner would have to earn the title.

Will inbounded the ball to Marc at about mid-court. Marc moved forward with little pressure as the Big Red sat back in a zone to guard the two big men inside. Marc had one eye on the movement going on under the basket and one eye on the clock. Seconds ticked off. Marc moved to his left, and then sharp right with a smooth motion lobbed a pass inside to Ron on the left side.

Ron made the grasp, and went up from four feet out. The ball hit the back of the iron, came off high. Ron had missed. Spider tipped the ball back to the rim. It came off again. Spider made a second attempt. The second tip was too hard. The rebound came off long, bounced once short of the foul line right into Marc's hands at the top of the key. There was no time left, Marc had no choice, he went up for a shot. At the peak of his jump, Marc finger rolled the ball back toward the basket. The game ending buzzer sounded as Marc watched the ball swish through the net.

The Red Riders had won.

The gym that one moment was rocking and screaming, suddenly and instantly, had its breath taken away, moaned, groaned and went silent. The only sound came from the Weirton cheerleaders and the few dozen fans who had braved going into the rival's den. The small group was cheering, yelling and running across the floor to mob the team.

Marc was getting hugs, handshakes, pats on his back, plus kisses from all the cheerleaders and finally a real kiss from Jamie. It would be a joyful ride home across the Ohio River. *Winning is such fun,* thought Marc as he sat in the locker room. Everyone was laughing, joking with each other, showering and getting dressed. But Marc sat, still in his uniform, savoring the moment. "Winning always feels good. I'll miss this next year," he said softly to no one in particular.

Well, when I was a young man and never been kissed ...

"That's me, never been kissed," Marc whispered in Jamie's ear.

"Clear off," was her whisper back.

So I got me a girl and I kissed her and then, Oh Lordy, well I kissed 'er again, because she had kisses sweeter than wine...

"Your kisses are sweeter than a coke," Marc murmured with his mouth at her ear.

"You're daft!"

Well, I asked her to marry and to be my sweet wife...

"What do you say; will you be my sweet wife?"

"Are you asking?"

"Sure, why not!" They continued to dance to the *Jimmie Rodger's song, "Kisses Sweeter Than Wine"* bantering with each other light-heartedly enjoying the bubbly give and take.

The Community Center teen room was full. The mood was jubilant as yesterday's victory over Steubenville was still being celebrated. A snow storm was roaring outside, snowball fights were underway with some overflow into the building. Marc had picked Jamie up just as the storm was starting. Her parents were reluctant to let her go out, but had agreed in the end with the caveat that she be home early and then agreed to a revised curfew of ten o'clock.

As the dance came to an end, they found seats along the side as they had been dancing continuously for a half hour. "You didn't tell me how the visit with the Army recruiters went," Jamie queried.

"Well, there were two sergeants who gave out information about their careers, details about boot camp and…"

"What in the world is boot camp?"

"Boot camp is the first place you go when you enlist. It's your training to become a soldier, marching, learning to shoot guns, making your bed, stuff like that."

"Ah think we call that basic training in England," Jamie countered.

"We do, too, boot camp is just another term."

"What did you think? Are you interested?"

"Yes, I think so. I want to hear more, especially about the advanced training, maybe in mechanics or something. Yeah, I'm interested."

"So what are you going to do next, enlist?"

"No, not yet. I'm not enlisting until I know more. The sergeants were from the Steubenville office so I am going over there sometime to learn more. The Navy recruiters will be here in a couple of weeks. I want to talk with them also. What about you and your applications to college?"

"Well, I have sent my application to West Virginia and I have one for Marshall and Pittsburgh at home to fill out. I'm not sure what to do about those two. Miss Darnie, my counselor says you should apply to at least three colleges in case you don't get accepted by one or two. So, I think I should send in the other two. America is so different from England where you just take a test to qualify for different schools. That makes sense, not here."

"Well, you will get into all three. Your grades are great and with your involvement in advanced classes and various activities, there should be no problem. Don't worry," Marc wanted to change the subject. She's talking college; he's talking the armed services, not much togetherness planning. "When do your grannies head for home?"

"On Monday. Da is going to take them into Pittsburgh to catch a train to New York. There they will board a liner for home, ocean liner, a boat," Jamie explained as she could tell Marc was unsure about "liner."

"Yipes, just a few more days then, just a few days."

"We had better go, with this weather n Ah 've to be home by ten.

They grabbed their coats, waved to the gang and ran through the deepening snow to the coupe. Snow made all the cars look the same. When they finally distinguished Marc's black Chrysler, it looked like a large snow mound. The snow was inches deep covering the top including the windows which had a sheet of ice underneath. Actually, the entire car had a coat of ice, and they found the doors iced shut. Finally, Marc was able to wedge the driver's side door open and they crawled in. Marc placed the key in the ignition, turned it hopefully. The eight cylinder engine came to life with gusto. Marc, jokingly raved, "Old Faithful."

"Let's sit here and let the engine run awhile. I need to get the car warm to melt some of the ice on the windows so I can clean them enough to even see."

"Okay, hold me, Ah'm so cold," Jamie snuggled up close, placing her head on his chest. They sat together warming each other while the car's heater struggled to do its job. The windows were deeply encrusted with the wintry mix, so, they weren't going anywhere for awhile. Marc squeezed Jamie a little closer, and looked down at her cute little red cap pulled tightly over her ears. She knew he was staring at her, so she lifted her head looking into his dreamy blue eyes. They smiled, smooched and went into a long passionate embrace. Their passion ebbed and slowed with each being both the aggressor and the submissive one. Marc moved and Jamie laid back into the seat, her head resting on the top. He kissed her with boldness and she returned the zeal by pushing him into the door.

Marc started to move his left hand to feel more of her body, but she stopped him, moving his hand to her hip, still returning his kisses. Finally they were both breathless and their embrace loosened.

Jamie was the first to speak. "Marc, that's as far as Ah want to go. Ah really fancy being frisky, making out, as you say," she smiled, as did Marc. "But doing the 'Full Monte,' or that whole sex thing is just not for me."

Marc sat very still just listening. "I understand. You are right and it is alright with me. You're my, my, I don't know, my girl, my everything. Kissing and hugging is fine. That's fine with me."

"Ah knew you would understand. That's why you are my chap, my lad, my boyfriend."

They kissed, hugged and sat for a few minutes. Finally Marc said, "I think I can clean the windows now, and then we can head for home." She gave him a smooch and he grabbed a small broom from the back seat, cleared the snow and ice as best he could.

As they approached the Marland Heights hill, they discovered it had been plowed and slag and salt had been spread. With the new used snow treaded tires, they made the climb with no problem and arrived safely at her home. As Marc opened the door, Jamie tumbled out the passenger door into a snow drift. She looked so cute, he began tossing snowballs at her and they ended up in a real snowball fight until her mum turned on the porch light, calling her in.

The snow did not let up as he drove slowly down the steep hill. Marc decided to take the Cove Hill Road home; it was not as steep as the only other way up the Weirton Heights hill. Keeping a steady pace, he made the trip easily. Along the way, several cars and trucks had gotten stuck. He remembered his dad had suggested over the holidays that he get snow tires for his car. He had done just that, and the advice had been right on target three or four times already this winter.

"Knock, knock."

"I said, knock, knock," Sarah repeated a little louder this time.

"Ok, I'll bite," Amanda replied, "Who's there?"

"Boo."

"Boo who?" Niki replied in a disinterested tone.

"Gosh, don't cry. It's just a knock, knock joke."

A few half-hearted giggles; one very loud "boo," and the dozen or more girls returned to their conversations.

Sarah again, even louder this time, "knock, knock."

"Another one? Sarah, 'please'," Niki scolded.

"This is a good one, a really good one, knock, knock."

In unison the four girls answered, "who's there?" That caused a group chuckle.

"Annie."

Again in unison, "Annie who?"

"Any one you like."

"Boo, yuk, what?" were the immediate responses and then a few mocking jeering expletives. Mr. Pfeiffer, the advisor to the National Honor Society, chimed in with, "Ladies, let's be a little more civil. I know you learned the profanity from the boys, but you ladies don't want to let them know they can influence you." His dry humor received the biggest outburst of the night.

The library was nearly full with over thirty members. The February monthly meeting was over and, as was normal, this was the happy hour when members brought pop, juice and snacks of all kinds. A few of the more ambitious had provided hot hors d'oeuvres for everyone. This was an opportunity to bring up topics for discussion. Some preferred to get the entire membership involved and some liked to form smaller groups.

Tonight's discussion concerned Alaska becoming the forty-ninth state. There were a variety of opinions on everything from "why do we need another state, especially one that is at the top of Canada almost one thousand miles away, cold and desolate," to "Why not make all the territories, Hawaii, Puerto Rico, and Guam all states," and "what is the flag going to look like," etc. The discussion was lively, just what Mr. Pfeiffer wanted, a good exchange of ideas on a current event, the National Honor Society at work.

The musketeer group of girls had no real interest in the subject, so they had drifted over to the research shelves of the library and created their own faction. The most important topic for them was the big Sadie Hawkins dance on the Saturday after the final regular season basketball game about two weeks away.

"What is a Sadie Hawkins Dance? Ah know it is a girl ask boy thing. Are there special things girls are supposed to do in inviting a boy?" Jamie asked.

"Nothing special. It's just a dance where you ask Marc to take you. It's informal or maybe semi-formal. You don't do anything special," Amanda answered.

"Ah don't buy him a corsage or one of those flowers for his coat?"

"A boutonniere," Sarah answered quickly.

"You don't do anything. The only thing that changes is that the girl gets to pick the boy that she wants to go with," Niki spoke directly to the issue.

"So, all Ah 've to do is ask Marc. What about dress? Formal dresses or just a nice dress you would go to school in or maybe go to church?"

Amanda and the others thought for a minute. Then someone said, "Just a nice dress, nothing with crinolines or a big puffy skirt, nothing like prom or homecoming, just a nice going to Sunday dress."

"Wear one of those dozen dresses you have in your closet. They are all beautiful. Maybe I'll borrow one," Niki snickered.

"You can borrow one if you want, come over, pick one. We are about the same size," Jamie offered.

The discussion of the dance continued about dresses, which boy to ask, who might be a surprise date. Out of nowhere, Niki made a rather unconventional comment, "What if we asked someone we are not dating?" She looked at Amanda and Jamie. "What if we changed dates, at least to go to the dance? We could change back to our boyfriends at the dance and go home with them; I mean get them to take us to our homes after the dance." The near slip made them all sneer.

"Can we do that? Are we allowed to do that kind of thing?" Jamie asked with concern.

Niki looked at her in disbelief. "There are no rules; the only rule is that we have to ask the guys."

"I think it would be fun, that would really cause the boys to think, as long as we get back together with our own guy at the dance," Amanda was warming up to this novel idea.

"Yeah, that would be fun! Really fun," Sarah had joined the side conversation.

"What about me?" Danni was another joiner.

"Well, I guess a couple more would be okay. We don't want too many. Let's keep it just to us five, well; maybe it depends on who you are going to ask." Niki took charge, directing her question to Sarah and Danni.

"Right, the idea is brilliant, but Ah don't know everyone that well to ask someone Ah don't know. Who are you going to ask?" Jamie stared at Sarah.

"I was going to ask Sage, Scotty Stockdale. You know Sage; you're always talking with him."

After a moment, Jamie said, "Right, right, Ah know Sage. That would be okay. Ah could ask him."

"Danni, who are you asking?"

"Well, I talked with Tom Kec about the dance, but I haven't asked him as yet. Tom and I have been friends for a couple of years."

"That might work. Tom is in our lunch group. He plays basketball and football. That's a good choice," Amanda smiled. "Let's do it. Remember we get together with our own guy during the dance."

"We know that, together at the dance. Okay, does everyone agree?" Niki asked the other four. Heads bobbed affirmatively.

"Now, the big question, who asks which guy?" Sarah queried.

"Well, Ah guess Ah could ask Sage for Sarah," Jamie offered. "Ah know him well enough."

"I want to ask Will for you, Niki. He is always trying to kiss me," Sarah jumped in.

"He always is kissing you, not just trying!" was Niki's come back. "Okay, you ask Will, three to go."

"Well, I have Tom in a couple of classes. We have been friends since junior high. I could ask him with no problem. My parents also know him and they will understand his coming to pick me up," Amanda offered.

"Danni, is that alright with you?" Niki looked at Danni.

"That's a good idea. Amanda and Tom are a good fit. Fine with me," Danni responded.

"That leaves Ron, Marc, Danni and me. That is going to be zany. I feel odd about both of them," Niki stopped in mid-thought. "It would seem hard to ask either of them because of you two," she added looking at Jamie and Amanda.

"Well, it's okay with me if you ask Ron. He will enjoy the attention," Amanda laughed, made the compromise so the joke could continue. "Ron will have fun with the idea."

"That leaves Danni with Marc. That's a good match. Oops, I'm sorry; I didn't mean what I said. I mean the way I said that. Sorry Jamie," Sarah finally realized that she may have been insensitive.

Jamie was quite accommodating, "Blimey, it's fine. Ah know Danni and Marc were once going together. It's okay. Marc will be fine with it as a brilliant wicked stunt. It is cool as long as they aren't getting off with each other, Ah'm not gagging. Ah'll have him back at the end."

"What does 'getting off' mean?" Sarah butted in.

Niki just looked at her, shook her head, "Never mind, just think about it."

"My parents also know Marc. You know my mother; she needs to approve of whoever I go out with. She's comfortable with both Tom and Marc, so the mid-dance switch won't bother her," Danni made the prank unanimous. The hoax was on.

The girls finished the meeting deciding on when, where and how they would make this happen: What they would and wouldn't say to the guys; how they would make them buy corsages; fancy dresses were to be worn; sports coats for the guys; no double dating, and each couple was to come to the dance alone!

With that, they noticed the main meeting was breaking up. As they started to leave, Sarah continued with another "knock, knock."

"Not this again," Niki complained.

"It's the best one, the very best one," Sarah begged.

"Who's there?" All four voices chimed in.

"Cows go."

"Cows go who?"

"Cows go moo not who."

There was complete silence. Two muffled tee hees. Finally Danni spoke up for the sisterhood, "Sarah, you are many things, but a comic is not one of them."

Why did the New Deal work, or did it?

The question was on the black board in bold letters,. The discussion was fifteen minutes old. Marc's mind was wandering over the lyrics of the Marine Hymn, *From the Halls of Montezuma, to the shores of Tripoli…* He thought, *I think I know where Tripoli is, Africa, on the coast, but where is Montezuma, what is Montezuma. Being a Marine, that might be an idea. Where is their recruiting office?*

Marc's mind was far away from the 1930s and the New Deal. Twentieth Century American History usually kept his attention, but not today. Lunch was next. He was hungry, tired, upset and wanted to see Jamie; American History would have to wait.

This had been a very difficult week, or really the past ten days. After the high, lofty victory over Steubenville, reality returned with a devastating loss to Farrell High. Again, the score was close, but there never seemed to be any doubt of the outcome. Farrell was the better team. They were taller, with their center about six foot eight, in addition, their team boasted two forwards six five or taller. It was not just height, however dominant that was, the real overwhelming advantage was they could run, run and run. Everything was up tempo. The pace was non-stop fast. The Red Riders could not get back fast enough to play organized defense. Farrell won by nine.

In recent days, Marc felt like he was sitting in a tempest with everything moving faster and faster. His father had asked for his help in rewiring the entire electrical service in the garage. He had been told by his dad that he was not doing enough around the house and what he did do was less than perfect. His mother was upset with his sisters who were now growing into being independent thinkers. He had to work a full eight hours at the filling station on Sunday of all days, and he had been tired ever since. Jamie had been busy all weekend so they barely saw each other. Yesterday he took a four hour bus trip to play a basketball game in the middle of the state at a new country consolidated school, Harvest.

With all that, the most upsetting event took place during the game at Harvest High School. The school was all new and had only been open for two years. The student body came from four smaller schools that had been consolidated into one large high school.

The gym was phenomenal: big, spacious, with bright lighting, a gleaming wooden floor, state-of-the-art stands, a large visitors' locker room; everything first rate. There was a large crowd; Weir High had brought only the varsity. No cheerleaders had made the trip. Their only fans were a few administrators.

Everything started out well. Marc and the entire team were playing at their best. It was obvious that they were the better team and at the half they held a double digit lead. The second half was quite different. It was ugly, repugnant and revolting to the small Weir contingent, not because of what happened on the court. The Red Riders won easily, but the ugliness came from what the opposing fans said and yelled at them.

Harvest was an all white team. The players and their coaches were fine. Not so, a small, but loud group of students and adults. Since Weirton's team was integrated, the fans began shouting every racial name they knew. Racial slurs were shouted directly at the players by referencing their numbers. The white players, noticeably Marc, because he had the ball a high percentage of time, were also called some very rough names.

At one point a time-out was called by the officials. A discussion was held by the coaches and the security staff about ending the game. The result was a decision to finish the play, but the police were called in for more support.

After the game, both Coach Warren and Coach Romeo stood at the front of the bus, apologized to their team, and complemented everyone for controlling their emotions. It was a very long, silent ride home. Marc never made it to bed until about two am, slept in a little, and made it to school for second period and now he was hungry, tired and confused. *Where do people get such anger? That should be the topic of today's class.*

When at last the bell rang, Marc exited quickly, went straight to his locker, got his brown lunch bag and started to eat his sandwich even as he was getting a coke from the student store by the stage. By the time Jamie reached her seat, he was half finished and greeted her by asking her what she might have to eat that she did not want.

As they sat back on the hard seats and talked about the busy weekend, the Honor Society meeting, the basketball game trip, he did not say anything about the racial comments and the fans. He thought, *maybe some other day.*

All of a sudden Jamie stood up. So did some of the other girls and they started to move around. "Where are you going? The bell didn't ring," Marc asked. "Where, why, what's going on?" were questions from all the guys. Just as suddenly Danni was sitting next to Marc.

"Hi," she grinned at him.

"Eh, hi…"

"Marc, will you take me to the Sadie Hawkins' Dance next weekend?" she pleadingly looked up at him.

"What! You asking me…me?"

"Yes, you Marc. I'm asking you to the Sadie Hawkins' Dance at the Community Center."

"You're asking me?" Marc questioned again, mystified.

"That's what I said," was Danni's answer.

Marc looked around, could see this scheming plan was being played out with all the other guys. He smiled curiously and answered loud enough so that he could be heard four or five rows away. "Yes, Danni, I accept your invitation. I will take you to the Sadie Hawkins' Dance."

A chorus of "Yeses" rang out. Danni, as did the other girls explained to her date a few of the rules the girls had cooked up, emphasizing that they would be reunited with their true date sometime during the dance. Everyone seemed happy. Partners returned to their rightful places. All afternoon the entire school was buzzing about the loony happening. Marc told Jamie he thought it was "foxy."

He wondered how he would be greeted by Mrs. Taylor. He had not been around her except to see her in church since he and Danni had stopped dating. He liked Mr. Taylor, but Mrs. Taylor was very reserved. The front of the house was well lighted as he approached the door. One of Danni's young brothers opened the door and led Marc across the living room to sit with Mr. Taylor. They talked basketball for a few minutes. Mrs. Taylor entered and said hello, asked about his family and told Marc that Danielle would be down in a few minutes. Marc could see she was already standing at the bottom of the stairs, stunning as always. She smiled, showing her adorable dimples, her hair sparkling, just like old times. He walked over and told her she looked beautiful and presented her with the red/pink corsage. Her mother helped her pin it on as she inserted a boutonniere into his lapel. As they went out the door, her mother added, "I guess we will expect Tom Kec to return you home."

"That's right, Mother."

"Have fun you two. It's nice to see you again, Marc."

"Thank you, Mrs. Taylor." To Danni, he whispered, "I guess she likes me now."

Danni responded, "She always did. She just didn't trust you."

"Thanks, that makes me feel great."

"Just kidding. She just wants me to be safe."

As they sat for a moment in the car, Marc looked at Danni. "You are a beauty."

She blushed, touched his shoulder, "thank you that was nice."

He stopped at the door, looked for the bell, decided to knock. Jamie answered, "Come in. My parents want to meet you."

Sage stepped into the foyer and followed Jamie into the living room. Her parents were waiting to greet him. The four of them made small talk about the unusual evening, the school and something about England and the weather in the U.K. Jamie's mom wanted to take pictures so Jamie and Sage posed in front of the fireplace. Sage was charming to Jamie's parents, well dressed in a new sport coat, but Jamie was the star. She looked angelic. Her hair had been styled earlier in the afternoon. The crimson bangs framed her face and embellished her piercing blue eyes. The dress was stylish, light blue, accented with bluish red piping around the lace collar, midriff and bottom of the puffy skirt. The cherry rose wrist corsage complemented her outfit. Sage was stunned by her bewitching beauty and winning smile. He had seen her in school, at parties, dances and many other events, but this was different. She was a dream. However, she was also Marc's girl.

The Sadie Hawkins' Dance was sponsored by the Community Center, the city and many of the churches. It was open to all high school students, not only Weir High, but Madonna, Follansbee, Steubenville, Central, Lindsey, and St. Mary's schools. This was the tenth year for the dance and as usual it attracted a large crowd, mostly couples, but singles were welcome.

The five sisters of the farce, as they had been dubbed by their classmates, all met with their dates in the community room where the church groups were providing food, beverages and a respite from the packed gymnasium. Here the ten sat exchanging stories about parents, friends and strangers reactions to the experiment. The plan was to stay with your invited date until nine-thirty and then switch. That would be the half-way point through the dance.

"The gym looks nice with all the decorations and the colored lights. It's different than on basketball night," Danni ventured into conversation as she and Marc danced to a *Conway Twitty song*; "*It's Only Make Believe:*" *People see us everywhere. They think you really care, But myself, I can't deceive, I know it's only make believe…* "Those lyrics sound like us," was Danni's next comment.

"You're right, it sounds like our love story."

"Was it love, or just puppy love?"

"Some of both, I believe," was the return whisper as Marc brought Danni closer. The bouquet of her hair was intoxicating to him as her ringlets brushed his cheek. Marc pondered what could have been. *You are my every dream, but it's only make believe.* That set the tone for the first half of the dance, a great reunion for Marc and Danni.

Meanwhile, Jamie and Sage were on the other side of the dance floor. Their first dance as a couple was more of an introduction to each other. They discussed school, Honor Society, teachers, favorite classes, best books, travel adventures and compared England with the States. The time went almost too quickly with the last song before the nine-thirty bewitching hour beginning, a *Brook Benton* piece; *"It's a Matter of Time:" Someday someway, you'll realize that you've been blind, yes darling, you're going to need me again. It's just a matter of time…* The two were finally smooth together in this last dance as they started to become comfortable with each other's style. *Until you reach the end of the line, Well, I know you'll pass my way again. It's just a matter of time…*

It was time to convene, so the sisterhood brought their initial dates back to the community room. The switch was made with laughs, hugs, a few smacks on the cheeks and foreheads and transfers were completed. Everyone headed for the food table for punch, and a never ending variety of snacks. As they grouped around a large round table, they all agreed that the pretense had been fun. After the brief pause, the reunited couples returned to the dance floor. Strangely, the group stayed together during the second half of the evening. There were constant jokes and wisecracks. The final dances were slow and romantic. At last the couples drifted apart as the last dance of the evening *"Come Softly to Me:"* by the *Fleetwoods* ended the evening. *Come to me, stay, you're my obsession, forever and a day…I want, want you to know, I love, I love you so. Please hold, hold me so tight. All through, all through the night…*

The boys went for girl's wraps and then sauntered towards their cars. Marc opened the passenger door, helped Jamie in, went around to the driver's side, slid in quickly, and started the coupe. It was chilly, but not cold, a late February night.

They sat for a moment, held hands ogled each other. "I have something for you," Marc said provocatively.

"What, what do you 've? For me?"

"Yes, you! Open the glove compartment," Marc motioned with a nod.

"This?" She put her hand on the latch.

"Yes, open it. Go ahead. It won't bite you," he chuckled.

Jamie opened the door. Inside were two wrapped small packages. "Open the smallest first, the white one."

Removing the paper, she found a box. She took the top off and inside was a ring.

"It's my class ring. I would like you to have it, wear it."

"Oh, Marc, bloody me, your ring. Are you sure?" She was looking at him, then the ring, back and forth her eyes traveled. "Yes, yes, Ah'll wear it. Ah'm so very, very happy. Thank you, oh, thank you." She hugged and kissed him over and over and over.

"Open the red one now."

"Another one for me?" Off came the red paper. Another box. This time inside was a gold chain and a miniature gold football from the State Championship game a year ago.

"I want you to have my State Championship Football. You can wear it around your neck, maybe put the ring on the chain, too," Marc whispered.

In those few minutes, their relationship had moved to another level.

Chapter 11

Madness

Marc sat quietly in his room unable to sleep for some unknown reason. He could see the half orange moon high in the night sky. What would March bring? February was over, and March seemed to be coming in like a lamb, but as Marc thought about the new month, he knew it was going to be a lion.

This was the start of the last grading period, his last chance to achieve a better graduating average. Did a higher four year grade average really matter, maybe not? He's not going to college.

March meant the start of the West Virginia State basketball tournament. The Sectional games would be this week on Tuesday, Thursday and Saturday if you win. If you lose, the season is over! This would be followed by the Regional games in the second week of March; the state finals in the third week of March. All you had to do was win!

At school Jamie would be working with the Weirite staff to finish the year book. She had told him about all of the work that needed to be finished by April so the book could be printed, sold and distributed by mid-May. Jamie along with the seniors going to college needed to decide which school they would attend and ensure their acceptance. Marc needed to get to the Army recruiting office, talk with the Navy recruiters, start looking or making applications for jobs.

He looked at his alarm clock—one-thirty—still not sleepy. He was restless as he thought about Jamie. It had been a big step for him to give her his class ring and gold football. But, what did it mean? Marc was now thinking about a future with Jamie, something more than just a friendship. Sleep was finally beckoning him as he headed toward his bed with a last look at the moon that was now partially hidden by mist. Tomorrow, March 2nd, would start his final high school dash.

"This place has more cigarette butts than bricks," Ron commented.

"You're right, some of these guys come out here between almost every class," Marc replied as he stepped lightly around a rather large mound, seeing some cigs still alive with a spark flashing. They continued to walk down the alley behind the main school building towards the band's temporary practice building. The building had been an unused army hut made of steel and had the acoustics of a drum.

They were solo for Monday lunch as the girls were all involved in deciding on a play to be presented at the early April Class Play Festival night. Each class was to put on a twenty minute, original play, and a large number of seniors were starting to plan, write and eventually perform in their class play. Ron, Will and Marc were not interested so they were left alone for lunch. As it was an unusually warm March 2nd, eating outside was in order. As they rounded the corner of the building, they found Will, Spider and a few others sitting on the stone wall outside the band building.

"Hey, where "you'ens" been? Nice day; maybe we should skip school," Will greeted them.

"Skip school, great idea with the tournament game tomorrow night," Ronnie answered with some attitude.

"Coach would understand our need for spring, that almost rhymes."

"Rhyme my ass," someone in the group rebuked him causing a series of lewd comments thrown at Will.

Marc, leaning against the wall shared some news, "coach just told me in the hall that we play Wellsburg tomorrow night. All the games this week will be at Follansbee. I like that floor, it's big and well lit."

"Wellsburg certainly is a team we should beat," Spider chimed in.

"Well, we beat them twice already; should be an easy win," was Will's response.

"Yeah, you're right, but let's not think it's going to be that easy. If we play like we did against Charleston, it could be a different story," Ron cautioned.

"Charleston was a terrible game for us. I have thought about that game—even just last night. If we had played a decent game, we would have won. They may be number one in the state, but we are better when we show up and play like we should," Marc was preaching. Heads nodded in agreement.

Just a week ago! The next to the last regular season game, Charleston had come to Weirton and beat the Red Riders by six points. It was not even that close, with just two minutes to play, Weir was down by twelve, when Melvin hit four straight shots to cause a final score of 56-50. The Riders had been terrible all game. They needed to and had usually played better. What a disaster!

"There were some really dumb ideas in there. We need to do something with a little more thought, less slapstick," Amanda grumbled. She was not pleased with the discussion of the possibilities for the senior production.

"Don't worry. Everyone was just making wild statements. The school will not let us throw water on the stage or some stupid stunt like that," Niki tried to calm her down a little as they walked into the library. They crossed the room to the back of the stacks where a few tables sat empty. Opening their binders, the girls began writing down ideas. The two of them along with Jamie had been designated by the class president to bring the three best ideas before the class council. At first they concentrated on their task, but the discussion soon drifted to the discussion of the Sadie Hawkins dance.

"Willy said he really liked our switcheroo. He had a lot of fun with Sarah. He said they laughed most of the time they were together," Niki sputtered as she slammed her notebook shut.

Amanda grinned as she thought about Will and Sarah. They truly had been laughing each time she had seen them. "That's because they don't take life very seriously. They are both jokesters. They are fun loving kids—not ready to grow up."

"That's a bit harsh!" Jamie rushed to their defense. "They are both bloody nice."

"I agree. I didn't mean anything mean by that. They are my friends. I love them, but they do like their jokes and like laughing."

Jamie smiled, "Ah know, sorry to 've jumped. They both do try to be fun, but they are not really very good jokes." She continued, "Ah really had a great time Saturday. What a great night. Sage was very nice; very polite, talked very smoothly with my parents. They liked him a great deal. He n Ah talked about so many different things."

"Well … it sounds like he made a big impression on you. Is he a new love?" Niki teased.

"No, don't be silly. Marc is my lad, my guy. All Ah was trying to say is that Sage is very pleasant. We did not know each other except here at school, n Ah was surprised that we had such a good time together. It's always nice to find someone who talks about the things you like, that's all."

Niki looked at Amanda, then back to Jamie, "sounds like the start of a new American friendship."

"Oh, bugger off!"

"Ouch, that hurt."

"Sorry, Ah'm kidding. Ah'll show you why you are daft," Jamie reached inside her collar pulling out the gold chain Marc had given her with his gold football and ring attached.

"What is that?" Niki exclaimed. Amanda stepped close. With a muffled scream, she exclaimed, "It's a ring and one of those awesome footballs." She jumped a little in place, squealing, "Marc gave you his class ring, his football from last year and the necklace!"

Jamie was wiggling, dancing, crying, laughing all at the same time. "Yes, yes, look at them," she exclaimed as she pulled them out so they could see them better.

Congratulations were repeated louder than permitted in a library as the three girls hugged. Mr. Pfeiffer moved quickly between the stacks warning the three. "Quiet down or out you go."

As the final bell for the day began its ringing, they left the library, went to their lockers and headed for the bus. Sitting in the very rear of the bus, they picked up the conversation where it had ended.

"What does this mean?" Amanda questioned. "It is really special to have a guy's ring and football. What did he say?"

"Well, Marc did not say much. He wanted me to've them n wear them. That's all."

"He must have said something more. What did you say? This is like a step before you get engaged. You're engaged, that's what this is, you're engaged!" Niki continued to press for answers.

"No…no, he just gave me the ring and ball. We did not talk about, you know, anything else. He said he really liked me n wanted me to be his girl, officially his girl."

"That sounds," Niki searched for the word, "that sounds…"

"I have Ron's football. I don't think he has a ring, but I do have his football," Amanda admitted.

"What does that mean to you, to you and Ron?" Jamie asked.

"Well, we have spoken about the possibility of getting married after we both graduate from college, not now, after. The football is like a pre-engagement thing for us."

"Niki jumped in, "Wow, I was right. Jamie, have you told your parents? What did they say?

Jamie hesitated, in deep contemplation. Finally, she said, "No, Ah haven't; Ah did not tell them."

"I'm tired. My shoulder's killing me," Ron stretched out as best he could on the narrow, short, rather hard school bus seat. The bus was just leaving the Follansbee High School parking lot, heading back to Weirton. As it moved along Route Two, it passed the massive Follansbee steel plant along the Ohio River, the bus and everyone in it bouncing up and down. The road was not in good shape, but the real reason was the lack of, or at least the worthlessness, of the shocks. School buses were built for kids going to and from school, not for tall athletes and lengthy travel.

"I was dragging that fourth quarter. That last shot was a brick. The ball felt like a brick, a very heavy brick," Will supported Ron's comment. The river could be seen on the left, Steubenville beyond with some lights, but the scene was extremely bleak.

The final Sectional game was history. They had won and were now the 1959 North Sectional Champs. Three victories, in just five days, a very tough five days! The first two games, Tuesday and Thursday had gone as expected ending with victories without much challenge. Tonight was a different story. Triadelphia was better than their record had predicted. The sectional championship game started with some quick, easy baskets. By the end of the first quarter the Red Riders were up by ten points. The second and third quarters were just the opposite. Poor passes, poor defense, terrible shooting turned the score one hundred and eighty degrees in the other direction. At the start of the fourth quarter, Weir was down by six. It took the entire fourth quarter for them to take the lead back. In the very last minute, they had rallied to a lead of five points to win the championship and the chance to go to the Regional Tournament.

"The only thing that saved us tonight was that they got tired, too," Ron added. "At the end that tall number thirty-two was breathing so hard, I thought he was going to keel over."

Marc, sprawling in the seat in front of Ron, raised his head just above the seat back to add, "I thought I was going to fall over at the end, too. Playing three games in five days is just too much for me."

"Well, we did this last year, also. Was it this tiring then? Maybe, we are getting older," Will laughed at his own joke.

"Yes, but last year we didn't play the entire game. We had five or more subs who could rest us. Not this year. I played the entire game—never came out. I think you did, too," Marc looked at the other two. He was right; they had played the entire game as had Spider, who was already sound asleep across the aisle.

"Yeah, I remember now. We had more subbing last year. I only started in half the games. Could have used some help tonight," Ron's voice trailed off as he also disappeared into his seat.

"Are you going to church tomorrow or not?" was Niki's mother's question, asked for the third time.

"I'm tired, just want to go to bed right now. Ask me in the morning," Niki answered as she dragged herself up the stairs toward her room.

"If you don't decide right now, I will just let you sleep in."

"Alright, let me sleep. If I wake up and want to go, I'll come down."

"This pace is going to get you sick. You can't do everything. You cheer, go out almost every night, and stay at school to do this or that. You need to slow down. What about Penn? Is it a yes or a no?"

"You know it is a yes," she stopped on the second step and sat with her elbows on her knees and face cupped in her hands. "I will write Penn this week and accept. I am going there just like you and Dad and everyone else in our family."

"I shouldn't have brought that up at this late hour. I am just concerned about your doing too much and getting yourself sick."

"There is so much ahead. All of us, Amanda, Sarah and all the girls want to be a part of everything as high school ends. This is the last few months that we will all be together. It is fun, but frightening, too." Niki was looking up at her mom with sad, tear filled eyes.

"I know, hon. Remember, the world doesn't end with graduation. It just becomes bigger, more friends, more to do, the whole world opens up."

"You sound like Jamie. That's what she says. She talks about her world falling apart when she left England to come here. Happiness was gone from her for weeks, and then suddenly there was a new school, new chums, as she calls us." Niki had the start of a grin.

"She would know, leaving all that she held dear, a new land, for a different life. That would be hard, but she did it."

"Yes, she did. She has been a 'cool cat' here."

"A 'cool cat.' Yes, that is a good description of her. And, you will be, too, as this school year ends and you wake up in some Penn dormitory. Think of all the cute boys who will be there."

"Mom! What kind of a comment is that!"

"Well, that's how I met your father. It turned out good for me and your father. We had you and your brother. That's what love brings."

"Mom, you don't have to get so personal. I'm going to bed."

"Well, life is personal. Good night dear. Sleep well and sleep late."

Principal Paige was the last one into the conference room at a very early hour on Monday. He took a seat among the coaches, the few staff members who oversaw the athletic program and with Coach Baker, more correctly, the Dean of Students, sitting at the head. Coach Baker had been the Weir High coach of every sport during the 30s, 40s and early 50s. Retired from coaching, he was now the dean, but still very involved as an advisor with the athletic program. Everyone still called him coach, his gray well-trimmed hair and weather worn face, made him the obvious senior stateman in the room.

Coach Baker opened the discussion: "Congratulations to Coach Warren and Coach Romeo on a fine sectional victory. The team played great. This week begins the regional tournament and we have a good chance to win it. For a team that was not thought to be exceptional before the season, they surprised everyone. The only concern is that once we get past the five starters, we are weak. As long as they stay fresh and play their game, they can play with anyone. Coach, what do you expect this week?"

Coach Warren glanced around, "I expect to win the regional. We have not played any of the other teams, but we have played some of their opponents, and have beaten them all. You are correct, we do rely on the five starters with maybe two subs. We could go deeper on subs, but we would greatly reduce our play. The top five players work so well together, and they play team ball better than any team I have ever had. We play Moundsville on Thursday on their home court. We should beat them. Coach Romeo, do you want to chime in?"

"Yes. We may have a big advantage by not having played these teams before. That is our defense. All three teams have one star that does most of their scoring. They each have someone who averages twenty or more points a game. We have seen single manned teams before; we played a box and one very effectively. I think we can do that here. They may never have faced someone playing that type of defense, or a team such as ours that plays it so well. It will be our surprise for them."

The discussion went on for an hour covering travel, meals, fans, tickets, even the possibilities of new uniforms. Everyone was excited. It had been a very long time since Weir High had gone to the final four in the state tournament. This might be the year.

"Can't you just relax? All you've talked about on the phone last night n now here at lunch is basketball, basketball and more basketball. Ah know it's important, but there are other things going on, too!"

"Sorry birdie."

"Don't call me that! You are not English. Ah'm not a 'bird.' You don't even know what that word means in England. It is not nice," Jamie was furious with Marc. However, the reason was something besides his conversation about basketball.

"Alright, I never wanted to make you mad. I was just joking with you. 'Bird' is probably not a nice thing to call a girl. I am really sorry. Please let's not fight."

"We're bloody not fighting, and Ah'm not mad. You just get on my nerves sometime with all of these American things," Jamie's voice was frosty and caused the others to stare at them. "Now I'm sorry," she tried to change her tone. The group looked away. Jamie placed her head against his. "Sorry. There is just so much going on. Ah can't keep track of it all. Last week everything was basketball. The layout for the year book is not done. Ah'm in charge of all of the activities pictures. Ah 've to get those done before the end of the month."

"Slow down, it will all ..."

But she wouldn't slow down or even listen to Marc. "Ah'm responsible, not you. You're never responsible for anything. It's all on me!"

"Wait, wait, now, I'm mad," Marc's volume was up a couple of notches and heads were again turning towards them.

Jamie adjusted the back of her hair, undid the clasp on the necklace, reached over and dropped it in Marc's lap. "Here is your ring n football." Marc's face was suddenly ashen. Jamie picked up her books, rushed out to the main floor and started to trot towards the auditorium door.

Marc rose partway in his seat, and then collapsed back down. She was gone before he realized what was happening. The bell rang ending lunch time. Eyes from everyone sitting close enough to hear their exchange were fixed on him. Marc sat completely still. Amanda, Ron, Will, Niki and even Danni gathered around him. A few questions were raised: "What happened? Why were you arguing? Did you really give her your ring and your gold football?" Marc answered none of the questions. His only comment was "Leave me alone." One by one, they started for the next class leaving him alone.

At the start of practice, the coaches discussed the past week's win, gave them information about the Regional tournament, the Moundsville team, travel times, etc. The coaches were proud of what the team had accomplished and predicted a successful outcome in the Regional semi-finals.

The actual practice was very dissatisfying. Passes were sloppy, shooting was dismal. The starting five were just lethargic. Part way through the practice, the coaches called a break, sat everyone down to see if they could muster some improvement. This proved unsuccessful and practice ended early.

Coach Warren sat down with Coach Romeo on the bleachers and just looked at each other. "Not the same team. Are they tired? Are they played out after the tough game Saturday?"

"I don't know, Jim. You're right; they are a different bunch than they have been all year. It seemed to me the big problem was Marc. He didn't seem well, or maybe not awake. He is the leader—as he goes, so goes the team. Any indication that he is hurt or sick?" Coach Warren asked.

"None that I have heard about," Coach Romeo answered.

The two sat for another fifteen minutes trying to figure out what just happened and what to do about it.

"Hello Mrs. Toliver, this is Marc. Is Jamie there?"

"Oh, hello, Marc," she answered in a friendly voice. "Ah heard you played very well in the basketball tourney. Very good of you boys to win!"

"Thanks Mrs. Toliver. Can Jamie come to the phone?"

"Yes, right. Ah'll get her." Marc could hear her calling for Jamie. He waited, hearing more calling, but no one picked up the phone. Finally, she returned to tell him, "Sorry Marc, she can't talk right now."

"She can't talk on the phone?" Marc stammered.

"No, she said she would see you in school." After a long silent moment on both ends, Mrs. Toliver said sympathetically, "Sorry Marc, Ah hope you two can talk tomorrow. Good night."

Practice on Tuesday was not much better than Monday. Even Coach Baker stopped to watch. He had told Coaches Warren and Romeo that Marc had not been in class Monday afternoon and had skipped his last two classes today. They suspected a couple of problems, but had ruled out illness or injury. They decided to let it sit for one more day before trying to intervene.

As practice ended, showers were taken and most of the team dressed quickly and headed out of the locker room. Ron stopped at Marc's locker. "Jamie gave me this note for you as I left school. She told me to tell you to read it before you leave practice. So here it is. You two had better settle this thing before Thursday's game."

As Ron headed out, Marc opened the note, it was short. *I'm sorry. Please come to my house right after your practice today.* Marc just sat by his locker pondering what to do. Should he go? It might be best to just not answer the note. What else could she say now? It was clear she wanted to break-up. He did not know why. Maybe, he should at least try to find out, and talk with her.

Jamie was waiting for him at the front door. Her greeting was warm and friendly although she did not ask him in. Instead, she stepped outside, took his hand and asked, "Can we sit in your car? It's cold outside."

"Sure, the car is nice and warm."

As she entered, she remained over on the passenger side against the window, her head down, her eyes semi-closed. She shuddered, "Ah need to apologize. Ah don't know what made me explode like that. Ah don't even remember what Ah said or what you said. Ah remember everyone looking at us…Ah'm so ashamed of myself."

"No one has said anything to me about it…" Marc attempted to say.

"Ah know. No one has asked me either. They just all look away, don't say a thing, but, Ah can't stand that either."

"That will change. Hopefully things will return to normal."

"That's what Ah want. Ah want to go back n erase that day. Do you think we can just forget about it? Please?"

"We can," he smiled and reached for her hand. She moved closer. "I have already forgotten, forgotten everything about Monday."

She leaned over and kissed his cheek, "you are so sweet; so wonderful to me. Ah don't know how Ah deserve you." She kissed him again. They nuzzled up in each other's arms as dusk settled in.

Jamie spoke first again. "Ah had a long talk with my Mum last night after you called. Ah had not even told her you had given me your class ring n golden football."

"Why on earth not?"

"Ah don't know. Ah really loved them. They made me feel special, very special. Ah just didn't tell her. Ah wore them under my clothes n only told Niki n Amanda a few days after you gave them to me."

Marc was stunned. "I thought you were pleased and excited about them," he stammered.

"Ah was, Ah really was, but, Ah was unsure of what they meant."

"What they meant? What, what do you mean? They meant you and I are going together. You are special to me. I had hoped I was special to you."

Emotions had started to rise again. Jamie attempted to keep the conversation from getting out of hand. "Right, all that is true. We are going together, n we really like each other, but a ring n your football is a big step. They mean something more." She paused, looked up at Marc, "Just going together as a couple, boyfriend n girlfriend is enough without these gifts."

"Well, yes, you are right, but…"

"When Ah showed Niki and Amanda, Amanda told me she has Ronnie's gold football. To her it means they are more than a couple. She says it means they are, as she put it … pre-engaged. They want to remain a couple after high school while they go to college n maybe get married afterwards. She told me the gold football is a long term commitment. Is that what you meant when you gave me your ring n football?"

"Wow, eh, I…"

"Your answer is very important to us both. When my mother asked that question, Ah didn't know what to say."

Marc looked around at the darkening sky. With the night closing in, the coupe became an isolated cube. "I gave them to you for a number of reasons; first, because I want to be with you now and in the future, maybe forever… maybe. You are very special to me. I would use the word 'love,' but I'm not sure what 'love' really means. You are more to me than just a high school girl friend. I know I want to be with you after high school…"

"That was awesome, brilliant. Ah don't know what to say. You're spot on."

"What do the ring and football mean to you? What do you want them to mean?" Marc pressed.

"Ah thought that was what you meant. Ah... Ah got scared a bit when Amanda n Niki reacted so, n then you were so involved in basketball n Ah couldn't really talk to you. Ah think that is what they mean to me, too."

"Is that alright with you?"

"Yes Marc, yes it is," Jamie's eyes were shining. Tears were starting as she gave him a passionate kiss. "Yes, it means all that to me, too, and much more."

Marc reached into his pocket, pulled out the necklace, ring and football. "Would you consider wearing these now?"

"Yes, my love, yes." The knot that had been deep inside each of them started to loosen, untie and passed away.

Thursday night's game was too easy. The Red Riders dominated from the start. The starting five shared the scoring almost evenly. The box and one defense really destroyed Moundsville's offense. Their top scorer, who was also their point guard, playmaker and leader, rarely touched the ball as Marc followed him all over the court. That win meant they would move on.

Saturday evening's game was against New Martinsville, a team that had won fifteen consecutive games during the regular season. They had two very high scorers, a guard and the center. Fans from both schools filled the Moundsville gym to overflowing. Most anticipated the game would be a down to the wire finish. They were wrong. The box and one defense created havoc. Ron had a great night with twenty-one points, Spider followed with seventeen. The Red Riders won their first Regional tournament in almost twenty years. They were going to State! They were in the final four in 1-AAA in West Virginia.

As the game ended, fans rushed the floor and the team. Someone cut the nets down; the team was mobbed by friends and strangers alike. The bus ride home was a celebration. As they stopped in front of the school, Coach Warren stood at the front of the bus and the team fell silent.

"Wonderful victory, but it's not over. Next week is your week. Rest up. Enjoy the win, but think about Friday night in Huntington." He nodded to the driver who opened the door and he jumped out.

"Not many made it to church today. I know my bed felt very comfortable, but my mother said no."

"Mine, too. Ah came because Ah wanted to see Marc, so Ah hope he shows," Jamie answered.

Jamie and Sarah were the only two teenagers sitting in the community room of Cove Church. Usually there would be at least ten or twelve in their Sunday school class. It was a self-run class with no instructor, just open discussions about religion, and current events as they related to religion. The youth, mostly seniors and juniors, even some home from college, could discuss what was important to them and their religion. Some days the religion part proved to be a stretch.

"Hi," it was Marc.

"Hi you," answered Sarah, "I can't believe you got up for church."

"Well, for church and to see you two."

"Sure, to see me. I think you mean Jamie."

"Well, maybe Jamie." The two touched hands as he sat across from them. "Quiet morning."

Sarah answered, "Very quiet. What time did you get home?"

"About one, late, very late, a very slow bus ride."

"Ah'm so proud of you n the others," Jamie told Marc and squeezed his hand.

Sarah mocked Jamie, "I'm proud too. I really am. It was an exciting night. Next week will be even more exciting," Sarah's tone changed the more she talked. "Winning is fun. Everyone is happy when we win."

"Certainly, I'm happy," Marc added. "This week is going to be so busy with much to do. Then we'll be traveling to Marshall, staying in a hotel. I am discombobulated. It's just like when you went to Charleston. It's a travel game."

"Ah know, Niki has invited me to go with the cheerleaders again. They will 've rooms for Friday n Saturday nights, just like Charleston."

Sarah jumped in, "We already have rooms, and many of the mothers are going with a big bunch of girls. It's all been arranged already."

"Why are you asking me then? You are all set. I don't even know when or who we play," Marc muttered.

"We just want you to know we are ready to go to support you. A big community group is planning to be there. These arrangements started on

Friday even before your game on Saturday," Sarah blurted out. "Everyone knew you were going to win."

"So did I," Marc stated matter of factly, "so did I."

Marc was at a side basket practicing foul shots. Others were spread out across the gym when the whistle blew. Everyone gathered around the coaches at mid-court.

"We are leaving for Huntington tomorrow at eight a.m. at the school. Make sure you are not late. Hate to think of you walking the two hundred plus miles." Smiles, smirks and mostly stone faces greeted the lighthearted comment. "We will have a Greyhound for the trip this time." This time several "yeses" were heard.

"Have clothes for three days; athletic stuff, again for three days. As usual, our team will arrive in coats and ties. We will arrange getting things washed between games, but bring extras just in case. Try to have a few dollars with you for spending money. You don't need much, but try to have at least ten dollars or so. If that is a problem, please see Coach Romeo."

"For the trip tomorrow bring some fruit, crackers or something to munch on. We will have drinks on the bus. We plan to eat lunch in Parkersburg and will be staying at a motel in Huntington. We should get there about two in the afternoon. There will be two to a room, rest during the afternoon. Dinner will be at five at a nearby restaurant, and the game is at seven. After the game, we will go back to the same restaurant for an evening snack. Lights out tonight at eleven, no exceptions. Coach Romeo, any comments?"

"None coach, except I will say, if anything is unclear or something unexpected happens, talk to us directly."

Coach Warren looked around. "I have been coaching for twenty-five plus years. I have never coached a state championship basketball team. You will be my first. You will win it all this weekend! You have everything it takes: talent, drive, confidence and above all … team! Enjoy what you are about to experience. Now, let's have a good practice. Everyone home early tonight and get a good night's sleep."

The predictions proved right. At seven on Friday in the semi-final game, the Red Riders started strong and ended strong leaving the Marshall University Field House with a lopsided victory. The flow of the game went their way, so much so that the starters were all rested at different times in the first half and still led by eleven points at intermission. The second half was much of the same with a final victory up by seventeen points.

With the final seconds finished, the fans cheered at full volume. Some came down on the floor to personally congratulate the team; others waved, shouted and threw confetti. The team members took it in stride, resolved to take the next and last step. Real celebrations would have to wait until tomorrow.

The final game of the evening would determine who the Red Riders would play for the state title. Undefeated Charleston would play a new county consolidated high school from near Shepardstown. They had been a "Cinderella" team in their Regional tournament and they would be again in the state semi-final game. Charleston was defeated by one point and was out of the finals. The Red Riders and their coaches watched some of the game, and realized that the "Cinderella" team was very dependent on a fast, quick point guard to run their offense. The Red Riders would play a box and one defense again.

"That was a good crowd tonight. A lot of Weirton people made the trip," Spider mused as they lounged while eating their after-game meal.

Will put down his coke, picked up a french fry, "more than I expected, and a lot of girls."

"You would notice the girls! What about Niki? I thought she was your love," Spider joked.

"She is, she is. I was just making an observation, that's all."

"That's never 'all' with you, Will. Niki knows you're always looking," Ron entered into the conversation.

"Well, she's always looking, too. We have no close ties or commitments like you two," he was looking straight at Marc and Ron.

"I'm too tired to deal with this 'nothing' baloney," Marc took a last swallow of his drink, stood, and walked towards the door and the waiting bus.

Ron stood and walked out, too, yelling, "Marc, wait up."

Everyone else followed suit with someone saying, "bedtime."

Their coaches and administrators had been sitting watching and listening to their conversation. Coach Romeo looked at Coach Warren. "They never talked about tonight's game or tomorrow," he paused, watched the team climbing into the bus. "They know the importance of what they did tonight and the opportunity they have tomorrow."

Coach Warren looked around the table, "They are all business."

A mid-morning breakfast started Saturday followed by a short tour of Marshall University campus, as spectators watched the first of four title games for the different school divisions, followed by a short afternoon rest, and dinner at five and finally the Division I-AAA title game.

As Weir took to the floor for warm-ups, the field house was nearly full. Weirton fans were there in droves, many more than last night's game. Their cheers, shouts, and yells were loud and supportive. Finally, the last game of the season was underway. It started, progressed and ended with the Red Riders in control.

With an eleven point victory, the Red Riders were the West Virginia Division I-AAA State Basketball Champions for 1959! The Weirton High School basketball team had done what had not been done before in the school's forty-plus year history.

Coach Warren waited until the last minute to substitute en masse, a new team to replace the five starters, giving the stars an opportunity to experience a standing ovation from their fans. They exited the floor with ear to ear smiles, and arms raised.

At the final whistle, fans rushed the floor towards the entire team. The excitement was electric with hugging, jumping, kissing, running, laughing, mobbing. The whirlwind of jubilation continued as the coaches and team made their way to the center of the floor, where they were presented with the victor's trophy. It took nearly a half hour for the crowd to exhaust themselves and begin to disband.*

*It is appropriate to acknowledge, that the real history of the West Virginia Division I-AAA 1959 State Basketball Championship records the Charleston High School Mountain Lions as champions who had an outstanding 1958-59 season.

The five hour bus ride home was under way early the next morning. Everyone was still sleepy, subdued from a very short night and a very large breakfast. After their lunch stop in Parkersburg, the atmosphere livened up with a lot of chatter, even a few songs, a number of silly jokes and a lot of ribbing. They were going home as state champs. Could there be any greater reason for being cheerful. Just watching the Ohio River out the window seemed to bring joy and crazier joking. Boats, barges or a rusty scow brought comments like: "look at that, that's what I want, a speed boat or maybe a job on a barge would be fun."

As they passed Wheeling, Marc drifted into a philosophical state. With basketball now over, the final stage of high school was starting. Only two more months left - then what? He still had not settled on any course of action. He really did not need to decide anything. So what if he had no plans for after graduation. He could take his time and just wait to see what happens. The only thing he really had to decide was his future with Jamie. He had already decided that he wanted her in his future. Wanting to be together was a decision they had made together.

Marc was sidetracked back to the present. They were at the Weirton city limits. Police cruisers, two fire trucks and dozens of cars, vans, and pick-ups were waiting to escort them into town. Horns and more horns were filling the air, sirens blaring, bubble lights, red, green and blue flashed. People lined the street as the parade moved like a horde of snails toward the center of town.

Two blocks from City Hall and the Community Center, the bus stopped. Everyone got out, walked down the center of the street while spectators greeted them from both sides. The Weir High band, "The Biggest Dance Band in the Land" led the way, almost the entire student body of Weir High joined in the parade. As they reached the Center, the band led them through the multiple doors into the gym where even more of the community waited. The team was led to the stage to be recognized, congratulated, praised and made into heroes.

After nearly an hour long vigorous welcome, the team could finally make its way down into the crowd and search out close friends and family. Marc and Jamie found each other quickly. They stood wrapped in each other's arms, laughing, crying and dancing simultaneously. Finally they looked adoringly at each other, kissed and kissed again, only to suddenly break apart when they realized both sets of parents were standing beside them.

"Whew, every class has held a celebration. It's like a bash. Ah'm 'aving a blast with this winning thing. Even the professors are even into it. We spent one entire class just talking about what we did at the tournament. Ah'm on cloud nine. It's been crazy for a couple of weeks around here," Jamie was still enjoying the jubilation of the weekend.

Afternoon classes were canceled and a pep rally scheduled in the stadium. In the alley, the band was already marching their way to the demonstration. The entire school was preoccupied with whooping it up over the championship.

Niki, who had been leading the cheers during the twenty-five game season, was in burn-out mode. "This is my last cheerleading thing. I am tired, my voice is gone, my legs are sore, enough already!" The excitement of the past three weeks, especially the last five days, had Niki exhausted; one last pep rally was all she could take.

They made it out the side door, across the parking lot filled with school buses and into the stadium. "You are right. Ah'm ready for some down time. There is so much to do about the yearbook, going to university, just graduating. Maybe we will be able to rest after today," Jamie was suddenly less confident. "Ah need to finish my job on the Weirite. All of that is due at the end of this week. Right now, all Ah have is a big stack of pictures."

"Well, for me, the big problem is prom. Will has not asked me yet. For all I know, he will decide not to go. You know him. He is, or can be, a real jerk," Niki complained.

"Blimey, Marc hasn't asked me either. Everything is about him, his basketball, his car, his job. Everything is Marc this, Marc that."

"You're right. Everything is about them. We spent three weeks running to their basketball games. It's time they did something for us, us girls." Niki was back to her old frisky self, "Let's get this pep thing over with."

The band had already started to play the fight song: *"Weir High School Victory March," words and music by Theodore A. Whitaker: Let's give a cheer for Weir High 'til victory and let us make Weir High our pride. For we will sing and cheer forever, through all kinds of weather...and raise the Red and Black high o'er our heads, and lead and we will follow on.*

The teen room was packed. Weather was warm for a late March evening. The entrance way to the outside was in constant motion as kids ran in and out keeping the party atmosphere going. Marc and Jamie finally were able to sit down after dancing for the last half hour. It was their first real date for almost a month, and it was comforting to have nothing to attend and be alone with each other.

Jamie was thinking it was just fun to sit quietly in their corner watching people come and go when Marc grabbed her hand, "C'mon, let's go for a walk. I want to show you something."

"What?"

"You'll see. It's not far just over by the baseball field."

"Oh no, Ah know. You want to go to that covered seat area n make out!"

"No, I just wanted to, well, you know," Marc answered sheepishly.

"Ah know what? Ah know you!" Jamie teased, recognized his motive.

"Yes, you do know me. All I want to do is hold you. It has been a long time since we have really been together. What is wrong with that?"

"Nothing except that you were trying to trick me," she leaned in and kissed him on his forehead. "There, that is enough until we say good night." They continued mocking each other, clowning around while eventually strolling over to the baseball diamond. Shadows of other couples could be seen scattered among the stands. Still joking with each other, they pretended to be having quite a torrid rendezvous complete with groans and heavy breathing when someone called out their names. It turned out to be Will and Niki out doing the same thing. The four of them sat in the dark enjoying each other's company beginning with a lighthearted discussion until finally delving into the more serious issues that were important to each of them. Life suddenly seemed full of hope. With luck, the future would fall into place.

As Marc drove Jamie home, they were silent, having talked everything out with their friends. Only the radio and the hum of the engine broke the silence. *Does she love me, with all her heart? Should I worry when we're apart? It's a lover's question, I'd like to know. Does she need me as she pretends? Is this a game...It's a lover's question. I'd like to know; I'd like to know when she's not with me...* the words of the song by *Clyde McPhatter* asked.

As they turned onto Jamie's street, Marc asked, "Would you like to go behind the club and park for a little while? It's still early."

"Still wanting to make out, huh"

"Of course, don't you?"

"Ah do, but let's just go home. Ah don't trust myself. We may become too involved too soon."

Marc said nothing for a moment. He kept driving towards her home adding, "I guess you are right, but…it's just that I think about you all day, and all night."

Skittishly, she answered by resting heavily against him as they pulled into her driveway and ended the evening.

Jamie sat at a small, white desk in her room. The family had just finished Sunday dinner, later than usual. They had gone to church in the morning, a family ride in the afternoon; an unusually quiet day. She and Marc just finished a short non-productive phone call. He was ready to eat following a long double shift at the gas station, so the conversation was restricted.

She picked up a pen, began writing to a Birmingham address on the envelope addressing the letter to Tommy Shelby, a long time friend from Birmmie.

Hi Tommy,

Thank you for the post. I assume you got my address from granny. We had a great visit with them over the holidays. I am fine here in the U.S. Very different, but it is fun to see and learn new things.

It sounds as though you and your mates are having fun at University. I am in what they call a high school here. Classes are easy, and there are many more activities than in our Birmmie school. We just won the State basketball tournament. Hope you understand American basketball. We travelled with the team—that is, I and all the cheerleaders—great fun.

I will be coming home to England for most of the summer! Then the plan is for me to come back here to the States to go to university. I will go to a very, very big university called West Virginia State University.

Please try to see me this summer in Birmingham. Write again soon.

Your good friend, Jamie

Jamie finished the letter, put it in the envelope and would give it to her father to post in the morning. She turned on the radio, laid on her bed and listened to *Connie Francis* crooning: *I'm sorry dear, so sorry dear. I'm sorry I made you cry. Won't you forget, won't you forgive. Don't let us say goodbye. One little word, one little smile...one little kiss won't you try. It breaks my heart to hear you sigh. I'm sorry I made you cry.*

Chapter 12

Passion

The library was ghostly, almost empty. It was the last period of the day, and everyone seemed to have left school or was hiding. Marc was searching for the library copy of the social studies textbook. He was behind in the class and needed to read a number of chapters. He searched the usual location, but no book. He considered finding a classmate with a book he could borrow.

"Are you looking for something, Marc?"

"Oh, hi Mr. Pfeiffer; yes, I'm looking for the copy of the social studies book for class. It is usually in this section, but I can't find it."

"No, you won't find it here. It's on my desk. I'll get it." He walked over to his desk near the windows, reached into a stack of books, picked out the one he wanted and returned to Marc.

"You never bought a copy, did you? That's why it would disappear for weeks at a time isn't it? Well?"

"You know I always have used the library's copy when I can," Marc said sheepishly.

"Have you ever owned a text book?"

"Yeah, a few…when the library didn't have a copy. I don't like carrying books around all day. It's easier to come to the library, read the copy and leave it for the next time."

"I will miss you next year. You are a regular customer." Mr. Pfeiffer started to walk away, turned suddenly, "Bring that copy back tomorrow, tomorrow."

"Yes sir, tomorrow," Marc acknowledged the order, knowing he would need it for at least a week. Out the door he ducked before the librarian could say anymore, and headed out the front door of the school as the end of the day bell rang. He spotted Will sitting on the top step of the stairs to the parking lot. He walked up to him, scaring him with a sudden comment, "You look lost!"

"Damn, you scared me," Will stated as he twisted around with a lurch. "Hell, you bastard, you could have given me a heart attack."

"You have to have a heart first, Jackass," Marc was taking a seat next to him, "but you do look lost."

"Well, maybe, I'm bored. No more practices; Niki is off doing something with the senior play, whatever that is."

Suddenly people were rushing past them, running for their buses, cars or just scurrying to get off school property as fast as they could. A traffic jam was building up behind Marc and Will as they blocked part of the staircase.

"Hey, get out of the way, dipstick," someone yelled.

"Sit on it, Bozo," Will yelled back.

Marc glanced at Will, wrinkled his face, "You are down, way down."

"Not really, I just need to be doing something. I seem to be upset about doing nothing…do you sometimes get an uneasy feeling someplace deep inside, way down inside," Will's voice trailed off and he stared into space.

"I've had that feeling. Usually at night if I can't sleep. I get kind of…I don't know, concerned about everything and nothing at the same time," Marc shrugged his arms with his hands open to the sky.

They looked at each other, and then searched the scene in front of them.

"That mill is really big. It covers everything, even the horizon, one big black monster. My mother calls it the black coffin. Men go in there each day, come out looking like death," Will philosophized.

"Just look at it. It is Weirton. Anywhere you look, all you can see is mill, always black, gray, and dirty. It never sleeps. It has a life of its own. Boy, thinking like that can be depressing," Marc continued to gaze at the dark mountainous structure. Straight ahead and to the west, the mammoth buildings strangled Weir Avenue and Weirton Heights in their shadows. To the south, Marc could see houses, roof tops and more of the mill. The stadium was to the north, surrounded by a ten foot high privacy fence, and boxed in by more of the mill. Beyond the stadium, the mill stretched on to infinity.

"The mill is everywhere. You can't escape it. It is so large it seems as though it has been here forever. It makes us what we are, what we will become. I want to be a part of it. At least I think I do," Marc was talking to Will and maybe to himself.

"Are you staying here after school?" Will looked quizzically at Marc.

"I still don't know. I still have to talk to the Navy. The Army turned me down because of my physical and that heart thing. What about you, is it Marshall?"

"I signed the scholarship papers about a week ago. Got a football scholarship that pays about half the cost."

"Good for you. Marshall looked like a nice place. Congratulations."

"Thanks, I think. I'm not completely sure. If it doesn't work out, I can always come back to the mill or else sell cars with my uncle."

"You're right. The mill will always be here. They can't pick it up and move it," Marc mused. "The mill is always a fall-back."

"Ron told me when we were in Huntington that he has a full ride to Tennessee. Must be nice to have everything paid for."

"Yeah, he told me that, too. He's excited."

"Carl Miner has a full ride to some big ten school. He may even leave school early and enroll up there for summer classes."

"Heard that, too," Marc added as he continued to watch the sun lowering over the hills.

"Carl's not going to play baseball this year since the college does not want him to risk getting hurt. So, no baseball for Carl and now no catcher for us," Will looked hopefully at Marc. "You are going to come out for baseball, aren't you? Practice starts Wednesday."

Marc thought for a moment and finally answered, "I'm not going to play baseball this year. Just like last summer, I really don't have any interest in baseball. I'm not that good."

"Come on, you have to play; without Carl, we don't have a catcher!"

"Yes, you do, I'm sure there are some underclassmen who can play."

"What are you going to do, just sit around the last two months of school? You need to do something."

"I will. I'll spend time with Jamie."

"I just can't go with you after school. We are working on the senior play. It is only two weeks away and the script isn't done yet. Someone has to work on the set so I can't just leave after school."

"But, Jamie, we should be taking time for ourselves, not this stupid show."

"It is not stupid to me. It is going to be fun, and besides, you said that you would be part of the cast, remember? Not a speaking part, but part of the scenes."

"I will; I told you I would and I will."

"Now we have a new name for the play," Jamie was excited. "You know, it is about visiting countries around the world, so we are going to call it, 'Around the World in Twenty Minutes'."

"In what?"

"Twenty minutes. That's how long the play is going to be, twenty minutes."

Marc and Jamie had been talking on the phone for fifteen minutes about school, people and now, the upcoming farce of a senior play. Marc wanted to spend more time with Jamie, but she wanted to be part of as many school activities as possible. Once the play was over, she would start working on arrangements for the prom which he had finally remembered to invite her to. All of a sudden all the girls wanted official confirmed dates, something the guys had assumed was taken for granted.

"I have to go now. I have to talk to Niki about, ah, the play. See you tomorrow, Marc."

"I love you," was Marc's unsolicited comment.

"I thought you weren't going to use that word. You said that you didn't really know what it meant."

"Well, I still don't. That's love without a capital letter, all lower case."

"That makes a difference?" Jamie puzzled.

"It does to me, my love,"

"Goodnight Marc."

"Goodnight, my love."

As she hung up the phone, Jamie looked as though she were looking directly at Marc. She paused for minute, then picked up the receiver and started to dial Niki.

"Wait just a minute. You have been on the phone long enough. I am waiting for a call, so just put it back down, Lassie," her Dad interrupted.

"Oh, all right. I'm tired anyway." Jamie left the phone and went upstairs to her room. After looking through her clothes and picking out an outfit for tomorrow, she flopped on her bed. The radio was softly playing and she began to think about what was happening. The school year was ending. Suddenly, the pace was slowing; it was "walk, not run." In less than two months her American school experience would be over. The only things left were prom and the senior play, which was nothing but a farewell evening of vaudeville plays, the last buffoonery of the school year, then, graduation.

She was drifting off to sleep, still fully dressed thinking of England, listening to *Frankie Avalon singing, When a girl changes from bobby sox to stockings, and she starts trading her baby toys for boys…Then she's old enough to give her heart away.*

She wondered if she was old enough; was she giving up bobby sox?

"How's the Chrysler running?"

"Fine, just purring right along."

"Haven't seen you changing the oil recently. Are you keeping up with your maintenance?"

"The oil was changed at the gas station a couple of weeks ago. It's easier to crawl under the car in their garage. Do you want me to change yours?"

Marc's Dad was still not completely finished with dinner. He sipped his coffee, "No thanks. I changed it recently. By the way, where are you with the Navy? You said about a week ago that you were talking to a recruiter."

"I spoke with them Friday by phone. They want me to wait until I graduate and then take their physical. It's different somehow from the Army, and the guy thinks I can pass it. So, guess I'll take it in Steubenville."

"Marc, are you sure you want to go into the armed service? You don't have to," his mother joined into the conversation. The three of them were sitting at the kitchen table leisurely finishing their meal. Marc's sisters had already left without actually finishing everything and were back upstairs playing.

"I know I don't have to go into the Navy, but I have to start someplace! The Navy could be that place. It's a three year enlistment, training, could be ok."

"It could be if you want it to be. Just don't go because you think it is the only choice," his mother added.

"Your mother is right. Only go if you want to. You don't have to. I spoke with Mr. Gilbert from church. He says colleges are still looking for people. He could help."

"Dad, college is not for me. I'm through with going to school. I want to do something; earn money, be out on my own, maybe the Navy, maybe the mill or something."

Marc's Dad sat back in his chair. Every single time college was mentioned, Marc would bristle. It was time to stop pushing and let him make his own decision. After a moment, he asked, "How's Jamie?" changing the subject.

However, Marc was still offended by all the questions and said prickly, "she's fine, just fine."

"Don't take that tone with your father or me," his mother quickly dampened his rebellious spirit.

"Sorry. She is good. Sorry, I'm, I'm upset that everything is going so quickly, and I'm not sure where I am going."

"Marc," his mother laid her hand on his arm, "the decision will happen—maybe not today or tomorrow, but one day. There are decisions all throughout life. This one will happen. Enjoy your final weeks at high school." She attempted to impart some of her wisdom to him.

"Everyone seems set but me. I'm the only one with no place to go after school. Jamie and I have decided to stay together. She will be leaving for England right after graduation and then college. I will be stuck here waiting for her. I should do something so we can be together when she finishes."

"This sounds serious. What does 'stay together' mean? How are you going to stay together?" his father asked.

"Well, just being together, you know—going steady. We can't be together right now, but after, or maybe during her going to college we could."

"Being together sounds like, like you're talking about living together or marriage—or something else?" his father stumbled to find the right words.

"Not living together if we aren't married, but maybe we will get married soon. We haven't decided yet," Marc's answer was guarded, almost like a riddle. The quandary continued between the parents and their son, both sides trying to tie down clarity, both failing.

At that point both sisters pranced into the kitchen, bringing the discussion to a standstill—unfortunately before his parents had a chance to caution Marc about the slope he seemed to be sliding down. Marc immediately made an excuse about needing to go to the library, and was up and gone before his parents could corral him.

Back stage was crowded with nearly twenty girls. Some were sitting in the few chairs but most were just sitting on the floor trying to finalize the details of the senior play.

"I don't think we need many props. We could use signs with the nation's names on them, scattered around the stage, like street signs."

"That would work. They would be easy to make and move around."

"Let's arrange them by continents with the continent's name on a larger sign."

"That sounds like a go and not much construction needed. Is that okay with everyone?" Darby Shaw, the chairperson of the play committee attempted to get yet another detail settled. As everyone nodded in agreement, she checked that off her list and raised the next issue. "Girls, we need to get more of the guys involved. A few have said they will do something to help, but they never show up. How can we persuade them to help?"

"How about we set up a kissing booth?" Laughs followed the comment from someone in the corner.

"Well, maybe, but this is serious. We really need their help!" she tried to keep the discussion on track.

"Let's each bring a boy or even two to next Monday's meeting?"

"Sounds okay," Niki responded. She continued, "we could have the meeting later than right after school. The guys don't like to stay after school. They have sports and some have jobs. Some just like to leave school."

Amanda spoke up, "we always have to feed them." Everyone laughed.

"Please, quiet! We have to make this happen," Darby interjected. "Sounds like a good idea. We need to move quickly as the play night is only two weeks away. Niki, will you organize this for us?"

"Why me?"

Darby answered very businesslike. "It's your idea. Another issue settled." At that point, the restlessness of the group brought an adjournment to their meeting.

Niki had one of the family cars so she gave Amanda, Sarah and Jamie a ride home. It was almost five o'clock and all agreed the meeting had lasted way too long. They were all tired, hungry and frustrated.

"How did I get myself another job to do? Every time I open my mouth, I get stuck with something to do?" Niki asked of no one in particular as she drove out of the parking lot.

"You get stuck because people know you will get the job done. Fail once and they won't ask you again," Sarah analyzed.

Amanda agreed, "She's right, Niki, you're too good."

"I wish I were good at something," Sarah whined. "I can't even get a prom date. I still don't have one!"

"It is still early. The only reason we have dates is because we are going steady with someone. Not many of the other girls have been asked either," came the honeyed response from Amanda.

"It's hard waiting, not knowing if you're going to be asked. Maybe I will have to go stag, I don't want to go alone." Sarah began to cry.

"You are not going alone. There are a couple of great guys who still don't have dates. One of them will ask you, for sure," Niki tried to quash the blubbering.

"Who?" Sarah asked.

Niki was trying to drive and calm Sarah down. She looked over at Amanda, sitting in the passenger seat, "Tell her who they are."

"I'm not sure, but I know there are guys who don't have dates yet, really nice guys."

"You don't know any, you're just saying that," Sarah mumbled.

"Well, I know that Sage doesn't have a date. He says that he and Tom don't have dates. You know Tom Kec, or Rick Schild, Alex, Bruce, none of them has asked anyone. At least that is what Sage says, how about one of them?" Jamie joined the hubbub.

Niki was the first to respond to Jamie's roll call. "How do you know all about these guys? Are you playing matchmaker?"

"Sage and I talk after second period. He tells me things. That's all."

"Could you? Jamie? Could you just hint to him? He and I had a great time at the Sadie Hawkins dance. He owes me a date!" Sarah answered.

"Right, maybe, I don't know."

"Please Jamie? Please!

"Well, I'll try."

Amanda leaned over the front seat, "I'll help too. I know all those guys; Ron can talk to them. It will be okay. You'll have a date." She spoke directly to Sarah.

"Thanks, you guys. Thanks."

Niki and Amanda started a different topic in the front seat, Sarah became quiet. Jamie sat thinking about how she would bring up the subject with Sage.

They had been talking more since the Sadie Hawkins date rotation. She could tell that he liked her, so he probably would be willing to do her a favor.

"Get the basket to center stage, the reporter's desk on the right in front of the curtain—all the country signs in the wings! We only have five minutes," Darby Shaw was trying to get props, character actors and extras in their places for the final play of the evening, the last hurrah for the seniors. She thought the play, a cleverly written comedy about two Weirton High Seniors circling the globe in a hot air balloon, needed to move quickly to be funny. The opening featured Red Rider Rita, played by Amanda and Colt Chief Chad as her side kick who made mistakes in identifying countries as they passed over them in their basket. The trip was narrated by two reporters, Will and Niki, who followed them in a helicopter.

Most of the jokes were not funny, but the auditorium laughed anyway, or in truth, laughed at how corny the jokes were. As ninety percent of the audience was fellow students, the quality was not a priority. Making a fool of yourself was! Poor humor was part of just being a teenager. Each class was awarded a "Tony" by the so-called faculty judges.

The entire cast had been invited over to Darby's house for the traditional cast party. They were all anxious to see her new home. A new development had been built in Weirton Heights near the Pennsylvania border. The cast was in awe finding themselves walking up to a very large, well landscaped colonial home tucked into a woodsy site. It proved to be a great place for such a party as it contained an entire wing called a family room—an entirely new concept that none of them had ever seen before. Music was piped throughout the home and Darby's parents had laid out a feast on long tables across one side of the party room.

"This home is a monster and so beautiful," Jamie was speechless.

"They call this area Kings Estate, a lot of doctors, lawyers and executives live here," Marc's voice revealed his intolerable feelings. "My parent's entire home could fit into this one room."

Jamie punched him in the ribs, "I doubt that, but it is like a castle. You Americans want everything to be new and big, the bigger the better."

"Don't you want new things? Look at your home. It is bigger than mine, newer and with all new furniture. I know you are enjoying living in it."

"Yes, but we didn't have a choice. It was found for us and we did not bring our own furniture. I had to get all new clothes because what I had was all wool stuff. That's different than wanting things just to have them. We needed the things we bought," now she was a little touchy.

"I wasn't criticizing you or your family. It's just that everyone likes new things," Marc tried to avoid a clash over a simple observation. "I would like to own a home like this when I get older, wouldn't you?"

"Well, it would be nice," she shrugged off her scolding nature. "You and I could buy a home like this when we are rich."

"We better be real rich real soon or all we will have is a one room shack."

"Well, I'll need more than one room if I'm going to live with you," she teased.

"If I don't decide what to do after graduation, a one room shack is all we will have."

"Let's not talk about that subject again tonight. I'm tired of thinking and talking about graduation and what comes next," Jamie drew the line.

They were sitting on the top step of a three step entrance into the sunken family room watching their friends dance and devour the feast that had been laid out for them. Marc and Jamie each had a full plate, but there would be no chance of seconds.

Amanda and Ron joined them lounging on the step just below them. Ron's tall frame and long legs looked uncomfortable stretching out onto the floor. "You should sit on the top step so you'll be more comfortable," Amanda urged him.

"I'm just fine," Ronnie drawled.

"No, you're not. Sit up on the top step."

Ron pulled his large frame up and slid up a step, "Just to keep the peace …"

Jamie smiled, "You two are so funny sometimes."

Amanda looked at Jamie, "What do you mean?"

"You're like, like really tight. I mean, it's just that you know each other really well. You can say anything to each other."

"Well, we have been going together for years. Even in grade school, I think we were attracted to each other, and started dating as freshmen."

"Right, you can count on each other, brilliant," Jamie suddenly felt uncomfortable with her nosey comments.

Ron stood, stretched his legs. "We better cut out. We have our first baseball game tomorrow if it doesn't rain again. It's on a Saturday due to all our rain-outs. We need to leave, Marc."

As they drove down Cove Hill, Marc leaned over the back seat, "Hey Ron, when will you have your car back?"

"My dad is having his truck fixed next week, so I should have my jalopy back then. It seems I have been without transportation for a month." He and Amanda were cradled together in Marc's back seat as he drove towards Marland Heights. "That is a real bummer. I would be lost, no buses for me ever again." Marc looked at Jamie. "Maybe you can drive me around now that you have your license, Jamie, if I need a ride."

"My dad won't even let me drive downtown yet. He wants me to stay his little girl forever."

"Well, you are my big girl," Marc joked pulling into Amanda's driveway. As Amanda and Ron climbed out of the back seat, Ron looked over at Marc, "Ten minutes, no longer than ten minutes."

Jamie called out, "Don't worry, he'll be back quickly. My parents said we can't sit in the driveway any more. If we want to spend more time together, we have to come into the house." Marc backed out of the driveway and headed towards Jamie's. "Did they say anything else? You never told me what your parents said."

"It was my Mum who talked to me. She said she could see us having a go at each other. She was mad because we were making out and she didn't want me to be known as a fast girl or something worse. If she sees you, I'm sure she will give you the one-two."

Once in the driveway, Jamie kissed Marc quickly and got out of the door. Marc did not make a fuss; he watched to make sure she went in the front door and left immediately. As he approached Amanda's again, he found Ron waiting for him at the end of the driveway.

"I've been wanting to speak with you, Marc," Ron began as soon as he jumped into the car. "I know you said you didn't want to play baseball, but we really need you. I'm not sure I want to play either anymore. With all this rain, we haven't even had batting practice. Now we have to play two games on a Saturday. Damn rain, I just can't get excited about the game and even playing."

Marc paused for about five minutes before answering. "I still don't want to play. High school is over as far as I'm concerned. I have decided that I will come out just for something to do. Coach Warren has been good to me, and I don't want to leave him stuck. Guess I wouldn't feel good about backing out on him."

Another assembly? What's this one all about?" Will was complaining as usual.

"You know it's about graduation stuff. Now sit down and shut up!" Sage emphasized the "shut up."

"More information about graduation, why…"

"Will, shut up!" came a chorus from everyone at once.

Ron and Marc were sitting behind Sage and Will, as Ron, more to quiet Will than anything else, asked, "who's starting today?"

"I think it will be the sophomore, the lefty, I don't remember his name," Marc answered.

"He could be good, especially as a lefty, we could use a good lefty in the starting rotation. I heard that his brother was a lefty and very good four or five years ago."

"You don't see many lefties," Marc added. "We should have won both of those games Saturday. You pitched great in that first game, but nothing went right in the second. We must have had a dozen errors."

Ron corrected him, "six actually, two in just one play in the sixth."

"We didn't hit well, either. I couldn't get even one hit, zero for six, not a good day at the plate," Marc admitted.

"That's because we haven't had any batting practice—not even once this year! Today we…"

"Please close the doors. We need to get started. If a few of the faculty would stand in the halls to keep the noise down, that would help. Thank you staff," Mr. Paige tried to quiet the crowd so the assembly could begin. "Good morning to all. This is probably the last assembly for you as seniors, but not the last time we will all be together. In about a month, you will be graduates of Weir High, looking back on what I hope will be good memories of your past four years." A few cheers and also boos greeted his last remark.

"Regardless of your sentiments, by the end of May, high school will be over for you. To make sure you have a complete picture of what will happen over the next thirty days, we are going to move quickly to review what will take place leading up to graduation.

Before I turn the podium over to Mr. Baker, I want to say a few words about some academic matters. Throughout these last weeks, we will be announcing one National Merit Scholarship, the Valedictorian and the top ten academic seniors. There are twenty-five honorary scholarships to be awarded to your class members. At least one class member has been appointed to a military academy and nearly sixty percent of the class of nineteen fifty-nine plan to go on to colleges. This is the highest percentage of any previous class.

Please watch for these announcements and congratulate your fellow seniors as they are identified. The package of material that is being distributed is for you and your parents. It contains the guide to a smooth graduation so please don't lose it. Enjoy your last few weeks of high school. Mr. Baker, the podium is all yours."

Mr. Baker addressed the students in his usual matter-of-fact manner, dealing with each topic thoroughly from academic awards, to the procedures for renting cap and gowns. When the assembly ended, the auditorium was like a mad house. Everyone was trying to get out or else to get into their seats for lunch. Marc eventually found Jamie, rushed outside with their brown lunch bags, and found seats on the long stone waist-high wall in the front of the school.

"What confusion, too many people in the same place. It's good to be outside in the fresh air. Wow, I'm tired," Jamie exclaimed.

"If you're tired, think of me. I worked yesterday at the pool and the gas station. Saturday I had to catch at two baseball games, and now I have another one this afternoon."

"I don't even know why you decided to play that baseball game thing," Jamie almost sneered at him.

"You're right. Guess I got forced, no, maybe shamed into it; that's a better word. I could kick myself for letting Will and Ron talk me into it. Now I have to finish the season because of them, and most of all, for Coach."

"Well, don't kick yourself; just don't complain."

"I won't complain." They sat, as what seemed like the entire school walked by, quietly eating their lunches. Marc started an old conversation. "I was really impressed by part of the assembly, all those honor scholarships were something. Just about every club or community organization gives scholarships." He was paging through the material that had been distributed. "Look, there are a dozen or more that provide one thousand dollars or more. Holy molly, that's a lot of prize money just for being smart."

Jamie's reaction was discerning, "I kept telling you that all year. You wouldn't listen. All you wanted to do was play your games. I have only been here a year, and I'm being considered for some of them. You could have qualified!"

Marc hesitated, "You're right. I just didn't know or understand how this worked. Our entire family never knew about this, no one has ever pursued going on to further education. In truth, I will be the first one to graduate from high school. My family is all about working, not about schooling. I just didn't know these opportunities existed."

"Listen and learn; you do not do much listening."

"Yeah, and now in less than a month, it's graduation. Hell, the prom is only two weeks away and I still need to rent or buy a tux. You're right, I need to listen more, especially to you."

"There's the bell," Jamie broke the spell of regret that had fallen over Marc, "Cheerio-O," and off she dashed.

The song was a new release by *Elvis Presley*, "*A Fool Such As I*:" *Now and then there's a fool such as I. You taught me how to love and now you say that we are through…I am a fool, but I'll love you dear. Now and then there's a fool such as I.*

Marc and Jamie were dancing in the darkened corner of the teen room at the center. The crowd seemed sparse because the day had been so beautiful, ending with the first really warm evening of the year. Most of their friends were no-shows at this final evening of teen dances held by the center. "Too quiet tonight," Marc mused while nuzzling Jamie's ear.

"Very and not much fun without Niki, Amanda and the others," Jamie murmured back.

"Do you realize that Prom is just two weeks away now? It is going so fast. I got a tux today."

"A rental?"

"No, I bought one. The price wasn't that bad."

"Where are you going to wear a tux after Prom?"

"Well, maybe I'll get married this summer," Marc joked.

"Just hope you find the right chick!" Jamie was quick to respond.

"I thought that would be you. What do you say?"

"You are far out in front of my thinking. You never asked or gave me an engagement ring. Why would I marry you?" kidding him with her eyes, her smiling face and a kiss on his cheek.

Marc smiled back, kissed her forehead just as the music stopped. "Since there's no one here, let's go for a ride."

"Where?"

"No place special. It's nice outside. We can just ride around, talk, maybe get an ice cream."

"Right, brilliant."

As they left, the last glow of the sunset was fading revealing a star-filled sky. Jamie sat close in the coupe, as they talked about tomorrow. Marc had another double-header. Jamie was going to a "hen night" at Niki's.

"Where are we going?" Jamie suddenly asked as she noticed them winding down a road she had never noticed before.

"I'm taking you someplace you have never been—King's Creek."

"What is a King's Creek?"

"King's Creek is a creek; you know, a small stream. It's in the country, in a valley behind Weirton Heights. There are a lot of country roads including dirt roads that go through the farms along the creek."

"Why do you want to go there now, at night? We won't be able to see anything."

"Well, that's what makes it fun. The stars and moon are out tonight. Don't worry, we'll be able to see the creek just fine. It will be romantic."

"Romantic, that's all this ride is about?"

"There's a special place down here called "Devil's Den." We all go there in the summer to swim; there's a deep water hole with a bridge over it. The guys go skinny dipping there."

"What about the girls? Do they skinny dip, too?"

"Not the girls, they swim in their underwear."

"They do not. You're lying again. I always fall for your stories. You're just a big story teller!" Jamie poked him in the side and curled up against him.

Suddenly, they were on a dirt road. Marc slowed down for the rough surface. The creek that was about twenty yards wide ran along the passenger side. As they wound slowly along the creek in the moonlight, an occasional house came into view. Marc turned into one of the more rustic side paths and stopped, backing into a more secluded spot. He shut off the lights and looked down at Jamie.

"What are you stopping for?" Jamie looked up at him and deep into his eyes. He was just too cute—too hard to resist. She reached out, put her arms around his neck and kissed him long and hard. Without a word, they reacted to each other finding the atmosphere of the solitude and the enticing babbling brook luring them to each other.

Chapter 13

Commitment

"That was a hell of a game!"

"Funny way to win; I almost felt sorry for their pitcher, seven no hit innings and then you lose. That would be hard to take!"

"Three errors on one play. That ball was flying all over the field. But a run is a run no matter how you score. One to nothing is all it takes. You only need to score one more run than the other team to get a win," Marc patted Tom Kec on his back as they walked toward the library. "Your curve was really moving that seventh inning. You deserved the victory!

"Yeah, as you said, a win is a win. I'll take it, the arm felt strong the entire game. It had been almost a week since I had pitched. That rest helped. Who do we play tomorrow?"

"Wintersville, at least that's what Will told me this morning, but Will is not the most reliable source," was Marc's answer as he crossed the on-coming traffic of the crowded hall and ducked into the library with a closing remark, "Need a book…see you at practice."

Marc headed for his favorite window seat. He needed to find the Social Studies text book. He was four chapters behind and there was a test at the end of the week. He always seemed to be behind in the class, and there was always reading to do, especially as they raced toward the end of the year and the final grading period. Without a book, and with his nonchalant attitude toward the course, Marc was always behind and cramming everything academic into the last minute.

Even though graduation was only weeks away, he still had to pass the course. Therefore, reading the chapters was a must, or at least skimming the chapters was needed. He put his notebook down on the chair nearest the window and walked toward the shelf with the textbooks.

"Well, Mr. Floreau, back to take one of my books? Looking for a textbook I see. Do you read any novels, or the newspapers, or just my textbooks?" Mr. Pfeiffer, his nemesis over the years, but also his kindred spirit, was standing by his side.

"Yes, yes sir, Mr. Pfeiffer. I need the Social Studies text. I have some chapters to read.

"It's on my desk. Follow me." Mr. Pfeiffer moved towards the back of the library with Marc in tow. The head librarian walked around his desk. He was a tall slender man in his 40's, always dressed in sport coat and tie. Very formal in his manners and appearance, but also much respected by both faculty and students, a firm, but fair individual. He sat motioned for Marc to take a seat on the other side of the desk. "You have a moment Mr. Florant? I would like to speak with you."

"Yes, I have time, but I do need the Social Studies text."

"Yes, in a minute. It is right here, you can have it. I was wondering how prepared you are for graduation? You realize that it is only a few weeks away?"

"I am ready. All I have to do is finish these last few weeks of classes and pass. I'm ready."

"Good, but what about after graduation? I didn't see your name on the college enrollment list. That surprised me. What are you going to do after graduation?"

"That's not settled yet. It's not college. School is over for me. You know how I stumble through. I'm not going to college, maybe the Navy. The Army said no because of my heart illness, but the Navy is still possible. I'll take the Navy physical after I graduate."

"I'm sorry to hear that you are rejecting the idea of college. The Navy is all right, but it does not sound like you are sure it is going to happen. What is the next step if the Navy says 'no'?" Mr. Pfeiffer was speaking softly and very directly to Marc with probing eyes.

"Not sure what I will do then. Get a job here in Weirton, probably the mill or someplace else close by. Not many choices after the Army and Navy say no.

"There are always choices Marc. You need to be open to other possibilities. There are some very good apprentice type trade possibilities right here in the Ohio Valley or in Pittsburgh. There are two year trade schools in Wheeling, Pittsburgh, Youngstown—many different chances to create a career for yourself. But you need to look for them and search them out."

"I know. You sound like my dad. I haven't had time to look at a lot of these."

"You haven't taken the time. You're too busy doing everything you can to avoid the responsibility of becoming a young adult with plans and decisions about your future. I have known you since I was your teacher in the sixth grade. Do you remember that year?"

"I remember you almost flunked me again. I had already taken the third grade twice, and you wanted me to do sixth grade again. I remember."

"I'm glad that I didn't hold you back! That would have been wrong. You proved that to me ever since. You are a very bright fellow, although you play the role of the dull tarnished one. You are not—not even close. You show that in athletics. Did you note when there was some hole that needed to be plugged or something unusual that needed to be done, who the coaches turned to? It was you. You are honorable, with integrity and smarts. You are selling yourself short. You can tackle anything you want. But first you need to decide what that is or at least what you can do after high school that will give you the chance to explore your possibilities."

"I don't know what to say Mr. Pfeiffer. Thank you for those kind things you said. I will think a little more about other options. Thank you."

"Here is the book are looking for. Keep it till the end of the year; you are the only one that ever uses the library copy. If you want to talk before or after graduation I would be glad to have another conversation."

"Thanks Mr. Pfeiffer!"

"I had the oddest conversation with Mr. Pfeiffer today."

"About what?"

"He was talking to me about what I was going to do after graduation. He asked questions about college, the Navy, going to some trade school. It was just a different conversation with him then I have ever had. He seemed to be telling me that I should plan to do something special after high school."

"You should. If you go to the Navy, that will be something special. What did he say about college or the Navy? Did you tell him you were planning to join the Navy?" There was silence from the other end of the phone. Jamie didn't say anything either, waiting for Marc to answer her question. Finally the silence began to annoy her, "Marc are you still there? Did you go away?"

"No, I'm still here. I was thinking about your question and the conversation. It was a short talk and he did most of the talking, but I'm not sure what he thought about me going to the Navy. He said that it was all right, but seemed to be questioning that choice. He is the only one, well maybe with the exception of my dad, who has really ever questioned me about joining the Navy or even the Army."

"That's not true. Ah've talked to you about the Navy, n the Army, n college n everything else about after graduation. You don't listen when Ah ask you about them. You just tell me what you're going to do. You're like most boys. You never really talk about anything. You tell us things, but you don't ask for our opinion. We have talked about the Navy, about you being so far away, you being gone on some ship for months and months. Ah think that is stupid, unless there is a war, some reason to go," Jamie sounded cross in her response.

"It is not. It will give me a start in a career of some kind. I can get free training in some profession and get out and find a good job here or someplace else."

"Why do you always talk about coming back here, to Weirton to live?

"It's my home. My family is here, my friends, you are here."

"Well, home can be many different places. Look at me. Weirton is my home now, but a year ago it was Birmmie. It was England not the states. Family will always be family, but where they are will not always be the same place," Jamie was irked and her high pitched voice made that clear.

"I know that. I know you have experienced leaving your home town and your family, friends and everything you knew. I guess I'm not, I don't know, maybe I don't want to do or see other things."

"When we first met, you talked about travelling, seeing England, seeing where Ah came from. You seemed to be excited that Ah was English, different from the others even though you made fun of my language n words that Ah used. You talked about doing something different with your life than what was going on in Weirton. What happened to those thoughts? Where did they go?"

"I still feel that way, well, sometimes I feel that way. I just can't find a way to make it happen."

"Maybe that is what Mr. Pfeiffer was talking to you about. It sounds like he thought you were not looking outward enough. Maybe he was trying to encourage you to think about things beyond the Navy. Ah want you to think about things beyond the Navy, beyond Weirton. My Da is telling me to get off the phone. We have been talking for a long time."

"Yes we have. Sorry, but I really need to talk. You know me so well. You have helped me so much this year. I depend on you to keep me going in the right direction. I do love you and wish I could kiss you goodnight."

"Well you can't, so we need to say goodnight."

"Goodnight my love!"

"Goodnight Marc." Click.

Jamie and Marc walked to his car sitting in the Toliver driveway and were about to get in when her mother came out the front door with a sweater for Jamie. "You will need this sweater as the evening comes on. It's warm now but it will cool down when the sun is gone. Where is this place?" She looked at Jamie on the other side of the car.

"It's close to downtown on Colliers Way. It's a big picnic area with a covered area and picnic tables spread in the grassy area. It's called the Police Park or Lodge, something like that. Very nice. All the city picnics are held there," Marc replied.

"You 've a good time, but be home early Jamie."

"Yes Mum," Jamie sat in the passenger's seat, waving to her mother as Marc backed the car out of the driveway and started down the street.

"What did she mean about being home early? This will be over by nine; does she mean to come straight home?" There was concern and disappointment in Marc's voice.

"They were concerned about how late Ah got home last Friday. My Mum was waiting for me when Ah came in door. Ah told you that. We were so far away at the creek place, and then you got lost coming back. They were mad. When Ah went into the house Ah looked a mess, Mum asked all kind of questions. She n Da want me home early tonight."

"I know, you told me. We will be back by ten, will that be okay? I don't want them mad at us with prom next week."

"No later than ten, earlier would be better. Ah don't think they trust you or me n you right now. My Mum had a long talk, girl or women's talk, as she called it, with me last night, so we need to follow their rules."

"We didn't do anything. You told her that didn't you?" Marc's question was defensive.

"Yes, Ah told her we were good n all that, but she was still concerned that we were on 'thin ice.' Those were her exact words," Jamie was firm in her answer.

"I understand. We will come straight back to your house. Is that alright with you?"

"Yes," and she scooted closer to him as they passed the Community Center and their church, heading to the Senior Class Picnic at the Police Lodge. This would be a big event sponsored by the Parent's Association, the Christian Alliance, and most of the clubs, lodges, and business associations. There would be food, games, dancing, prizes, rewards and a large ice cream social at the very end. They were expecting over 250 attendees and dozens of volunteers. Marc had volunteered last year so he had experienced the size of the crowd and the fun of the event.

They quickly found their group of friends who had already picked out two large picnic tables off in a large wooded area. The food lines were long, but regardless of the slow pace, when they finally arrived at the food tables, they found the choices and quantity riveting.

"Ah've never seen so much food," Jamie said with eyes glancing down the double table pathway. Ah don't know what to take or how Ah'm going to get everything on my plate."

"Told you it would be overwhelming."

"It is brilliant. This is a jumbo bash. In Birmmie we would call this 'fat city.' Can we take some and come back?"

"Yes you can, dear. You can have more after every one has gone through the first time. They want it all eaten. So dig in!" was the advice from one of the servers behind the food table.

"Right, thank you it looks wonderful. Thank you."

Marc, Jamie and their friends finally filled their plates, stopped to talk to Marc's and Niki's mothers who were helping with the pop, ice tea and other drinks. They joined the others at the two reserved tables and devoured the meal. Everyone went back for seconds when the announcement was made that the first pass was over. Finally full, they sat on the grass to enjoy a band concert by a select group from the high school band and a few light remarks from Mr. Paige.

There were a few games. A team of twenty girls won the tug-of-war against ten boys. A spoon and raw eggs race, also was won by the girls, in fact, this time it was Niki, followed by a boy/girl sack race and a few others events. A raffle was held with the grand prize being a camera. A couple of scholarships, apprenticeships and cash rewards were announced. Both Amanda and Ron were winners, as everyone expected. Finally dessert was served, another gigantic offering of ice cream in twenty different flavors, plus all the trimmings.

As the evening turned to dusk, the park started to empty. The gang all left together walking out to their cars, saying goodbye, heading home. "Should we go to your house of maybe stop someplace, just to talk?"

"When we stop, you n Ah never really just talk. We better go home. My mother would really like that."

"It's only quarter to nine. You will be getting home really early."

"That's okay, we can sit in the back yard n talk if we want to. Ah'll need that sweater Mum gave me. Do you 've a coat, its cold now?"

"Back seat. I'll get it when we get out, if I get cold," Marc started for Jamie's.

They drove for a few minutes. "I had another conversation with Mr. Pfeiffer on Thursday. He showed me some apprentice programs available through Weirton Steel and other steel companies. There seemed to be many in Pittsburgh, Cleveland and other places. You have to apply, and pay some, but you have a job when you finish. I am going to look into them. I have an appointment with a guy at Weirton Steel next week. He is director of training."

"What's his name, maybe my Da knows him."

"I forget, but I have it written down. My dad says he knows who he is, but has never met him. When I talk with the guy next week, I'll let him know that I know your father."

"Give me his name tomorrow n Ah'll tell my Da. He knows a lot of people in the company. Phone me with his name."

They drove on towards Jamie's talking about the Picnic, the food and the fun of being at such a large function. WEIR was playing: *"Bye Bye Love," by the Everly Brothers*: *Bye bye love, bye bye happiness, hello loneliness, I I think I'm-a gonna cry-y, bye bye love, bye bye sweet caress, hello emptiness. I feel like I could di-ie, bye bye my love goodby-eye.*

Jamie looked up at Marc as they turned onto her street, "Ah like this song but it is very sad. Not our story. Ah love walking out with you, you're my baby n Ah want to caress you daily."

"Ditto, you're my cute baby," Marc squeezed Jamie closer and pulled into the driveway. *There goes my baby with-a someone new, She sure looks happy, I sure am blue, She was my baby till he stepped in Goodbye to romance that might have been. Bye Bye Love.* They sat for a few minutes in the fading light, kissed, exited the coupe, and strolled to the front door.

"Marc is here. He is driving his parent's car just as he said. It is very shiny, just like new. You will be going prom-ming in great style, your silver chariot awaits," Ellen Toliver was watching out their front window. She turned to look again at Jamie. "My, my dear you look beautiful. Marc is going to be smitten even more than he already is. Your dress is enchanting; you are radiant like a joyful sunbeam. The fit is perfect; you are perfect n my angel," Jamie's mother couldn't help but hug her daughter again as she stood next to her father in the living room.

The doorbell rang, Marc had arrived. Mrs. Toliver greeted Marc with a wide grin, "Welcome, handsome, you look sharp in that white sport jacket."

"Thanks Mrs. Toliver. I feel good in it, even enjoyed buying it. Is Jamie ready?"

"She surely is; come in. She's in the living room."

Marc moved from the foyer into the living room. At the other end, in front of the fireplace, was Jamie. He slowed his pace, memorized by her beauty. Her golden ruby hair was shoulder length, reflecting the light in a shining sheen. The hair appeared to be suspended, floating effortlessly, curling tightly, and accenting her cheeks and face. She had a beaming smile, deep red lips that trailed to her deep set blue eyes. Marc searched for the right word to describe her. "You are gorgeous, divine, stunning. I don't have the right words to describe you. You are everything, absolutely everything."

He stammered again as he approached her. He was flabbergasted by her appearance. "Your dress is magnificent, just as you said." The dress was a very light powder blue, with a thin strapped lacy top, a wide mid-drift panel of slightly darker blue that brought her waist inward, the skirt flowed out in a bell shape, but was layered to permit ease of movement while allowing a broad flowing pattern. The entire dress was accented with shading of bluish patches, darker blue piping, complimented by lace gloves.

Jamie's father was standing next to her holding her hand and her elbow lightly. He grinned proudly at her and took her hand and placed it in Marc's hand, "Take care of my precious Princess!"

"I will sir. She is my Princess, too. I'll take good care of her. She is gorgeous sir!"

"Yes she is!" Jamie's father replied as he moved aside.

"You are dressed to the nines! Very handsome. Love that white jacket. You look like you are part of the King's Court."

"Thank you my beauty. Here is your corsage just the color you asked for."

Marc made a sophisticated appearance in his white tux sport coat, with velvet lapels, blue satin lining, red bow tie, red cummerbund, midnight black pants with a satin stripe on both legs, and shoes with a deep black shine.

After the blue orchid wrist corsage was in place, and the red carnation pinned on the left lapel, pictures were taken of the couple, each alone, and then with family until the film and flash cubes were finished. An over the shoulder shawl was put on, goodbyes were said and prom night commenced.

"Ah love your parent's car. You must 've polished it recently." Jamie said as they approached the white, olive striped, Plymouth Belvedere with trendy pointed back fins.

"Recently was this morning. That was part of the arrangement with my dad."

Once inside Jamie surveyed the space age front dash. The seats were smooth leather and comfy. "This is brilliant, like riding in my Da's car. We are going to enjoy this," she ran her hand over the red leather.

"It is nice, roomy enough for your billowing skirt with lots of room in the back for Ron's legs and Amanda's dress," he commented as he looked over at Jamie. "Are you ready?"

"Yes Ah'm ready for a wonderful night, a very long night with my knight in shining armor, my Sir Lancelot!"

"Here we go."

The first stop was Amanda's home. Marc had left Ron there on his way to Jamie's. They went inside for more pictures and so that Amanda's parents could see all four of them together. Next stop was the Williams Country Club where the prom's dinner and dance would be held. This would be the first of a three pronged celebration that would be the Prom experience. After the dinner-dance, prom night would continue with an after prom party at the Community Center that would last until three A.M. Following a short night of sleep, most of the seniors would make their way to Kennywood Amusement Park in Pittsburgh for a day of rides and fun.

As they entered the country club, the evening turned magic. Decorations were impressive throughout the entire building. Each of the gathering rooms was adorned with a theme from the four years of high school. The main color was red with white and black embellishing the displays. Balloons were everywhere, most floating to the ceilings with long tails of ribbons. Music was being piped through the sound system. The extravagance of the setting reminded Marc and Jamie of the New Years Eve Dance they had attended just five months ago.

Dinner was fine with good adequate servings. The girls complained about "too much food" and the difficulty of eating in their prom gowns. But they ate anyway with just as much enthusiasm as the guys. Like Jamie, the gals were in flowing skirts, colorful glittering gowns, hairdos of all types, and corsages. Their fellows were in a tux or suit: many in white jackets, but a few in very fancy colors, even blue and red.

Following dinner, walks around the country club or outside near the golf course seemed to be the post meal choice. The dining hall was quickly transformed into a dance floor with chairs circling the room and a few small tables set in each corner. A stage was set-up and the band was ready to go.

The evening was filled with dancing: fast, slow, romantic, funny, line and stroll. Everyone seemed to be in the mood to strut their stuff, even a few who never danced. As the bewitching hour of eleven o'clock for this first phase approached, the songs took on a sentimental quality. The last was "*Good night sweetheart:" Good night sweetheart, till we meet tomorrow, Good night sweetheart, sleep will banish sorrow, Tears and Parting may make us forlorn. But with the dawn a new day will guide you…*

"Ah hate to 've this evening end," Jamie whispered in Marc's ear. "It has been a grand night, just a grand night."

"For me, too. We still have more to do and this will not be our last grand night."

"I know, I'm looking forward to many more."

Good night sweetheart, still my love will guide you, Dreams enfold you, in each one I'll hold you, Good night Sweetheart, Good night.

From Williams Country Club, they headed for the Community Center. This venue was going to be completely different. It was casual. Most of the girls changed into more comfortable dresses and the guy's removed their jackets and ties. Between mid-night and three, the center was open for the entire senior class to swim, play pool, handball, basketball, and even a volleyball court was set up. An open buffet was provided by the churches and the parents' association, and the opportunity to dance some more was provided in the teen room or couples could just sit and talk. The post Prom event would close with a raffle.

The constant friends: Jamie, Marc, Ron, Amanda, Will, Niki, Sarah and Sage started with a mid-night swim, followed by a one am snack, some volleyball, more dancing and finally the raffle. They started strong, but by the end of the post Prom, they were exhausted. But they didn't go home empty handed: Jamie won a movie camera and Niki a small TV. Everyone headed home for six or so hours of sleep and then a trip to Kennywood.

"I'm so tired I hope I make it home to find my bed," Marc complained as he and Jamie reached her front door.

"Ah'll sleep with my clothes on," was her reply.

"I can help you get undressed."

"Go home, we will see each other around noon," Jamie answered, kissed him, went in the door and found her mother waiting for her.

Noon came almost too soon for all eight, but they met at the center and took off for the two hour drive to Kennywood Park, located southeast of Pittsburgh.

They had decided to go in two cars with Marc and Sage each driving their parents' cars. The decision about who would drive with whom was easy. Ron and Amanda would continue to double with Marc and Jamie while Will and Niki would double with Sage and Sarah. There were at least two dozen other cars loading up at the same time so the park would have a good representation from Weir High. The Park had a special post Prom promotion each Saturday in May which attracted hordes of seniors from all over. The weather was perfect.

Marc led the way since his father had given him directions on how to avoid as much traffic as possible. Even so, the trip took two hours, and to the tired riders it seemed like four. Once there, the fun was worth the long ride. The eight rode everything they could: roller coasters, the Racers, the Jack Rabbit and the Speed-O-Plane, Ferris wheel, the park circling train, bumper cars, Noah's Ark, the carousel, even the Looper and the Rotor—the two rides that scared everyone, along with anything that moved around and went up and down.

The guys won a few trinkets for the girls at the midway games. Niki, as usual, won the biggest prize, a large stuffed rabbit. They had hot dogs, cotton candy, snow cones, French fries, and gallons of lemonade, and pop. Finally, around eight pm, out of energy and money, they headed home.

About half way home Marc realized that the other three were sound asleep. Ron and Amanda were cuddled in the back seat and Jamie had her head on his lap with her face very near the steering wheel. The last hour Marc did everything he could do to keep awake: he listened to the radio, opened his window, and sang along with songs. Finally he pulled into the Community Center parking lot and woke everyone when he stopped next to Ron's car.

As they made the climb up Marland Heights hill, Jamie started to liven up. "That was a brilliant day, a brilliant Prom, everything was brilliant," she continued to talk about all they had done in just over twenty-four hours. At her house, they sat in the darkness and held each other kissed and kissed and kissed again. They were both thankful to the other for such a fabulous time. It had been all they expected and more.

"Time to say goodnight my knight," Jamie said.

"Yes."

They walked to the front door. Mrs. Toliver was there. "You're home safely. Thank you Marc. Everyone 've a good time?"

"Ah will sleep forever," were Jamie's last word as she kissed his cheek and went inside.

"Me too," Marc answered

"Ah slept until noon. No church for me."

"I didn't make it either. My mom tried to wake me, but I was too tired to move, still tired. Think I'll go to bed early tonight, we have another game tomorrow afternoon."

"Ah had a great time at Prom, it was unreal n that tank of your parents surely helped with all the riding we did. It all seemed to go so fast n was over so quickly. Ah would like to do it again. Ah've been telling my Mum all about it—she never experienced anything like that when she finished her comprehensive school. She said they just finished n either went to work or to university."

"My mother didn't have a Prom either. She and my dad never went to high school; they ended their education in elementary school. Boy! Times sure were different," Marc responded.

"We've been lucky, no war for us n Ah 've graduated twice: once in England n now in America."

"Well, we haven't graduated yet. We have another week and a half before we get our diplomas."

"Right, what are we going to do this week in class? We've finished all the work, taken the final exams, there's nothing to do in class. What a bummer! Ah hate just sitting in class n talking about a lot of old stuff."

"That is a drag. I won't be in class much tomorrow anyhow. We have a baseball game in the afternoon."

"More games, when is this baseball thing going to be over?"

"It could be over tomorrow, if we lose. This is state tournament time, if you lose, you are finished; if you win, you play again the next day."

"Guys get all the opportunities. We never 've a chance to play sports n miss classes. We 've to go to class even if there is nothing to do. That's a class society thing."

"Hey, don't get mad at me. That's just the way it is. Don't forget, if we lose tomorrow, we have to go to all those meaningless classes too. Tomorrow we can have lunch together. We don't leave until one thirty."

"Ah didn't mean to be a wet rag. Ah'll see you tomorrow. We are 'aving supper in a few minutes n Ah need to help Mum."

"See you at noon. What does 'wet'," Marc heard the phone click, "'rag' mean?" Another one of those English words or phrases he thought.

As he sat on the couch, he agreed this was going to be a wasted week at school. Not much would be done in the classes. Teachers would sum up the past year or semester and hold open discussion on related topics. If the days were nice, some classes would be held on the school lawn. Five days of nothing.

For Marc, he could avoid some of the boredom because of the state baseball tournament. Marc didn't even know who they would be playing or where. The baseball season had been a short one caused by days of bad weather. They had played better than he expected them to, but what the tournament would be like was a guessing game. It may be a one game tournament.

Commencement activities were still ten days away. That would be the last event in his high school years. Now with Prom over, he and Jamie had settled on continuing to go steady even though she would be gone all summer in England, then off to college in September. The next three months seemed settled. They had decided they wanted to remain dating as a couple, looking forward to something more promising in the future.

Marc was starting to look forward to graduating. He had talked to a few people and felt that his search for a path after high school was going to have a good conclusion. Nothing was certain yet, but there were opportunities. Right now he was going to relax and watch some Sunday evening TV, Maverick, Ed Sullivan and The Rebel.

"Jamie can you help me clear the table n get these dishes washed?"

"Right, eh Right Mum, Ah'm coming."

Sunday supper was over at the Toliver's, everyone was attempting to get settled in for a quiet evening. Harry was sitting in front of the TV and Frances was reading something in the corner lounge chair of the living room, now that he had forced Harry to turn the volume down to a whisper.

As they stood at the sink, Ellen asked her daughter about her packing plans for their trip to England. They, including Harry, would be gone for seven weeks, traveling by train to New York City, then by boat to England, so they had to take enough clothes, probably two suit cases each, for the extended trip and the different weather.

"Are you as excited as Ah am?" Ellen asked.

"Yes, well, Ah guess. It would be fun to be here for the full summer, but it also is exciting to see the grannies, the family, n some old friends. Ah'm excited, but Ah don't know what to expect; it has been a long time, n Ah 've changed so much."

"Right, you 've certainly changed. You are a young woman now. You're a world traveler; everyone will be impressed with all you 've done this year,"

"Ah…Ah hope so."

"Keep in mind that we leave the Monday after graduation, so get done what you need to take care of. Don't let things wait until the last minute."

"Right, right everything will be done."

"Want to go for a ride, we could get something to eat."

"Okay, Ah'll tell my parents n be right back."

Marc leaned against his Chrysler Coupe and waited for Jamie to return. It was early Saturday evening after the final week of school, and there was a baseball game nearly every day. Surprise was the theme of the week for Marc and the baseball team; they continued to win and would play in the sectional finals on Monday. Graduation day would be next Wednesday. Only four days away.

Jamie finally returned, "Let's go. Da said Ah needed to be back by ten o'clock so we need to stay close."

"By ten, eh, ok, we can get a hamburger or pizza. Maybe ice cream."

"Ok, let's get ice cream. Is that alright with you?'

The Dairy Cream on Freedom Way became the destination. To their surprise, they found Will and Niki there with the same idea. The four sat at a picnic table in the grassy area at the back of the parking lot. All four were in a holding pattern waiting for commencement to end school and for the summer to begin. The conversation was rather subdued as each expressed reflexive thoughts about the past year and the things they would miss. With the ice cream finished, they separated and Jamie and Marc headed back to her house.

"It's only nine o'clock, we have an hour before you have to be back, want to go someplace and talk?" Marc asked Jamie as they started toward Marland Heights.

"Are you sure you want to talk or make out," Jamie teased smoothly. She knew him well.

"A little of both. We haven't been together for a long time and next weekend will be the last before you leave. Please, just for a few minutes."

"Ok, but just for a few minutes," Jamie cuddled close and put her head on his shoulder.

Marc drove to the south end of Palasades Drive, not far from Jamie's house, where a number of new homes were being built, creating a few isolated parking spots that they had visited before. They did talk, and did make out, embraced expressing the affection and desire for each other. Their brief tryst lasted for about thirty minutes and Jamie was home by ten.

On Monday the baseball team won again. Now they were one of the final four teams. Tuesday they won the semi-final game and were scheduled to play for the state championship of the Division 1-AAA on Wednesday—but there was a conflict. Wednesday was Commencement for Weir High School. The game was moved to Thursday at Davis and Elkins College in the middle of the state.

The Community Center parking lot was nearly full. Marc drove around until he found a spot towards the back of the lot. The ceremony would be held in the Community Center gymnasium. It provided the only place in town that could hold the three hundred plus graduates and their families. He hurried inside with the box holding his cap and gown. His fellow students were gathered in the large dining hall trying to get to their alphabetical placement. They were in black attire with a red tassel that would start out on the right side of the cap and upon receiving the diploma, be shifted to the left. They had spent an hour early in the day on the rules of marching in, when to applaud, when not, when to shift the tassel and what to do, and not do at the end of the ceremony.

Finally the processional started, they could hear *"Pomp and Circumstances," by Sir Edward Elgar,* filling the packed, standing room only gymnasium, and in reality, throughout the entire building via the sound system. The ceremonial atmosphere stirred everyone's spirit. The *tramp, romp, stomp* of the march was both a festive and solemn act. Marc thought he was attending a coronation.

With a packed house, warm weather outside, no air conditioning and the pageantry, it was temperate in the great hall. Everything moved along on schedule, the Valedictorian's words of remembering each other, the Commencement speaker with words of challenge and hope, the recognition of award and scholarship winners, the shifting of the tassel, names being called, diplomas in covers presented and finally the singing of the alma mater:

Among the hills of West Virginia
Stands My Fair and Lovely Alma Mater
For Light, for truth, for fair of play
Stands my fair and lovely Alma Mater
May thy days be ever free
May thy children bring thee fame
May thy teachings always be
Strong as the steel that bears thy name.
Though years may pass and time may borrow
Though wars may darken my tomorrow
My thoughts and prayers will always be

With thee my lovely Alma Mater
ALL HAIL! ALL HAIL!
HAIL TO WEIR.

They had graduated. High School was in the past. They shook hands, hugged, kissed cheeks, searched out friends, parents, family, teachers, coaches, and even people they did not know well. It was chaotic and undisciplined. It took another hour for the chaos to end. Caps and gowns were returned, but the red tassels were the graduates to keep.

Marc and Jamie finally said goodbye to their parents as did most of the graduates. It was early evening and there were parties at a number of the graduate's homes to attend. They would make the rounds, visiting as many celebrations as possible. Finally around eleven thirty both had tired, and Marc drove Jamie home. They had enjoyed the entire day. They snuggled for a while, walked to the door.

"I have the state final game tomorrow. I think Niki and a few others are going to make the trip, are you going to be with them?

"No, Ah told Niki Ah couldn't. Mum and Ah need to settle some things for the trip. Ah want to come, but Ah can't. Sorry, love. So sorry. Ah want you to win. Ah'll be thinking of you."

"It's okay. This is the last hurrah for this Red Rider."

"Right, but you are my Red Rider," Jamie gave him a warm embrace.

"I'll call you tomorrow, as soon as I get back."

They hugged, kissed and said good night. Jamie went in, Marc back to his car and home with his diploma in the back seat; a very early morning and long bus ride awaiting him tomorrow. WEIR was playing: *"Young Love", by Sonny James: They say for every boy and girl there's just on love in this old world, And I know I've found mine, The heavenly touch of your embrace tells me no one can take your place, Ever in my heart, Young love first love filled with true devotion, Young love our love we share with deep emotion... Just one kiss from your sweet lips will tell me that your love is real, and I can feel that it's true, We will vow to one another there will never be another, Love for you or for me. Young love first love...*

"Hi, I'm glad you answered the phone. You are still awake, I was afraid you might be in bed."

"Ah'm ready for bed, just waiting for your call."

"We won. We're the state champs in baseball. What a year! What a finish to high school."

"Ah heard that from Niki about an hour ago. It's brilliant! Congratulations. You n the others should be very proud. Ah'm very proud of you. You're my true Red Rider. Just wonderful."

"This championship is so different than the others. We won and it was just the team and maybe a dozen fans there. There was no one to celebrate with, no parade, no anything. I guess that is okay, but very different."

"Sorry Ah wasn't there, but you know Ah needed to be here."

"Can I come up and celebrate with you, now?"

"No it's too late. Ah'm sitting with my parents n talking about the trip n some things. Ah'll see you tomorrow, okay?"

"Sure, tomorrow. What time?"

"In the afternoon. About one. Ah'm really proud of you!"

"Ya, thanks." The phone clicked on her end.

Marc walked into the kitchen. His mother was making him some lunch or breakfast—whatever you call eggs and bacon at noon. His father was sitting at the table with coffee. Marc sat and ate while he told them all about the trip, the game, the victory, the trophy and the ride back. Everyone was upbeat and enjoying another success, if unexpected story.

"We also got our gold basketball charms for the championship. Coach Warren gave them out last night to everyone that was on the basketball team." He took a small box out of his pocket and showed the golden charm to his parents. "I'm going to give it to Jamie this afternoon so she can have it in England."

"Don't you think that it would be best to keep it while she is in England. It could get lost over there," Marc's mother cautioned.

"It will be fine with her. It means something special to me that she has it along with the other things."

"She will be staying in a lot of different places, it would be easy for her to misplace it or forget it."

"It will be ok with her. She will be careful. I have to go now. I'll be home later tonight," Marc added as he started for the door.

His father turned towards him and said, "Tell Jamie we said 'Hi.' Enjoy your last few days before she leaves, then we have a few things to do, remember!"

"I remember," he called back over his shoulder, anxious to head to Jamie's.

He parked the car in her driveway, walked towards the front door; spotting Jamie already on her way to meet him. They said "hi" as she took his hand and started walking to the back yard. Marc chatted about yesterday's game and told her a few funny stories about the trip. In the middle of the back yard she stopped and looked down at the grass and said: "Ah've something to tell you."

"To tell me. What?"

"Ah want you to know that Ah love you very much but in my own way."

"I love you too,"

"Ah think we love each other differently. You're my best friend n we 've had a great year together."

"Yes we have."

"Ah need to go my own way n you need to go your own way now. We can't go steady any more. You don't 've to be in Weirton waiting for me while Ah'm in England or at college. We need to see other people. Our lives need to go in different directions."

"What …what …what are you saying?"

"Ah'm saying 'good-by' to our being together as a couple. Ah'm breaking up with you."

"You, you are…what? Stop for minute. We are going to…"

"No, we are not going to do anything but continue to be friends. Here is the chain with the ring n football." She put her hand in his and gave back his class ring, the gold football charm and the long gold chain.

He felt them in his hand. Looked at them, looked up at Jamie, but she had walked away, she ran through the patio furniture and in the back door. He was stunned. He wanted to cry out to her. He stood looking at the back door. He stared at the house, the windows, and the door again. Where was she? She couldn't just disappear. What happened? Is it true? Is it a joke? Where is she? Why am I holding these things, they are hers! He stood there for a long time. He was unable to move. He started to cry. Finally, he walked around the side of the house. He started towards the front door—stopped short—then really started to cry. Tears filled his eyes, ran down his cheeks, fell on his shirt. He gathered himself together and started towards the front door for a second time; then he stopped short again, turned and walked to his car.

In the bright light he sat in the car just looking at the front door. It was a beautiful spring day and the car was warming in the direct sun. Finally he tossed chain, ring and football onto the passenger side of the seat. He started the car. He backed out of the driveway, put the car in gear and slowly, very slowly moved down the street away from Jamie's.

Chapter 14

Footnote

Jamie and her mother-in-law sat on the vinyl covered seats of the chrome breakfast table set. They had been up for over an hour, both on their second cup of coffee, sharing a couple pieces of practically burnt toast. Looking out the back two windows, they noticed the dew on the lawn, the row of blue spruce fir trees, and the garage roof. He mother-in-law complained about the cold chill in the house. It was the first sound from either of them for at least a half hour. Jamie acknowledged the comment, but she was roasting in the seventy-four degree temperature.

The creaking sound from the stairs announced Jamie's husband was finally awake and about to join her and his mother. A third coffee cup sat on the kitchen table waiting for him. His mother poured a nearly full cup, added cream and sugar. As he came though the doorway to the kitchen, Jamie noticed he had on a faded pair of blue jeans and an old deplorable shirt that she had threatened to toss out. He needed a shave; his hair had not been touched by a comb or hair brush.

He sat with a groan, took a few sips of coffee. His mother opened the conversation with questions about last night's football game. He told her that they had lost, badly. She wondered if he had seen anyone she might know. He mentioned a few names; she recognized one or two.

"Oh, one funny thing did happen. Someone called me 'Sage.' It has been years since that nickname has been used, hearing that name really made me feel old." He took another sip of coffee, looked at Jamie. "It was that old friend of yours from high school—that Marc guy."

Jamie tried not to show any emotion. It had been years since she had heard anything about him, many years.

"He was in town to sell his parents home. They both died recently. Jamie, do you remember him?" Sage asked.

"Yes, yes, of course I remember him."

"I don't," commented Sage's mother.

"He lives in Ohio, and you won't believe this, he is some big honcho executive for a Fortune Five Hundred company. Sure was different, I remember him when he could hardly get through high school," Sage elaborated.

"Still don't remember him," his mother added and changed the topic.

Jamie sat quietly, as mother and son carried on some meaningless conversation about nothing. Her senior year in high school materialized in her mind racing past like an out of control silent movie. The one keep sake she had from that fantastic nine months was a letter from Marc, Marc Floreau. She had kept the letter hidden in a special place at home, but she had read it so many times that it was a part of her soul.

Jamie – June 10, 1059

Sorry we did not have a chance to say goodbye. I wanted to see you before you left but I was hurting so much. Enjoy your visit with your family and friends. Please – Please, re-think your decision. I love you. I thought you loved me. I still want to be with you. Even if we don't marry right now we could still date and plan for a future together. Please think about us being together.

Here is some news I did not have a chance to tell you the last time we were together. I am going to college this September after all. I have a scholarship from a small school in Springfield, Ohio – Wittenberg. The scholarship pays only part of the cost, but I can handle what it doesn't. I will be playing both football and basketball for them.

Please write. Please come back to be with me. I love you. I'll always love you.

Your Red Rider
All my love, Marc

What readers say

Enjoyable story with messages for young and old. Fascinating characters that are true to life. Each is someone you know or have known. What I want to know now is what happens next in Marc and Jamie's lives?

Juliet, thirty's something

Rediscovered the joy of being faced with decisions about the future. Youth is filled with hope, passion, happiness uncertainty and above all their future. Red Rider fills the soul with all these emotion in a simple, but everlasting way.

Allen, a very senior, senior

Red Rider, Best book I have read this year. Compelling, entertaining and educating. Looking for more stories by the author.

Temple, a book club junky

Being from Weirton and in our 60s Red Rider brought back intense feelings of home, and a culture lost to another time. Thanks for the memories.

Bruce and Beth, Red Riders

Printed in the United States
By Bookmasters